ROUTLEDGE LIBRARY EDITIONS:
DEVELOPMENT

THE ECONOMIC AND SOCIAL
STRUCTURE OF MAURITIUS

THE ECONOMIC AND SOCIAL
STRUCTURE OF MAURITIUS

J. E. MEADE AND OTHERS

Volume 48

Routledge
Taylor & Francis Group

LONDON AND NEW YORK

First published in 1961

This edition first published in 2011
by Routledge
2 Park Square, Milton Park, Abingdon, Oxon, OX14 4RN

Simultaneously published in the USA and Canada
by Routledge
270 Madison Avenue, New York, NY 10016

Routledge is an imprint of the Taylor & Francis Group, an informa business

© 1961 Methuen and Co Ltd

British Library Cataloguing in Publication Data
A catalogue record for this book is available from the British Library

ISBN 13: 978-0-415-58414-2 (Set)
eISBN 13: 978-0-203-84035-1 (Set)
ISBN 13: 978-0-415-59438-7 (Volume 48)
eISBN 13: 978-0-203-83841-9 (Volume 48)

Publisher's Note
The publisher has gone to great lengths to ensure the quality of this reprint but
points out that some imperfections in the original copies may be apparent.

Disclaimer
The publisher has made every effort to trace copyright holders and welcomes
correspondence from those they have been unable to contact.

The Economic
and Social Structure
of Mauritius

Report to the Governor of Mauritius by

J. E. MEADE AND OTHERS

LONDON
Methuen and Co Ltd
36 ESSEX STREET W.C.2

Published in Mauritius by authority
of the Mauritius Legislative Council

Sessional Paper No. 7 of 1961
Port Louis

Table of Contents

CHAPTER 6

INDUSTRY

CHAPTER 9

CHAPTER 10

APPENDIX

List of Tables

List of Figures

Maps

To His Excellency The Governor of Mauritius,
Sir Colville Montgomery Deverell, K.C.M.G., C.V.O.,
O.B.E.
LONDON, SEPTEMBER 1960

Your Excellency,

In November 1959 we were appointed by you as a Commission with the following terms of reference:

"To survey the present economic and social structure of Mauritius and to make recommendations concerning the action to be taken in order to render the country capable of maintaining and improving the standard of living of its people, having regard to current and foreseeable demographic trends; and in particular:—

(a) to consider and make recommendations for the solution of the problems described in the Luce Report (Sessional Paper No. 7 of 1958) and the Government's statement thereon (Sessional Paper No. 8 of 1958); and to advise on the adequacy of the policies laid down in the latter document and on the degrees of priority accorded to them;

(b) to enquire into the economics of the staple agricultural industries of Mauritius and to report on the cost of production and the apportionment of the proceeds among the various agencies involved in production and to make recommendations in regard to the general organisation and future development of these industries;

(c) to survey the structure of the current development programme (Sessional Paper No. 4 of 1958 as subsequently amended) and to advise on the degree of priority accorded in it to the major projects and to recommend the broad lines of development policy in the future;

(d) to advise on the administrative and technical machinery required to implement the recommendations made by the Mission with particular reference to the numbers, qualifications, and availability of specialist staff."

We began our work at once before leaving the United Kingdom. We studied numerous published documents germane to our terms of reference, in particular the Gorvin Report of 1948, the Report of the 1955 Committee on Population, the Luce Report, and the reports on the structure and progress of the five-year Capital Development Plan. We also studied a number of memoranda sent at our request by various departments of the Government of Mauritius and about

170 letters and memoranda submitted by individuals, institutions, and business concerns.

With the exception of Mr. Lees who had arrived a little over a week earlier, we left London on March 11th and arrived in Mauritius on the following day. We remained in Mauritius for a period of 5-6 weeks and departed as and when possible between April 14th and April 24th. During these weeks we travelled the length and breadth of the island, sometimes together and sometimes separately. We had discussions with most of the important officials, ministers, and businessmen of the island, and listened to the views of nearly 70 private citizens. Our terms of reference were widely publicised, and we may claim with some confidence that we received evidence from all sections of the community.

We begin our Report with a brief description of the Colony of Mauritius (Chapter 1) and an outline of its fundamental problems and the solutions we propose (Chapter 2). We then go on to consider, in detail, the structure of the economy, the labour market, agriculture, industry, finance, and education (Chapters 3-8). We conclude with some suggestions on administration and government (Chapter 9) and a summary of our recommendations (Chapter 10).

Finally, we would like to acknowledge the hospitality and cordial co-operation which we at all times received, and to express our gratitude to Your Excellency, the Government of Mauritius, and to private citizens of all walks of life. We would like to express our particular thanks to Mr. Arouff, our Liaison Officer, for his continual and unfailing help.

We now have the honour to submit our report for the consideration of Your Excellency and Your Excellency's ministers.

We have the honour to be,

Sir,

Your Excellency's obedient servants,

J. E. MEADE (*Chairman*)
G. FOGGON
H. HOUGHTON
N. LEES
R. S. MARSHALL
G. M. RODDAN
P. SELWYN

A. K. RUSSELL (*Secretary*)

Explanation of terms used

CURRENCY

The currency of Mauritius consists of the rupee and the cent, one hundred cents making one rupee. The Mauritian rupee converts to the pound sterling according to the ratio Rs.40: £Stg. 3. All figures are given in the local currency, though in some instances conversions to sterling are added in brackets. All figures given in pounds, shillings, and pence refer to the pound sterling. The following list of (approximate) conversions may be useful in those cases where no conversion is given in the text.

Rs.	Cts.	£	s.	d.
1 million		75,000	0	0
1,000		75	0	0
100		7	10	0
10			15	0
1			1	6
	10			2

MEASUREMENTS

The situation in Mauritius is confusing since use is made of pre-metric French, metric, and British weights and measures, and there is no consistency of usage even as between official or semi-official documents. For instance, the figures for sugar *acreage* in Table XXIX (paragraph 5:3) derive from the Yearbook of Statistics and those in Table XXX (paragraph 5:13) giving the area in *arpents* from a memorandum produced by the Mauritius Chamber of Agriculture. We have not attempted to impose a consistency on the use of measurements and have in all cases kept to the measurements used in print or quoted orally by authoritative people. The terms most frequently interchanged are the acre and the arpent, and the long ton and the metric ton. These convert to each other as follows:

    1 acre   ..   ..   ..   1·043 arpents;
    1 long ton   ..   ..   1·016 metric tons.

They are, clearly, so close to each other that for the purposes of this report they may be regarded as interchangeable.

THE PAS GEOMETRIQUES

The Pas Geometriques is a strip of land along the seashore which almost encircles the island and was originally never less than 81 metres (about 89 yards) wide. It was first reserved by the French for military purposes and under the British became an inalienable and imprescribable part of the 'domain public' in 1899. It is now preserved as a protective belt of trees around the coast and may be leased to private individuals, who are obliged under the leases not to damage the trees.

REPORTS

We make a number of references to two reports in particular, the Report on Employment, Unemployment, and Underemployment in the colony (1958), by R. W. Luce, and the Report on Social Policies and Population Growth (1960), by Richard M. Titmuss and Brian Abel-Smith with the assistance of Tony Lynes. Henceforth we refer to these as the Luce Report and the Titmuss Report.

CHAPTER 1
Introduction

1:1. The Colony of Mauritius consists of the island of Mauritius and its dependencies, Rodrigues, the Chagos Archipelago, Agalega, and St. Brandon. The island of Mauritius is situated about 500 miles east of Madagascar and 200 miles north of the tropic of Capricorn. Rodrigues, the major dependency, lies a further 350 miles to the east, St. Brandon 250 miles and the Agalega islands 580 miles to the north, and the Chagos Archipelago 1,200 miles to the north-east, half way between the island of Mauritius and the Maldives.

1:2. Unfortunately we had no opportunity of visiting the dependencies and have not therefore included them within the scope of our report. We do not think this greatly detracts from our report, however, since the dependencies account for only 12% of the colony's area and 3% of its population, and play little or no part in the economic life of the island of Mauritius itself. Henceforward, when we speak of Mauritius we refer only to the island and not to the colony which includes both the island and the dependencies.

1:3. The island of Mauritius is volcanic in origin and covers an area of approximately 720 square miles. The land rises from the coast to a central plateau, varying in altitude from 900 feet to 2,400 feet, and bounded on the north, west, and south by mountains believed to be the rim of a vast volcano. (See Map I, facing page 2.) Once almost entirely forest and the home of the dodo, it is now largely covered with sugar cane, and the dodo has been replaced by the deer which live chiefly in the scrub and savannah of the south-east. It is almost surrounded by coral reef and its associated lagoons.

1:4. The climate is maritime, tropical in the summer, sub-tropical in the winter, and, with south-east trade winds blowing most of the year, is generally humid. Yet within the narrow confines of the island, it displays surprising variety. The mean temperature varies between 67°F. at 2,000 feet and 74°F. at sea level, and rainfall from 35 inches in parts of the northern and south-eastern coasts to 200 inches in the more westerly parts of the central plateau. In addition, the island is subject to cyclones, which usually occur in February or March. During a recorded period of about 100 years cyclones have caused gusts of over 60 miles per hour on thirty occasions and gusts of over 100 miles per hour on three, 1892, 1945, and 1960.

1:5. The population of Mauritius is even more varied than its climate and reflects the importance of its history and the require-

1

ments of its sugar economy. The first permanent settlement of Mauritius was made in 1722 by the French, who shortly afterwards brought in African slaves to work on the sugar estates, and with the exception of a brief period of virtual independence during the French Revolution, Mauritius remained a colony of France until 1810. In that year it was seized by the British on account of its strategic position as "the Star and Key of the Indian Ocean" and in 1814 it was formally ceded to Britain by the Treaty of Paris. Few British settled in the island but like the French they were concerned to ensure a supply of labour to the estates, and after the abolition of slavery in 1833 began a system of indentured Indian labourers which lasted into this century. A further and more recent addition to the population of Mauritius have been the Chinese—chiefly traders.

1:6. The result is a formidable mixture of races, religions, and languages, which is thrown into strong relief by a population density approaching 900 per square mile. The 1958 population of approximately 614,000, comprised about 177,500 people of European, coloured, or mixed descent, 414,600 Indians—including some 80,000 Moslems—and 21,800 Chinese. English is the official language, but French is the language most commonly spoken by the educated, and Creole—a basically French patois—is the lingua franca. In addition a number of Indian languages are spoken, the most important being Hindi and Telegu, and also Chinese.

1:7. The economy of Mauritius is dominated by the sugar industry which accounts for 35% of the gross national product (i.e. of the total production of goods and services) and 35% of the economically active population. Its importance is emphasised even more by the figures for exports, of which it accounts for 97%. The only other exports large enough to be expressed in percentage figures are molasses (a by-product of sugar), 2%, and tea, 1%. The gross national product for 1958 amounted to Rs. 658 million (or £49 million) giving a national income per head of approximately Rs. 1,080 (or £81)—considerably higher than in India or most African territories, but far lower than in developed countries.

1:8. Constitutionally Mauritius has progressed rapidly since 1947 from Crown-colony status to representative and largely responsible government. At present (1960) the Legislative Council consists of 55 members, 40 elected on universal adult suffrage, 12 members nominated by the Governor, and 3 officials, and the Executive Council, of which the 3 officials are also members, is selected by the Governor from it. The Executive Council consists of responsible ministers but there is no first minister and no party government in the strict sense of the words. Constitutional talks are to be held shortly to discuss further advances towards a fully responsible government.

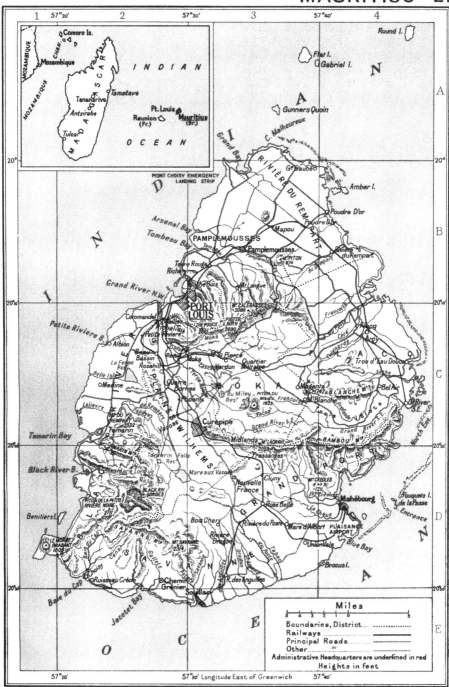

Published by Directorate of Colonial Surveys D C S 971
Third Edition.
10000/3/56 S PC. RE

Compiled and drawn by Directorate of Colonial Surveys.
Photographed by D C S and printed by G S G S 1956.

CHAPTER 2

The Issues in Outline

THE IMPLICATIONS OF POPULATION GROWTH

2:1. The future of Mauritius is at present dominated by its population problem. In the years immediately after World War II the elimination of malaria and other improvements in public health caused a revolution in the balance between births and deaths, the full implications of which have yet to be realised.

2:2. As the following figures show, the natural rate of increase of the population, which was about one half of 1% per annum in the years immediately before World War II, had risen to about 3% per annum by 1958.

Table I. Birth- and Death-rates in Mauritius
(per thousand of the population)

Year	Birth-rate	Death-rate	Excess of birth-rate over death-rate
1936-40	33·1	27·7	5·4
1948	43·4	23·8	19·6
1958	40·8	11·8	29·0

This demographic revolution is very sudden and very recent, and as a result of it the rate of increase of the Mauritian population has become one of the highest in the world. Recent calculations suggest that, if fertility rates remain at their present high level and if at the same time the progress of medicine and of public health in Mauritius bring mortality rates down to levels comparable with those in medically advanced communities, the population of the island will rise from its present 600,000 to no less than 3,000,000 by the end of the century.

2:3. This is a truly terrifying prospect. Mauritius is a small island dependent at present on agriculture, with a strictly limited amount of land and with an already existing pressure of population on it. If the population continues to increase there is a real danger not merely that the standard of living will not rise but that it will actually decline. The following figures suggest that such a decline may already have begun.—

3

Table II. National Income and Sugar Production per Head of Population

	1953	1954	1955	1956	1957	1958	1959
Real national income per head (Rs. per head at 1953 prices)	1,078	1,037	1,009	986	985	956	*
Output of sugar per head of total population (Kilos per head)	976	925	952	989	941	856	917

* Not available.

2:4. The urgency of the problem is underlined by the forecasts of population growth, 1957-72, made in the Titmuss Report under the following assumptions:—

(i) *Assumption A*, that mortality rates fall gradually over the next quarter of a century to levels comparable to those of medically advanced countries, while fertility rates remain at their present levels;

(ii) *Assumption B*, that mortality rates remain at their present level, while fertility rates return to the levels existing before the 1950s, which may be taken to represent the lowest levels to which fertility might conceivably fall without the adoption of voluntary methods of family limitation by a significant proportion of the population;

(iii) *Assumption C*, that mortality rates fall gradually as with Assumption A while fertility rates are rapidly reduced as a result of the acceptance of the idea of the three-child family and its putting into practice with complete effectiveness by 1972. The following figures show what would happen to the number of children, the number of persons of working age, and the number of old persons in Mauritius in the fifteen-year period from 1957 to 1972 under these three assumptions.

Table III. Forecasts of the Population of Mauritius

Age group	1957	1972 Assumption A		1972 Assumption B		1972 Assumption C	
	1000s	1000s	Per cent of 1957	1000s	Per cent of 1957	1000s	Per cent of 1957
Under 15	260	430	166	363	139	309	119
15—64	317	494	156	488	154	496	156
65 and over ..	17	27	157	25	149	27	157
Total population ..	594	951	160	876	147	830	140

4

2:5. These figures relate in fact to changes in population over the fifteen years 1957 to 1972; but we can safely use them to indicate the sort of population changes that may be expected over the coming fifteen years. There are three outstanding conclusions:—

(i) The working population in Mauritius will increase by some 50% over the next fifteen years (see paragraphs 3:4 and 4:6). This rise is totally unaffected by the question of family planning; all persons who will be of working age fifteen years hence have already been born. Moreover, the increase in the number of persons of working age fifteen years hence will be only marginally affected by any probable changes in mortality over the period; Table III shows that if mortality continues to fall, the number of working age might rise by 56%, instead of by 54%, between 1957 and 1972.

(ii) The figures in Table III do not show what may happen thereafter. The number of persons of working age in the following fifteen-year period (1972 to 1987) will, of course, be very greatly affected by what happens to family planning in Mauritius in the years immediately ahead. It will be difficult enough to absorb a 50% increase in the population of working age into the Mauritian economy; if the rate of increase in the working population continues thereafter unchecked the problem will become virtually unmanageable.

(iii) While family planning cannot affect the size of the working population fifteen years hence, it can greatly affect the number of children and so the size of the total population over the next fifteen years. With unchanged fertility rates (Assumption A) the number of children would rise by 66% and the total population by 60% in the fifteen-year period 1957 to 1972; with the fully successful introduction of family planning (Assumption C) the number of children would rise by only 19% and the total population by only 40% over the same period.

THE PROSPECTS FOR EMIGRATION

2:6. To what extent can this very great population pressure be relieved by emigration? We have not ourselves been able to make a first-hand survey of the possibilities of emigration. We have, however, examined the history of attempts to find outlets for the surplus population of Mauritius and our conclusion is that the impact emigration could make on the population problem—even in the most favourable circumstances—is no more than marginal. Unhappy as it may seem, the fact remains and should be squarely faced that

5

countries are not governed as philanthropic institutions but as societies in which the real or imagined interests of their own inhabitants are always paramount. Many Mauritians will find difficulty in migrating on grounds of colour, race, language, lack of skill, and so on. These difficulties are well expressed in the I.L.O. Report to which we refer in Chapter 4 (paragraph 4:34).

2:7. We believe that the Government of Mauritius should continue to investigate all possible opportunities for emigration and we recommend that it should itself approach the governments of countries to which emigration might be possible, for instance Brazil and British Honduras.

2:8. In the case of the United Kingdom there would be difficulties of language and of assimilation to a totally different mode of life in a highly industrialized country with very different climatic, social, economic, and racial conditions from those of Mauritius. But, unless present United Kingdom policies are changed, there would be no legal restriction on the immigration of Mauritians into the United Kingdom, and the cost of such migration would amount to little more than the fare from Mauritius to the United Kingdom (say Rs. 6,000 or £450 for a man, wife, and three children).

2:9. But in the case of migration to underdeveloped countries the cost of movement may be very heavy, since the country of immigration is likely to require the newcomers or their government to provide the capital needed to establish them in their new country. For example, the cost for a five-member Mauritian family of travel to, and establishment in, British Honduras might amount to some Rs. 50,000 (£3,750), which must be compared with the capital required to establish such a new family unit in Mauritius of, say, Rs. 20,000 (£1,500). Thus, even though such emigration might provide some opportunities for the productive employment of some small part of the increased Mauritian population, it would almost certainly require more capital than is needed to absorb them into the Mauritian economy itself.

2:10. Moreover, as will be seen in Chapter 4 (paragraph 4:32) the prospects for emigration are much better in the case of skilled than of unskilled workers. For it is trained persons whom the countries of immigration desire to take in. It has been suggested that the Government of Mauritius should, therefore, encourage the training of workers in Mauritius in order to prepare them for emigration. We are opposed to this policy. The training of an artisan may cost some Rs. 2,000 (£250) and this additional cost must be added to the other costs of travel and settlement of a migrant family. This then becomes an expensive method of providing what must remain a very small alleviation of the population problem; for, as is clear from

Chapter 8, present facilities for technical training in Mauritius are lamentably restricted and it will be many years before there could be any substantial flow of trained Mauritians into the stream of emigration.

2:11. But our opposition to training for emigration goes much deeper than this. Even on the most optimistic assumptions emigration will account for only a small part of the increase in the working population. For the vast majority employment must be found in Mauritius. The prospect of finding such employment for a large mass of unskilled workers would be dim indeed, unless that mass were leavened with an appreciable admixture of trained artisans. As we argue later, particularly in Chapter 8, one of the most essential developments in Mauritius is to expand the facilities for technical training; but if the policy of finding productive employment for the increased population is to be a success, all the available artisans and skilled workers made available by such training facilities will be needed to facilitate the expansion of domestic agriculture and industry.

2:12. In brief, we believe that the Government of Mauritius might usefully make approaches to the governments of countries to which some emigration might take place, in order to seek whatever partial relief for the Mauritian population problem can be found by this means. But we have no doubt that emigration cannot provide more than a minor mitigation of the economic problems of Mauritius; and these problems are themselves so pressing that action on emigration must not be allowed to delay the other social and economic policies which are necessary to deal with the problem.

THE NEED FOR CAPITAL

2:13. The greater part of the increased population of working age will have to seek employment in Mauritius. If this is not to lead to growing unemployment, to a reduction in production per head of the population, and to a fall in the standard of living, the increased population of working age must be equipped with the additional real equipment (such as the tools, motor vehicles, machinery, buildings, etc.) necessary to provide productive employment for them. The purchase of such equipment requires capital finance which can come only from private savings by Mauritians, borrowing from overseas, or from public savings by the Government of Mauritius (i.e. an excess of current revenue over current expenditure in the government's budget). Thus the employment of an increased number of workers in Mauritius will require an increased supply of capital funds for what may be called "productive" capital.

2:14. But the increased population will put a further strain on the capital resources of Mauritius. In order to avoid a decline in standards of education the amount of school buildings must be increased *pari passu* with the number of school-children; and the amount of dwelling houses, the amount of hospital accommodation, the provision of electric power for domestic and social purposes, and similar forms of capital must be expanded more or less in line with the total population. The requirements of finance of such "social" capital must also be met out of private savings, borrowing from overseas, or budget surplus of the Government of Mauritius.

2:15. These needs of "productive" and "social" capital mean that the Mauritian community must borrow from abroad or save out of its own income large sums for capital development to match the growing population; and to this extent savings must be used not to improve standards of living but simply to prevent income per head from falling. It is not easy to give any precise estimates of these capital requirements. But it is probable that at least Rs. 4 million of new "productive" and "social" capital will be required to make possible every Rs. 1 million increase in the national income. If the population is growing at 3% per annum, then national income must also grow at 3% per annum to prevent a fall in the standard of living. This would mean that at least 12% of the national income must be devoted to capital accumulation merely to prevent a fall in the current standard of living. This rough estimate does not allow for any capital needed (i) for reconstruction of post-cyclone damage, not all of which is covered by the special grant from the United Kingdom, (ii) for the provision of "productive" capital needed to set to work any existing amount of unemployed or underemployed labour, and (iii) for the provision of "productive" and "social" capital needed to raise current standards of living.

2:16. The decline in the figures of real income per head shown above in Table II suggests that the position has already been reached at which the whole of current savings are insufficient to provide the capital needed to prevent a fall in income per head. The national income figures themselves which are examined in Chapter 3 below, suggest that in recent years *gross* capital investment has been about 15% of the *gross* national product. But the figures of gross capital investment include not only net new capital investments, but also the expenditures necessary to replace existing capital goods as they wear out. A ratio of *gross* investment to *gross* income of 15% may well correspond to a ratio of *net* investment to *net* income of less than 12%. We believe, then, that an increase in the level of essential social and productive investment is the first need of the Mauritian economy if average incomes are not to fall still further.

2:17. Before we turn to a survey of the various fields of agricultural and industrial production in which the increased population might find productive employment, we wish to make one point of general importance.

2:18. In some lines of activity there is at present some shortage of labour in Mauritius (see paragraphs 4:3 and 7). Moreover, there is likely to be over the next few years an exceptionally heavy expenditure of governmental funds on reconstruction of cyclone damage and on an infrastructure of capital development (see paragraphs 7:43 ff). Such exceptional expenditure will be financed largely by exceptional overseas finance (e.g. aid for cyclone-damage from the United Kingdom and the once-for-all running down of existing sterling balances). While such expenditure lasts at an exceptionally high level, there may be some temporary intensification of labour shortages due to the extra demand for labour to carry out these special works of reconstruction and public development. But it will not be possible indefinitely to maintain the level of such expenditure; and, whatever may be the position in the immediate future, with a 50% increase in the working population over the next fifteen years Mauritius is going to be an economy in which there is a large working force seeking work, but in which land is scarce and in which it will be difficult to raise all the capital needed to equip the whole of the increased population with the necessary "productive" and "social" capital. It is not easy to make quick changes in an economic structure; and plans must be made now for policies which will mature only after a considerable lapse of time. In such circumstances, in which there is a plentiful supply of labour but land and capital are scarce, the things which Mauritius will be best fitted to produce will be those which require much labour but little land and capital for their production; and the most economic methods of production to adopt will be those which require labour rather than land or capital for their fulfilment.

2:19. The importance of this consideration can be seen if we reconsider the requirement of capital needed to give employment to the increased working population which we discussed above (paragraph 2:15). In the United Kingdom in 1955 it seems that in the cement industry the amount of capital required per worker was some £13,000 (Rs. 173,333) while in the singlet industry it was not more than £100 (Rs. 1,333).[1] Quite apart from the problems of finding markets and obtaining raw materials for new industries, if Mauritius relied on the former type of industry to increase the number of jobs by 50 % over the next fifteen years, an investment in industrial equipment of no less than Rs. 1,300 million (£97·5 million) per annum would be required. If the latter type of industry could be exclusively used for this purpose, the figure could be reduced to as little as Rs. 10 million (£750,000) per annum. Obviously new industries would not be all of one kind, and it may be expected that they would cover a fairly broad range in terms of capital requirements. But we consider it important that special encouragement should be given to industries and to processes at the lower rather than the higher end of the scale.

2:20. In saying that Mauritius most needs new industries which require much labour, rather than much capital and land, for their production, we are not advocating the deliberate use of inefficient methods. We are not advocating that the government should fill the public service with unnecessary clerks, or that the Public Works Department should use uneconomic and inefficient methods merely to give relief to a larger number of unemployed persons, or that the sugar industry should incur high costs by refusing to introduce new labour-saving methods of production if these would in fact reduce their costs. Indeed, we consider that one of the essential conditions for sustained economic growth in Mauritius is the inculcation of a spirit of strict efficiency throughout the economy. Nor are we suggesting that the government itself and other public bodies (such as the Central Electricity Board) should avoid all projects of capital development simply because they involve the use of much capital and the employment of little labour. Hydro-electric schemes, reservoirs, and many similar public utility developments in fact involve a high ratio of capital to labour employed; but it is, of course, essential for the economic development of Mauritius to have fully adequate supplies of water and electricity.

2:21. What we are advocating is that in Mauritius in the coming years wage rates should be kept stable, so that automatically in the search for low costs throughout the economy all producers and employers (governmental as well as private) will have an incentive, whenever there is a choice, to introduce new products and processes which involve the use of labour rather than the use of capital and land.

[1] These figures would be higher today because of the rise in prices since 1955. On the other hand, in Mauritian conditions, methods of production might be adopted in each industry which required less capital per man employed than in the United Kingdom.

2:22. This is a hard doctrine, involving great statesmanship and restraint on the part of the trade unions. In countries like the United Kingdom and the United States if trade unions press up the money wage rate too rapidly this is likely to result in a general rise in money costs and prices. Wage earners may gain little or nothing because the cost of living rises with the wage rate; and the community suffers the disadvantages of a monetary inflation. But in Mauritius the danger of pushing up wage costs is much more serious. For in Mauritius the general level of money prices is set by the outside world economy; if wage costs rise relatively to selling prices, the main result will be a smaller field for the profitable employment of labour; a higher real wage may be obtained for those in employment, but only at the expense of mass unemployment. We have time and time again come upon cases of the immediate and practical importance of the wage rate in Mauritius in determining the volume of employment. Should the weeding of the cane-fields be done by manual labour or by the use of imported chemical herbicides? In making this decision the availability and price of labour to the planters will be decisive. Should sugar be loaded into the ships by a fully automatic bulk-loading process or by labour handling the sugar in sacks? In this case too the relative costs of labour and of the elaborate new equipment which would be needed for complete bulk-handling may well prove the decisive factor. Or, to take another example, the production of tea shows a real possibility of success in Mauritius. Such production demands a relatively high use of labour; thus its successful expansion could provide a substantial volume of employment in the Mauritian economy. But Mauritius has to compete on the world market with established producers in Ceylon and elsewhere; and just because the production of tea demands a relatively high use of labour the wage rate which is already higher in Mauritius than in Ceylon and East Africa (see paragraph 5:38) is of great importance in determining its future success or failure. Finally, will it be possible to establish manufactures of one kind or another in Mauritius? Mauritius has no raw materials, very little technical training, little experience in manufactures, and a limited home market. Her one advantage could be a plentiful supply of inexpensive labour. It is on such a basis that other territories (of which perhaps Hong Kong is the outstanding recent example) have based a flourishing and expanding manufacture. If Mauritius sacrifices this one advantage her prospects will be bleak indeed.

2:23. Over the next decade or so the emphasis of the Government and people of Mauritius must be on taking all the measures needed to promote economic expansion with the primary object of absorbing into productive employment at existing standards of living the increased working population. Only if this objective is achieved will it be wise to press for any appreciably higher level of real wage rates for each person in employment. It will indeed be a very great achievement if over the next fifteen years productive employment can be found for a 50% increase in the working force without any appreciable decline in present standards of living.

2:24. But a policy involving wage restraint does not mean that there can be *no* measures taken over the coming years to improve standards of living. One thing which it does mean is that such measures should, as far as possible, take forms which do not raise the cost of labour to the individual employer. This point is well illustrated by the policies outlined in the Titmuss Report which advocates various extensions of social benefits—family allowances, widows' benefits, unemployment, and health benefits. To the extent to which such benefits can be financed from general taxation by means which do not raise the cost of labour to the employer, some improvement in the workers' standard of living can be achieved without so much danger to the expansion of profitable employment for the growing labour force.[1]

2:25. The subsidisation of the cost of living is a second way in which the standard of living of the worker can be supported without any direct raising of wage costs. For example a subsidy on the price of rice would raise the *real* purchasing power of the wage earner without any rise in his *money* wage rate.

2:26. We are not suggesting that social-security benefits or cost-of-living subsidies can be used without limit to raise the standard of living. Such policies need additional taxation for their finance and the imposition of such taxation may well discourage domestic enterprise and savings or the investment of foreign capital in Mauritius. But there may be some way of raising a limited revenue (such as the tax on the production of sugar which we suggest in paragraphs 2:38 and 39, and 7:22 and 23) whose secondary effects (for example, in discouraging the overproduction of sugar) are to be desired rather than avoided. All that we are suggesting is that if some moderate rise in standards of living is to be achieved, it will be better to bring it about through the indirect means of social-security benefits or cost-of-living subsidies rather than by a direct increase in money wage rates. In any case we believe that neither social-security benefits nor subsidies should be contemplated as a means of

[1] The Titmuss Report proposes that unemployment and health benefits should be financed not from general taxation but by compulsory contributions by employers and workers, each paying an amount equal to 2% of the wages paid. On administrative grounds this compulsory levy may be inevitable, but on economic grounds it would be desirable to avoid it since it would directly raise the cost of employing labour.

supporting the standard of living unless it is probable that thereby a rise in money wage rates can effectively be avoided. In the conditions of Mauritius low wages (to stimulate expanded employment) plus a moderate dose of social-security benefits or of cost-of-living subsidies (to support the standard of living) together make up a very sensible policy. But high wages plus social-security plus cost-of-living subsidies would spell inevitable ruin.

2:27. In fact, as the following figures show, the cost of living has remained remarkably stable in Mauritius over recent years. This stability is in part due to the action of the government monopoly in the import of rice, the staple ingredient in the worker's diet.

Table IV. Cost-of-living Index for Unskilled Labourers, 1956-1959
1951 = 100

1956	1957	1958	1959
104·6	103·5	104·1	103·3

Imported rice has been sold at a stable price which for a time involved a loss; but at the current (1960) low world price of rice some part of this loss is now being recouped. We believe that such a policy is sound provided that a stable cost of living can reasonably be expected to promote wage stability.

2:28. But in fact over the last three years, in spite of a stable cost of living, there has been a very substantial rise in money wage rates. The following table shows that after a period of five years of virtual stability from 1951 to 1956 wage rates in the sugar industry rose by more than 40% in the following three years; and in the economy of Mauritius the sugar industry is of such central importance that these rates are likely to set the level that will be acceptable in other industries.

Table V. Wage Rates of Daily Employed Men Labourers in the Sugar Industry
1951 = 100

Class of labour	1956	1957	1958	1959
Class I	103	117	129	148
Class II	104	120	132	152

The trade unions have clearly had considerable success in raising wage rates; but if this rise continues, the prospects of expanding the

13

demand for labour in Mauritius will be seriously endangered. As we explain later (paragraphs 4:10 ff), there is much for the trade unions to fight for in the way of arrangements for the decasualisation of the employment of labour and for other improvements in the methods of recruitment of labour; and it is important that they should now concentrate their attention on these other matters rather than press up still further the money wage rate. This is all the more appropriate in the case of the sugar industry in view of our proposal that a duty should be imposed on the production of sugar. If current money wage rates are maintained one effect of such a tax will be to reduce profits in the sugar industry. We consider this a better way than a further rise in money wage rates to achieve any desired redistribution of the income obtained from the sale of sugar. Any additional burden which is imposed on the producers of sugar in the form of a duty on the sale proceeds of sugar will incidentally help to raise revenue to finance the expansion of other industries and employments in the ways which we discuss in Chapter 7. To discourage sugar production by a higher wage rate is likely indirectly to raise wage costs in other industries and thus to discourage the expansion of these other industries as well.

2:29. We have already indicated that Mauritius needs considerable capital investment before useful and productive employment can be found for the increased working population. It does not follow, however, that if funds are provided, then all the available labour will in fact be automatically employed. The provision of capital on the sort of scale required is a necessary but not a sufficient condition for the solution of the problem of employment. We must turn our attention to the question whether new fields of profitable employment can in fact be found for the increased working population and for the capital equipment which must be associated with it. In what lines of agriculture, industry, or commerce might such openings be found?

PROSPECTS IN THE SUGAR INDUSTRY

2:30. In Mauritius one turns one's attention rightly and properly first to sugar. This great industry with its by-products accounts for 99% of Mauritian exports; there is, in fact, no other country in the world which is so exclusively dependent upon the export of one single product. The industry accounts for more than a third of the national income of Mauritius. The factory estates are efficient, well-equipped with modern machinery, and imbued with a spirit of enterprise. The soil, climate, and traditions of Mauritius are pre-eminently suited to the production of sugar which is, and must in the foreseeable future remain, the backbone of the island's economy.

2:31. But the basic question to which we had to address ourselves was whether the sugar industry over the next decade or so was likely to expand in a way which would give employment to any large part of the 50% increase in the total labour force in the island; and the conclusion to which we were inevitably forced was that this was unlikely. On some assumptions it may in the future give rather more employment than at present; on other and equally reasonable assumptions it may even give less employment than it now does. We feel that there is little prospect of its being able to absorb any large part of the increased labour supply.

2:32. There is undoubtedly at present some shortage of labour in the sugar industry; this is especially so in the crop season but even in the inter-crop season the managers of estates find difficulty in obtaining all the labour which they require. The evidence for the existence of such labour shortages appears to us quite convincing. This unavailability of labour (even more, perhaps, than the level of the wage rate paid to labour) induces the sugar estates to adopt methods of production which economise in the use of labour. For example, it is an important factor in inducing estates to use chemical herbicides instead of manual labour in weeding the cane fields (see paragraph 5:22). This is a most unfortunate development. For, as we have already argued, there is likely to be a considerable surplus of labour in the Mauritian economy as a whole in the years to come and it is therefore most desirable to avoid present conditions which may lead to the more or less permanent introduction of labour-saving methods. In Chapter 4 we consider some of the reasons for labour shortages in the sugar industry and some of the ways in which the availability of labour to the industry might be improved.

2:33. But we do not think that it would be wise to plan on the assumption that the sugar industry will be able to employ any very substantial part of the 50% increase in the total labour force in Mauritius for which provision must be made over the next fifteen years. The following figures show the total output of sugar, area under sugar, and employment of labour in sugar in Mauritius in recent years.

Table VI. Output, Area, and Employment in the Sugar Industry

Year	Production of sugar (thousands of metric tons)	Total area under cultivation (thousands of arpents)	Average number employed (thousands)
1929-48	267	137	—
1950	457	164	55·5
1959	580	204	57·4

The figures of output, though subject to variations from year to year, show a very marked and rapid upward trend. This is due only partly to the extension of the area under sugar cane. Much of it is due to increased yields and productivity resulting from the use of improved variations of sugar cane, the more scientific application of fertilisers, and other technical improvements. Increased productivity has enabled the greatly increased output of sugar to be produced by a labour force which has remained more or less constant over the last decade. The industry is a progressive and enterprising one and much new research is being undertaken. There is no reason to believe that the process of increased output per acre and per man employed has come to an end. Indeed, if it had not been for the very great cyclone damage in the early months of the year, a record crop of 600,000 metric tons or even more might have been expected in 1960. Well-informed persons in the industry are of the opinion that an output of 700,000 or even of 750,000 metric tons could be reached in the next few years without anything like an equivalent increase in the labour force employed.

2:34. However the actual ceiling on output will probably be set not by these production possibilities but by the problem of finding a market for all the available sugar. At present under the International Sugar Agreement and the Commonwealth Sugar Agreement, Mauritius has the right to export not more than the following tonnages of sugar.

(1) She can export to the United Kingdom 359,000 metric tons a year at the stable and normally relatively high "Negotiated Price" at which the United Kingdom undertakes to purchase this quantity of sugar.

(2) In addition Mauritius may export to Commonwealth preferential markets (in fact to the United Kingdom and to Canada) a further 118,000 metric tons a year on which she receives the variable and normally relatively low world price plus the value of the tariff preferences in these preferential markets. If some Commonwealth producers are not able to meet their quotas under the Commonwealth Sugar Agreement the shortfall is reallocated to the other Commonwealth producers *pro rata* to the latters' quotas. Between 1953 and 1959 this enabled Mauritius to export an additional 15,000 tons a year but this figure has now fallen to 3,500 tons only and appears likely to disappear altogether.

(3) Finally Mauritius may export an additional 41,000 metric tons at the world price in non-Commonwealth markets.

These three quotas—a total of 518,000 metric tons—are all that Mauritius can export under the existing International and Commonwealth Sugar Agreements. But she has a domestic market for some 23,000 metric tons of sugar, which are sold in the home market at a more or less constant price which is normally below the world market price. Thus, in all, Mauritius under present arrangements can dispose of about 540,000 metric tons a year. In 1957 the International Sugar Agreement was temporarily suspended and Mauritius was enabled to export an additional 85,000 tons, but such windfalls cannot be relied upon to recur.

2:35. Mauritius may hope to increase this market somewhat. As the world consumption of sugar rises it is to be hoped that the total quotas under the International and Commonwealth Sugar Agreements will be increased; and Mauritius being so largely dependent on the sugar industry will, so long as her costs do not rise unduly, have a strong case for favourable treatment in the allotment of expanded quotas. But there are many other countries which are anxious and ready to expand their sugar output. We have not thought it useful to make any precise forecasts of the market for Mauritian sugar. There are too many uncertainties:—the future course of the world consumption of sugar; the future course of costs of production of cane sugar and of sugar beet in the main producing centres; the extent to which other countries will insist on increasing, or be prepared to decrease, the amount of subsidisation or protection of their sugar industries; the future of Cuban sugar exports; and the development of the International Sugar Agreement and of the Commonwealth Sugar Agreement. But we have reached two basic conclusions.

(i) We think that it would be unwise to assume that the sugar industry in Mauritius will employ a substantially larger labour force. Total production, even if it is limited by marketing possibilities, will no doubt rise to some extent; but output per head will also rise and probably will rise as quickly as total output.

(ii) We think that within the next few years the problem may well arise in the Mauritian sugar industry of preventing the production of sugar from outstripping the amounts which Mauritius will be able to sell domestically and on export markets. Indeed, in a sense she has already reached this situation, since her current output in the absence of cyclones would have been some 600,000 metric tons while her current markets will absorb only some 540,000 metric tons a year.

2:36. It will not matter if for a year or two there is some excess of production over permissible sales. The crop season in Mauritius is the second half of the calendar year; and the quota year under the International and the Commonwealth Sugar Agreements corresponds with the calendar year. This means that Mauritius can export during the first half of the calendar (or quota) year the whole of the stock of sugar which she holds at the end of the previous calendar year; she can export during the second half of the calendar year that part of her crop which is needed to make up the whole of her export quota for the calendar year in question; and the remainder of her crop after satisfying her domestic market she must carry over till the next calendar year. At the end of 1959 Mauritius held a carry-over of some 125,760 metric tons; the crop of 1960 will be exceptionally low because of the cyclones; but Mauritius can add to her low crop of 1960 the carry-over of 125,760 metric tons to meet her domestic requirements and to help to make up at least part of her permitted export quota of 518,000 metric tons for 1960. She would then end the calendar year 1960 with virtually no carry-over. This carry-over she might well aim at building up again by some excess of production over permitted sales to a figure of, say, 200,000 metric tons. For such a carry-over is the best, indeed the only, assurance that Mauritius will not at some future date need to sacrifice any of her permitted exports even in a year in which her production is temporarily gravely reduced by cyclone or drought.

2:37. The building up of the carry-over will give some period of grace. Nevertheless we think that attention should be given now to the possibility that production will soon exceed the outlets for the disposal of sugar. We are opposed to the policy of waiting until the last moment. If this is done, it may become inevitable that quotas should be imposed within the sugar industry restricting the tonnage of cane produced, or the acreage devoted to sugar cane, by each planter. At present there are no restrictions on acreage or production within the Mauritian sugar industry; and there are, in our opinion, two arguments against their imposition in the future.

(i) Such quotas are almost bound to be allotted on the principle of granting to each existing planter a quota which is related to his previous output or acreage. Such a system removes the competitive spur to efficiency within the industry. The dynamic, expanding, and efficient producer can no longer so easily expand at the expense of the stagnant high-cost producer. Each has his fixed right to a certain output or acreage. This disadvantage can in part be overcome if production or acreage quotas may be freely traded so that the efficient producer can buy up the rights of the inefficient. Such trading in quotas should, therefore, be permitted if quotas are introduced. But the granting of quotas provides a firm protection for the inefficient producer who refuses to be bought out; and, it is better, therefore, to avoid the use of quotas altogether.

(ii) If sugar production or acreage is held back by quota restrictions, there would be a grave danger of dividing Mauritius into two halves—a privileged half in the sugar industry and an underprivileged half outside the sugar industry. As costs of production fell in the sugar industry those citizens—small planters as well as large—who were lucky enough to hold licences to produce sugar would be assured a relatively easy and profitable way of life, while the greatly increased mass of workers outside the industry might be struggling with low rewards and underemployment to find some way of scraping a living in the rest of the economy.

2:38. For these reasons we believe that the best way to restrain too rapid a growth in the output of sugar is to impose a tax on the total output of sugar. Such a tax will restrain the output of the least efficient and high-cost producers rather than that of the most efficient and low-cost producers. The tax can be raised in the future if a still heavier levy is required to discourage too rapid a rate of increase in sugar production; and if the price obtainable overseas for sugar should so fall or the domestic costs of production of sugar should so rise, or if the total export quotas available to Mauritius should be so increased, that the tax was no longer needed to the same extent as before to keep production within the limits of what could be sold, then the tax could be lowered or, if necessary, abolished. Variations in the rate of the tax should be regarded as the main instrument for controlling the long-run growth of sugar output and for keeping output within the limits of what can be marketed. Such a tax on sugar production, combined with the positive measures of government support which we advocate below for other and new lines of agricultural and industrial production in Mauritius, would, we hope, restrain too rapid an expansion of sugar production and encourage alternative openings for productive employment in a way which would avoid the creating of a legally privileged class of licensed sugar producers in the island.

2:39. In the conditions existing in the Mauritian industry, there is a further argument in favour of this method of dealing with the possibility of an overproduction of sugar. In Mauritius all sugar is sold by the Mauritius Sugar Syndicate; the receipts from sugar sold at different prices in the different markets (the negotiated price, the prices received for the rest of the sugar sold in preferential markets, the world price, the domestic price) are pooled; and each individual producer is paid for his sugar by the Syndicate a single price which is the resulting average of these different prices. The relationship between these various prices over the last four years is shown in the following table.—

Table VII. The Price obtained for Sugar in Various Markets

Rs. per metric ton. Price received in:—

Crops	U.K. (negotiated price)	Canadian market	U.K. (free sugar)	International markets	Local market	Average price received by producer
	(1)	(2)	(3)	(4)	(5)	(6)
1954	483	401	368	424	278	459
1955	479	417	382	373	278	448
1956	484	584	422	401	278	480
1957	503	447	415	487	277	474
1958	521	417	336	330	277	463

As far as export markets are concerned the Mauritius Sugar Syndicate will first fulfil its sales at the negotiated price; it will sell the next part of its supplies in the rest of the preferential market; and it will sell the remainder of its supplies (up to its total permitted quota) at the world price. Thus the last tons of the Mauritian production and export of sugar are sold at the world price (column 4 of the above table), while the individual producer of sugar in fact obtains the average price for this as for all other sugar which he produces (column 6 of the table). The individual Mauritian sugar producer thus obtains for any additional output which he produces a price which is normally substantially higher than the price which the sugar industry as a whole (and so the Mauritian community as a whole) receives from the sale of that additional sugar in the world market. In 1958, for example, the world price of sugar was only 73% of the average price received by the individual producer of sugar. The Mauritian marketing arrangements for sugar thus give an incentive to the individual producer to produce more sugar even though the value of additional sugar to the whole industry and so to Mauritian economy may be below its cost of production. A tax on sugar would among other things reduce this uneconomic incentive to the expansion of high-cost sugar.

PROSPECTS IN OTHER BRANCHES OF AGRICULTURE

2:40. For the reasons given above it would be unwise to expect the sugar industry to absorb any very great part of the increased working population of Mauritius over the next decade or so. What are the prospects for the expansion of other forms of agricultural and livestock production? These are surveyed in Chapter 5, which makes it clear that the tea industry shows the greatest prospect of expansion in a way which might give a really substantial volume of additional employment on land which to a large extent is not at present being used for other lines of production (paragraphs 5:35—45). It also shows that the soil and climate of Mauritius are suitable for the production of a range of other food crops such as groundnuts, potatoes, and other vegetables. Moreover, on the average of the prices which could be received for these crops over recent years, the production of these crops would appear to be as profitable as that of sugar cane for many planters. And yet there is an almost universal tendency in Mauritius for producers to shun the production of these other crops and to concentrate whenever possible on the production of sugar cane.

2:41. There are a number of explanations of this phenomenon. The most important is the striking difference in the arrangements for marketing sugar cane on the one hand and these other crops on the other hand. The production of sugar cane is a more or less gilt-edged investment for the small and large planter. The planter has the right to sell his canes to the factory to which his output is allocated; the price which he will receive from the factory is more or less fixed, under the supervision of the Sugar Central Board, at the value of two thirds of the sugar content of his canes; and the price of sugar itself is supported by the more or less stable and favourable negotiated price paid by the United Kingdom authorities on a large part of the total sugar crop. This highly organised and certain outlet for sugar cane is in complete contrast with the totally unorganised and uncertain marketing of other agricultural products. The man who produces a good crop of potatoes, for example, may make a good return if they come to market when there is a temporary shortage of potatoes in Mauritius; but he will be ruined if they happen to come to market at the same moment that a shipload of imported potatoes reaches Port Louis. For this reason we consider that the institution of marketing organisations which will provide an assured market at guaranteed minimum prices for crops other than sugar cane is an essential prerequisite for the stimulation of these other lines of agricultural production.

2:42. Accordingly, in Chapter 5 we make proposals for a Central Agricultural Marketing Board which should be in a position to offer to take from producers the whole output of specified agricultural products at pre-announced guaranteed minimum prices (paragraph 5:144 ff). We are of the opinion that in operating these marketing schemes the Agricultural Marketing Board should avoid the use of production or acreage quotas to limit the output of these products. The Board should receive a limited annual grant from the budget to enable it to set its guaranteed minimum prices at reasonably generous levels in order to encourage the domestic production of the crops concerned; and it should be asked to advise the government on any restrictions on imports to improve the domestic market for a product. But in so far as producers persistently offered to the Board more of any one of the guaranteed products than the Board could sell (given the limits to its financial ability to subsidise losses and to the restrictions which the government was prepared to place on imports), the Board should discourage production by setting a lower level of guaranteed minimum prices for the product in subsequent years. The Board should at first restrict its operations to one or two of the most promising non-perishable crops in order to gain experience in such operations. We recommend that the Government of Mauritius should start the scheme by appointing a well-qualified man to be the first manager of the Board, and that the manager's first duty should be to prepare a scheme for approval by the government. This scheme should include proposals about the crops to which operations would at first be confined and about the limits which should be set to the capital funds and the current annual grant which would be allocated to the Board.

2:43. There is at present in Mauritius one marketing organisation, namely the Tobacco Board, which does take over the whole crop at a pre-announced guaranteed price, but which finds it necessary year after year to restrict by quota the output of the product. We believe that the same marketing principle outlined in the previous paragraph should be applied to tobacco and that, so long as the quota restrictions on production remains necessary, the Tobacco Board should gradually reduce the price at which it offers to take the tobacco crop. In this case the producers of cigarettes in Mauritius should be required to pass on to the consumer any reduction in the price at which the Tobacco Board sold tobacco leaf to them (see paragraph 5:47).

2:44. As a part of the need for improved marketing arrangements for other agricultural products, the provision of more cold-storage capacity in Mauritius is an essential requirement. To carry fruit, vegetables, fish, and other perishable products in the climate of Mauritius from a period of glut in the market to a period when the products can be sold cold-storage capacity is essential; and at present there is a serious deficiency of such capacity in Mauritius. There are, however, plans for the development of cold-storage capacity by private enterprise; and such plans are to be greatly welcomed and encouraged.

2:45. Another major contrast between sugar and other crops is the great difference in Mauritius between the amount of resources devoted to research and the improvement of methods of production in the case of sugar and in the case of all other lines of production.

The Mauritius Sugar Research Institute is a highly organised and efficient research institute consisting of some 20 research officers and supporting staff and devoted solely to the improvement of sugar production. On the other hand, in the Mauritian tea industry, for example, there is only one officer, with a small staff, who is responsible not only for such small amounts of "research" as he can manage to find time for, but also for the supervision and control of the governmental development plans for the tea industry, which are described in Chapter 5. A considerable expansion of research into the problems of agricultural products other than sugar is desirable.

2:46. Further, whereas there is in Mauritius a widespread and traditional understanding of matters connected with the production of sugar, the planter is apathetic and less well informed about the production of other crops. It was not until 1954 that the agricultural extension service in Mauritius gave help to the small planter of anything but sugar cane. A considerable expansion of the agricultural extension services in helping small planters to turn to other crops is greatly to be desired.

2:47. Many of these changes which are needed to stimulate the production of other crops in Mauritius will cost money. Expenditure on research and on expanded agricultural extension services must, at first at least, be a direct charge on the government's budget. But in our opinion the government should be prepared in the years immediately ahead to face also a considerable charge on account of the new marketing arrangements required to make the production of other crops attractive. Much inertia, ignorance, and prejudice against other crops has to be overcome. The minimum prices which should be guaranteed under the new marketing organisations should be set at reasonably generous levels, and the government should be prepared to face some appreciable losses in the early years of their life. Such subsidies to the growth of other crops may well prove to be an essential feature in the early stages of development of these other lines of production.

2:48. As we have already observed (paragraph 2:40), the production of tea—which is one of the most promising of the alternative crops—requires considerable amounts of labour. This makes it a peculiarly appropriate crop for the absorption of some of the increased working population in Mauritius. But at the same time it means that its profitability and success will depend largely upon wage restraint in the years immediately ahead; for a large part of the cost of tea is the wages of the labour employed and tea has to compete in quality and price on a very competitive world market.

2:49. These considerations of wage costs provide an important argument, in an economy such as that of Mauritius, for the encouragement of small planters who rely largely on their own work and on that of their families for production. Where the production of sugar cane, of tea, or groundnuts, etc., is undertaken by such small planters, the income earned by the planter and his family is automatically adjusted to the price at which the product can be sold and to the productivity of the planter himself. Thus in the case of tea the planters' income would be the result of the price which Mauritian tea could obtain on the highly competitive world market and of the efficiency of the small planter in production. The standard of living of the planter could be raised as his productivity increased; but there would not be the same danger that an inflexible money wage cost would make Mauritian tea uncompetitive on the world market. Production by such small planters is, of course, desirable only if it can be efficiently organised, and we discuss the problems involved in such efficient production in Chapter 5 (paragraphs 5:35—45). There must be an organised market for controlling the quality of the product and for ensuring a secure outlet for it; in the case of products like sugar, tea, and groundnuts the further processing of the product must be undertaken by large-scale factories run on efficient commercial lines; there must be adequate sources of finance for short-term, medium-term, and long-term capital for the efficient development of the small planters' land; and there must be a well-developed agricultural extension service to advise the small planter on methods of production. If these conditions can be fulfilled, there is great social merit in the encouragement of the small land-owning producer; and there is the additional economic merit that the development of such production will not be unduly hampered by inflexible money wage costs.

2:50. It is to be hoped that the expansion of these other lines of agricultural production will make a substantial contribution to the provision of opportunities for productive employment to the growing labour force. But because of the ultimate shortage of land, if for no other reason, the possibility of finding additional jobs on the land will always be limited. A number of agricultural developments are, however, desirable even if the amount of employment which they provide is strictly limited. The rapidly growing population of Mauritius will require equally rapidly growing supplies of foodstuffs, if standards of nutrition are not to sink below the rather low levels at which they now stand. Still further supplies will be needed if nutritional standards are to be raised. At present by far the greatest part of all food supplies is imported; and in order, therefore, to avoid an excessive increase in the demand for imported foods which it would be difficult to finance by means of Mauritian exports, it is desirable to increase the domestic production of foodstuffs. For example, the rearing of beef cattle on lands which are unsuitable for other lines of production will not itself give employment to any great number of persons; but it could make a useful net contribution to domestic food supplies. Similarly, the improvement and expansion of domestic milk supplies which is discussed in Chapter 5 (paragraphs 5:82—96) is greatly to be desired on grounds of nutrition and of increasing domestic food supplies; and it is on these grounds rather than as a provider of additional employment that such a development is to be welcomed. Its success depends, as in the case of other agricultural products, upon the institution of a scheme for the organised collection, processing, and marketing of milk which will be provided by a large number of widely dispersed owners of one or two cows. Private plans which exist for the institution of such an organisation for the marketing of milk deserve encouragement and support by the government.

PROSPECTS IN INDUSTRY

2:51. One cannot rely upon the sugar industry to provide any substantial volume of increased employment, and other agriculture is likely to provide employment for only a strictly limited, if appreciable, labour force. It is, therefore, to the institution and expansion of manufactures that one must turn to seek productive employment for substantial numbers. In Chapter 6 we make a survey of what industrial activities already exist in Mauritius, of what sorts of industrial activities have the best prospects for development in Mauritius, of the obstacles which stand in the way of industrial development, and of the measures which the government might take to encourage such development.

2:52. There is already some manufacturing in Mauritius. This is, however, for the most part at a rather primitive stage of development, carried on on a small scale and often struggling to keep alive against many difficulties and obstacles. Once again there is a complete and sharp distinction to be drawn between the sugar industry and the rest of the economy. The production of sugar from sugar cane carried on in the sugar factories of Mauritius is a highly developed industrial process. It is performed efficiently, on a large scale, with modern machinery, with enterprise, with good business management, with adequate research facilities, and with initiative and imagination. There could not be a sharper contrast with the conditions in which the greater part of the rest of Mauritian manufactures have to be conducted.

2:53. These other manufactures are handicapped in many ways. Apart from some timber, aloes, and the by-products of the sugar

25

industry, such as molasses and bagasse, Mauritius possesses no raw materials. Its domestic market is small so that until it can produce at low enough cost to enable it to export (as in the case of sugar), the scale of its manufacturing operations must be relatively small. It has little experience or know-how in manufacturing outside the sugar industry. There is a grave lack of technical or commercial education in Mauritius to provide the necessary cadre of skilled labour for manufactures. As has already been made clear (paragraphs 2:13 ff), the expansion of the Mauritian economy (including manufactures) on a scale sufficient to offer employment to the whole increase in the working population over the next decade or so might well be impeded by a shortage of funds to finance the necessary capital development. But, at present, more important perhaps than any overall shortage of capital is the absence of financial institutions and intermediaries which will enable the manufacturer with plans for development to raise capital from others who have funds at their disposal. This last problem is not due simply to the lack of appropriate financial institutions to bring lenders and borrowers together. In part it goes much deeper into Mauritian social structure. Nearly every enterprise in Mauritius must be, if not wholly the concern of one family, at least wholly the concern of one race. It would be difficult with present attitudes in Mauritius to conceive of a man with business acumen (who happened to be Chinese) managing a firm for which a wealthy person (who happened to be Indian) had provided the capital to exploit an imaginative idea of an engineer (who happened to be of European extraction). And yet it is from combinations of diverse contributions of this kind that much economic growth might spring.

2:54. All these handicaps are indeed serious. But they are not impossible to overcome; and the only real hope for the future of the Mauritian economy and for an adequate expansion of opportunities for productive employment is that the great effort needed to transform these conditions should now be taken.

2:55. Mauritius, it is true, can do nothing to alter the two basic facts that it is poor in raw materials and that the scale of its domestic market is small. But there are many countries, including the United Kingdom, Japan, Jamaica, and Hong Kong, who have based flourishing manufactures on the import of raw materials to be made up into manufactures for the domestic market or for export. There are also many cases in which manufacturing countries with very limited domestic markets have ultimately enjoyed all the economies of large-scale production by producing for the export market; indeed the production of sugar from the sugar cane in Mauritius is an outstanding example of this. While it is certain that the first stages

26

of Mauritian industrial development must be built on production for the limited domestic market, it may well be that some manufactures in Mauritius succeed to the point at which they can begin to be exported; and it should not be forgotten that Mauritius, like Hong Kong and Jamaica, enjoys free entry into the large United Kingdom market for any manufactures which she may export.

2:56. The other handicaps to manufactures are to some extent within the control of Mauritius herself. Though their removal will require effort and considerable changes in existing policies, they can be removed—indeed they must be removed if productive employment is ultimately to be found for the whole of the Mauritian labour force.

2:57. We have already stressed the vital importance of a policy of low labour costs and wage restraint (paragraphs 2:17 to 29). This is particularly important during the early stages of the establishment and expansion of manufactures in Mauritius when low labour costs is one of the few advantages that can help to offset the initial handicaps from which Mauritian manufactures will at first suffer.

2:58. We cannot lay too much emphasis on the need for early and effective action by the government to introduce opportunities for technical training into the Mauritian educational system. The technical institute for which plans, equipment, and some staff already exist should be built and opened for students without delay. We discuss this further in Chapter 8.

2:59. In Chapter 7 we make proposals for the development of the existing Agricultural Bank into an effective financial institution which can provide capital to those who need it for the expansion of suitable manufactures. Up to the present the Agricultural Bank has been the vehicle for providing capital on favourable terms largely for the development of the sugar industry. We believe that this emphasis has been mistaken. For reasons already given at length we believe that industries other than sugar should receive special encouragement.

2:60. Another way, discussed in Chapter 6, in which the government can relieve the lack of capital by small manufactures is by the provision of industrial estates. The government should use some of its own capital funds to prepare an industrial site with services of water, electricity, drainage, etc., and to erect on it suitable buildings to be rented to small manufacturers who need small factory or workshop buildings. Such an arrangement would mean that such manufacturers would not have to raise the capital needed to acquire the land and buildings for their factories and could devote the capital resources which they did command to the purchase of machinery and to the provision of the working capital for raw materials, goods in process of manufacture, etc. This would have the advantage that the government would be safeguarded against loss to the extent that, if one of its manufacturing tenants failed, it would still own the factory for renting to some new tenant. Any such industrial estate should be set up in the Port Louis area; and we hope that an effective town-and-country planning organisation will be started in Mauritius in time to make sure that any industrial estate forms part of a larger area reserved for industrial development. An industrial estate, by concentrating a number of small producers together in a suitable area, may have great indirect advantage in encouraging producers to learn from each other, to build up an industrial labour market, to produce component parts for each other and so on.

2:61. The introduction of new manufacturing business into the Mauritian economy will almost certainly require even more direct government financial aid. This can be given in many forms: by lending capital to manufacturers; by tax privileges of one kind or another; by direct subsidies of one kind or another; or by tariff protection. Such financial aid can be temporary or it may be designed to last more or less indefinitely. In a number of cases temporary aid, while the infant industry grows up, will almost certainly be needed.

2:62. At the present time industry is encouraged in Mauritius by a system of investment allowances under the income tax which give certain tax privileges to economic activities which involve the investment of capital funds in plant, machinery, and other equipment (see paragraphs 6:97, 7:9). We do not support this arrangement. It gives much help to processes and industries whose costs are mainly capital costs; and it gives little help to processes and industries whose costs are mainly labour costs. We have already argued that this is the reverse of what is desirable. Tax privileges should be given rather to processes and industries which employ much labour and little capital.

2:63. In many underdeveloped territories at present new industries are encouraged by means of a tax holiday under which a newly established firm is given exemption from tax for, say, the first five years of its activities. This principle is preferable to that of invest-ment allowances in respect of capital expenditure in that it docs not treat activities whose costs are labour costs less favourably than activities whose costs are mainly capital costs.

2:64. But all these forms of tax privilege—investment allowances or tax holidays—are only of interest to an industry which is in fact making a profit which would otherwise be assessed to tax. None of them will help to turn what would otherwise be a loss into actual profit. There are, however, forms of aid to industry which would have this effect. For example the payment of a subsidy to an industry may make an otherwise unprofitable concern profitable; and if—when such a scheme is administratively practicable—such a subsidy is paid in the form of a subsidy to the firm's labour costs, it will give special encouragement to activities and processes whose costs are mainly labour costs.

2:65. Government can also support domestic manufactures by undertaking to purchase its own requirements from local producers in appropriate cases. Such purchasers may contain an element of subsidy to the local producers, and they can provide some guarantee of a market for the domestic manufacturer.

2:66. In Chapters 6 and 7 we consider in some detail the measures which we think might be taken to encourage new manufacturing enterprises in Mauritius. In the choice of industries for government support many factors must be taken into account: the prospect of the industry that it will be able to obtain its necessary raw materials and to find markets for its products and, generally, the prospect that any losses which it will incur will not be excessive in amount and duration. But one factor which we would like to stress is the extent to which the industry seeking support is one with a high labour content. In the choice of industries for support special consideration should be given to those which require much labour relatively to capital and land for their successful operation; and in the choice of methods of support special consideration should be given to those means (e.g. by the subsidisation of the wage bill of an enterprise) which encourage methods of production that rely on the use of labour.

2:67. Such a bias in favour of products and processes which require the employment of much labour must, of course, be applied with care. For example, it is to be hoped that overseas firms or other interests will from time to time seek government support for the institution in Mauritius of plants which they themselves will erect, finance, and operate. Even if such a plant were an industry which used much capital and little labour (for example, a cement works) its institution would not put any strain on the existing capital resources of the Mauritian economy. For if the plant is constructed, the parent company will provide the capital finance; and if it is not constructed, the capital finance will not be available for other purposes in Mauritius. The institution of such plants should be unreservedly encouraged. Even if they do not give much direct employment in Mauritius, they will impose no strain on the capital resources available to Mauritius and will introduce into Mauritius elements of technical knowledge, of business experience, and of managerial ability which may well permeate other parts of the Mauritian economy. And similarly, there may from time to time be projects, the capital and enterprise for which would come from domestic sources but would in fact be wasted or used for even less desirable purposes if the project under discussion were not encouraged.

2:68. The successful development of manufactures in Mauritius thus depends upon a whole nexus of different policies. We are of the opinion that the guidance and knitting together of this general policy requires a strong central organisation in the present conditions of Mauritius. We think that this might best take the form of an Industrial Development Corporation or Board whose function would be to investigate which industries stand the best chance of success in Mauritius, to stimulate private individuals and concerns in Mauritius into taking suitable initiative to promote such industries, to help and advise manufacturers in Mauritius on their business problems, to act as a go-between between the government and domestic or overseas business concerns which were interested in setting up establishments in Mauritius, and to advise the government on the industries which it might aid and on the most appropriate form and extent for such aid in individual cases. We do not think that such an organisation need be on a large scale. Indeed, it should consist essentially of one man of considerable industrial experience and ability with perhaps one or two assistants. But we cannot emphasise too strongly that, in our opinion, the government should be prepared to pay the considerable salary which might be necessary to attract a really well qualified industrialist to such a position. Such a man might make the whole difference between success and failure in the initial stages of building an industrial sector into the Mauritian economy. We also recommend some re-organisation of the machinery of government whereby proposals for government support of projects for economic development may be automatically examined and submitted for final ministerial decision by a standing committee of representatives of the departments and other authorities principally concerned (see paragraph 6:101).

2:69. One of the ways in which the production of agricultural products other than sugar and the production of manufactured goods in Mauritius might be promoted is by suitable alterations in the tariff on imports. At present, Mauritius exports practically only sugar and relies on imports for much the greater part of her supplies of foodstuffs, of clothing, of other goods for personal consumption, and of the machinery needed for her domestic industries. If the policy of economic growth in Mauritius over the next fifteen years is successful, so that the 50% increase in the numbers in the working force are successfully absorbed into productive employment, there will be a corresponding increase in the demand in Mauritius for foodstuffs clothing, and other goods. It would be most unwise to rely on such an expansion in the exports of sugar or of other products as would be necessary to pay for the import of all the additional supplies of foodstuffs, clothing, and other goods which will be demanded in Mauritius. It is only if consumers in Mauritius are prepared to satisfy a large part of their additional requirements by purchasing these products from Mauritian producers that the necessary economic expansion can take place.

2:70. In order to bring this about it may be desirable to give some additional protection from imports to Mauritian producers, at least for a period of some years during which the new lines of production are being established in Mauritius. We understand that the Mauritian customs tariff is under review. In our opinion a thorough review of this kind is most desirable, and we suggest that in making it the following principles should be borne in mind.

(1) Relatively high rates of duty should be imposed on those products of which there is considered to be a good prospect of stimulating the production in Mauritius.

(2) Relatively low rates of duty should be imposed on those raw materials or intermediate products which are needed for the production of those goods of which there is good prospect of expanding the output in Mauritius. There are in fact in the existing Mauritian tariff, as a result of historical accident, a number of cases in which raw materials are more heavily taxed on import than the final products which are made out of them. Thus rubber sheet is taxed more heavily than the shoes in whose production the rubber sheet may be used. To be able to import rubber more easily in the form of finished shoes than in the form of unprocessed sheet is, of course, a serious deterrent to the production of such shoes within Mauritius.

(3) Relatively low duties should be imposed on the import of the machinery needed for the production of goods of a kind which might be made in Mauritius.

(4) Adjustments in the tariff must be such as to raise the cost of living as little as possible. This is desirable in the interests of a policy of wage restraint on the grounds which we have already discussed.

(5) Since the Government of Mauritius relies for a third of its tax revenue upon the receipt of customs duties, the adjustments in the tariff must be such as not to sacrifice any important part of this source of revenue.

2:71. These principles will, of course, in a number of cases be in conflict. Thus a particular product (cotton piece goods) may be the finished product of one industry (weaving) but the raw material for another industry (making-up of clothing). Whether the duty should be high or low will depend upon whether it is most desired to protect weaving or making-up. In another case a product which it is desirable to protect in order to establish an industry in Mauritius may be an important item in the cost of living; and in such a case it may be desirable to support the establishment of such an industry not by the raising of an import duty (which will raise the price of the product) but by some form of subsidy to home production (which will help to keep the price of the product down). In another case it may be desirable to reduce the rate of duty on the import of a raw material or intermediate product in order to stimulate the domestic processing of the material; but this may cause a loss of revenue which must be made up by a higher rate of duty on some other product.

2:72. We recommend that the customs tariff in Mauritius should be systematically revised on these lines. At present the government has powers to make *ad hoc* adjustments in particular rates of duty in order to give help to particular industries when, from time to time, requests are made for such help. We believe that this method of dealing with the problem is insufficient, and that a systematic revision of the whole tariff structure is necessary in order to establish within Mauritius the general conditions in which enterprising individuals or concerns are likely to find the existing relationships between the prices of what they can make and the prices at which they can obtain their materials favourable to domestic production. The revision of the tariff, however, is a complicated matter and, as we have seen, in setting a number of the rates of duty there will be a number of conflicting principles to bear in mind. The right policy in our view is to set the general structure in as favourable a manner as possible and to retain the power to make *ad hoc* adjustments in this new structure as conditions change or as experience suggests that further adjustments are desirable to stimulate the expansion of particular parts of the domestic economy.

2:73. The theme of our report is the need for the adoption in Mauritius of a whole series of policies all of which have the single purpose of stimulating economic expansion in various sections of the Mauritian economy in order to give productive employment to a much larger working population. This nexus of policies will involve government expenditure on various projects. Such expenditure and its finance can be divided into two main parts: first, capital expenditure on various projects of capital development and, second, recurrent expenditures in the ordinary government budget.

2:74. As far as capital development is concerned, there are certain works for which the government must be responsible in order to provide the "infrastructure" of public services without which private enterprise cannot perform its task of economic growth. There must be an adequate network of roads for inland transport and communications, an adequate provision of port facilities for external trade, a sufficient supply of electricity and of water for use by new manufacturing establishments, a development of irrigation works for new agricultural production, the provision by the government of small factories on industrial estates for renting to small manufacturers, the establishment of a proper technical institute for the training of skilled workers, and so on. Mauritius is not deficient in all such "infrastructure"; indeed, her road network is particularly well developed for an economy of her kind. But in many of these directions heavy expenditure on "infrastructure" is essential.

2:75. This type of government capital construction is essential in order to set a background against which private enterprise can expand; but all such "productive" capital expenditure must compete with other objects of governmental capital development such as the building of schools, hospitals, etc., for the improvement of "social" conditions and the rebuilding of houses and other structures to achieve the "reconstruction" of cyclone damage. The sum of such "productive", "social", and "reconstruction" capital expenditures must be kept within manageable limits. Its manageability must be judged from two points of view.

(1) The total must be one which can be financed from the funds which the government can raise (i) from private savings inside Mauritius, (ii) from the excess of the government's own current revenue over its expenditure on recurrent purposes, (iii) from the amount which the government can borrow or obtain in financial aid from abroad, and (iv) from the amount of Mauritius' existing balance of sterling assets which the government considers it wise to use up once for all on the building up of this "infrastructure" of necessary capital development.

(2) The total of government capital development must not be so large as to require more than the total supply of labour and other real productive resources which are available in Mauritius to carry it out. Although in the years to come there is likely to be a surplus of labour for whom productive employment must be found, at the present moment the labour market

is not such that an indefinite supply of labour could be found of a type suitable to carry out simultaneously all "reconstruction" house-building and all the other "productive" and "social" capital works that might be considered desirable.

2:76. The Government of Mauritius has already put into operation a five-year Development Programme for the years 1957-62 covering a large number of items of "productive" and "social" capital development. Owing to delays in the preparation of plans and the letting-out of contracts, to difficulties in some cases of obtaining vital supplies on time from abroad, and to similar bottlenecks, there has been—as is so frequently the case with such programmes—delay in getting expenditure on the programme up to its planned level. As a result of the two cyclones of 1960 a large programme of reconstruction must be superimposed on the initial programme of development. The government has, therefore, decided—and we fully approve the decision—to replace the initial development programme with a new capital programme, which will amalgamate the development programme and the reconstruction programme and will cover the five-year period 1960—65. The government has shown us a first outline of this new programme; and we consider it later in Chapter 7.

2:77. The outline programme is inevitably dominated by the needs of reconstruction and, in particular, of housing. A large part, but not the whole, of the finance for this will be met by the special aid which the United Kingdom Government is providing. But apart from the balance of reconstruction finance which adds to the net financial strain on the Mauritian economy, the very heavy reconstruction work will place a strain on labour and other real resources in Mauritius which will make it more difficult to carry out the rest of the programme.

2:78. As we show later (paragraphs 7:43 ff, 7:59 ff) the total programme involves a scale of expenditure which can be financed only if considerable additional sources of external finance can be found. We recommend that every effort should be made to find this external finance; but the government of Mauritius must be prepared to face a situation in which it may prove impossible to find the finance for the whole programme.

2:79. Moreover, we do not think that the present outline programme provides enough governmental finance for the development of the private sector of the economy, i.e. in particular for the provision of funds through the reformed Agricultural Bank for the development of new lines of productive employment in Mauritius. In Chapter 7 (paragraph 7:90) we recommend an increase in the allocation of capital funds for these purposes.

34

2:80. For all these reasons it is of the utmost importance that the outline programme should be reviewed in order to postpone all capital projects which can reasonably be delayed without seriously interfering with what must be the predominant objective of economic policy in Mauritius—to provide the capital and the other conditions which are necessary to give productive employment to a much larger working force.

2:81. The nexus of policies for economic growth which are proposed in our report will also involve some increases in current governmental expenditure. A technical institute will require current expenditure on its running as well as capital expenditure on its institution; the promotion of new manufactures may require direct subsidisation of one kind or another, particularly in those cases in which protection by tariff adjustments is not appropriate (for example, where an increase in import duty is to be avoided because of its effect on the cost of living or in the case of a concern which might be producing for the export market); a policy of wage restraint may require some subsidisation of the cost of living or some expenditures on social welfare benefits to defend the standard of living; and the policy of providing secure markets at guaranteed minimum prices for agricultural products other than sugar may involve some appreciable losses in the early years at least. Many of the policies for economic growth which we recommend will in fact involve in one form or another temporary financial aid to many new "infant" activities to help them to establish themselves in Mauritius.

2:82. Thus, an excess of government revenue over current expenditure of, say, Rs. 20 million (£1·5 million) a year will be needed to help to finance the programme of capital expenditure for economic development; and some increase in current expenditures will be required to give financial aid to new economic activities in Mauritius. To some extent this financial problem could be relieved by reducing government expenditure on some items in the budget. Strict economy is required on all heads of expenditure in order to concentrate the country's resources on the paramount tasks of economic growth and in Chapter 7 we discuss the possibilities of effecting economies in government expenditures.

2:83. There are some heads of expenditure on which we recommend direct economies. For example, in a country of many religions such as Mauritius, we consider that it is inappropriate that the state should give financial support to various religions. We also consider that the sums paid on overseas leave for junior civil servants are extravagant and unnecessary, and recommend their abolition.

2:84. It is probable too that substantial economies can be made by carrying out some of the services of government more efficiently.

We have not been able to investigate this problem fully; but we consider that there is *prima facie* evidence of the possibility of some waste in administrative methods and in staffing in parts of the public administration. We recommend that the Government of Mauritius should employ a small body of experts in organisation and methods of administration to achieve any possible economies in administration. We propose that such a body should not be inhibited from proposing changes which will reduce the number of persons in government employment who are needed to carry out the necessary functions of government; such redundancies of labour can as far as possible be reduced by not recruiting new staff to replace existing staff as it retires (see paragraph 9:7).

2:85. However effectively such a policy of economy in government expenditure is carried out it is unlikely to meet the whole of the needs of the government for net revenue to finance capital and recurrent expenditure for the stimulation of economic growth. We have, therefore, turned to a review of the tax structure in Mauritius. In considering our recommendations about taxation we have had three principles in mind:—

(1) the need to raise additional revenue;
(2) the need to have a system of taxation which is as favourable as possible to enterprise and economic expansion of a kind which will give productive employment to a larger labour force; and
(3) the need to discourage the large family.

2:86. In order to encourage economic enterprise throughout the economy in a way which is likely to lead to as much productive employment as possible, we recommend that the rate of tax on companies' profits should be reduced from 40% to 30%. But we propose that this substantial relief to profits and enterprise should be combined with the abolition of the present investment allowances, whereby remission of income tax is obtained according to the amount spent by entrepreneurs on capital equipment. As we have already pointed out (paragraph 2:63) this sort of relief gives help to industries and processes which use much capital and little labour, whereas in Mauritius it is particularly desirable to encourage industries and processes which use much labour and little capital. But in terms of revenue the lowering of the rate of tax on companies' profits would far outweigh the abolition of the relief from investment allowances; and these two changes combined will together cause a loss of some Rs. 8 million a year.

2:87. Some part of this loss of revenue we feel can be made up from the abolition of the reliefs given under the income tax for leave abroad and by limiting the children's allowances under the income tax to the first three children in the family. But these two changes would make up rather less than Rs. 2 million of revenue. There would then still be a net loss of Rs. 6 million of annual revenue.

2:88. We have already shown why a tax on the production of sugar is desirable on general economic grounds; and accordingly we recommend that a tax of 5% *ad valorem* should be imposed on the production of sugar. This tax should raise some Rs. 12 million of net additional revenue, and would thus, together with the other changes which we have proposed in the tax structure, leave a net increase in annual revenue of Rs. 6 million for use for the stimulation of economic growth and activity in other sections of the economy. Apart from its importance as a means of raising revenue, a tax on the production of sugar is in our opinion (i) the best method for holding the production of sugar within the limits set by the permitted quotas for the export of sugar, (ii) a better method than that of raising wage rates for any redistribution of incomes from profits in sugar, and (iii) a method of offsetting some part of the uneconomic stimulus given to marginal sugar production by the present methods of pricing and paying for sugar (see paragraph 2:39). We believe that this tax should be subject to future adjustment—in an upwards direction if the threat of an excess of sugar production over what can be marketed should persist, and in a downward direction if the available market for sugar should show signs of expanding more rapidly than its production.

SUMMARY

2:89. The economic future of Mauritius is dominated by its population problem. The review which we have made of this problem has convinced us that unless resolute measures are taken to solve it Mauritius will be faced with a catastrophic situation. Even on the most "optimistic" assumption (see Assumption C in paragraph 2:4) that the three-child family will rapidly become the general pattern in Mauritius, it will be necessary to find work for a 50% increase in the population of working age over the next fifteen years and to find school accommodation etc. over the same period for a 20% increase in those under fifteen years of age. The review of the economic problems of Mauritius in this chapter shows that, even with this "optimistic" assumption, Mauritius will have done exceedingly well if she can bring about sufficient economic development to prevent a decline in the average standard of living of her population. With the less "optimistic" assumption (see Assumption A in paragraph 2:4) population growth would be so great as to make the problem sooner or later completely unmanageable.

37

2:90. The purely economic conclusion from this is inevitable, namely that the maintenance, and still more the improvement, of economic standards in Mauritius is dependent on the success of family planning in Mauritius. We do not believe that this conclusion can be substantially altered by taking account of emigration, which can at best form a useful but only partial mitigation of the problem. Indeed, the population situation is so serious that, in order to solve the economic problems of the island, Mauritius needs not family planning *or* emigration, but family planning *and* whatever emigration is possible. Mauritians are thus faced with a choice on this issue which only they can make; but they should be in no doubt that by refusing to encourage effective family planning they will be choosing economic disaster. In this report we say little on this subject since Professor Titmuss and his colleagues have examined it with all the expert knowledge which they command; we wish only to emphasise that we regard family planning as a pre-requisite for any long-run economic advance and to endorse the recommendations of the Titmuss Report on this subject.

2:91. The economic recommendations that we make are many and varied: a policy of wage restraint backed by policies for stabilising the cost of living and for relying on new social-security measures for guarding the standard of living; improved marketing arrangements at guaranteed minimum prices for agricultural products other than sugar; increased expenditure on research and improved agricultural extension services for agricultural products other than sugar; the organisation of small planters working for centralised marketing and processing establishments in these other lines of agricultural production; the institution of a technical institute and of other facilities for technical and trade training; the reform of credit institutions so as to make long- and medium-term credit more readily available to small producers in agriculture and industry; the building by the government of an industrial estate to let small factories and workshops to manufacturers; the setting up of an Industrial Development Board to investigate the possibilities of establishing new industries in Mauritius, to act as a go-between between private enterprise and government, and to advise the government on the forms of aid which might be given in particular cases to new manufactures; a recasting of the Mauritian customs tariff in a way to stimulate new production domestically; adjustment of the Five-Year Development Programme to give more emphasis to capital developments which will be useful for the stimulation of new productive enterprise in Mauritius; the reduction of some heads of budgetary expenditure; the employment of an expert group on organisation and methods of administration to eliminate waste from the public services; the reduction of the rate of tax on company profits and the elimination of investment allowances from the income tax; the abolition of allowances for overseas leave from the income tax; the limitation of children's allowances in the income tax to the first three children in the family; and the imposition of a 5% *ad valorem* tax on the production of sugar.

2:92. This is a long and at first sight miscellaneous list of disconnected proposals. But we wish to emphasise that they make up a single whole, devised to meet the basic economic problem of Mauritius. Each one of our recommendations will present some difficulties of a technical or political character; and each of them, therefore, alone may be threatened with postponement or neglect. But unless something like the whole of them can in fact be successfully implemented the outlook for Mauritius is grim.

2:93. Moreover, these recommendations together amount to a revolution in economic policies in Mauritius, and their implementation will not be possible unless there is a strengthening of the administrative machine with a number of experienced officers at the top level. The Government of Mauritius must be prepared to offer terms of employment which will attract really well qualified persons from outside for some of the central posts in the reorganised economy—for example, for the head of the proposed Industrial Development Corporation or of the proposed Agricultural Marketing Board. In this connection we would also draw attention to the proposal, which we make later (paragraph 9:10) and to which we attach great importance, for the interchange of senior officers between the public services of Mauritius and of the United Kingdom.

2:94. In fifteen years time the number of persons seeking work will be 50% greater than it now is; it is not to be expected that the sugar industry which accounts for more than a third of the economic activity of Mauritius will absorb much more labour; and, therefore, productive employment in the rest of the economy must be increased by some 75% over the next fifteen years if a serious decline in the standard of living per head of the population is to be avoided.

2:95. If our recommendations are effectively adopted and applied, we believe that this disaster can be avoided. A period of austerity in laying the foundation for a growing and expanding economy will be necessary. But if these foundations are firmly laid, the further prospects will be much brighter. If the birth-rate is effectively restrained, the rapid rate of growth of population seeking work will ultimately be checked. Moreover, once the economy starts to grow, this growth will in many ways be self-sustaining. Once the total number of trained technicians has been raised, there should be a marked rise in the rate of technical progress in all lines of production throughout the economy. Once the level of output per head has been raised, real income per head will be increased; it should then be easier to save; and the higher rate of capital development will in turn cause output per head to rise. Once the level of real income has been raised, the market for goods and services will expand and economies of large-scale production will be easier to achieve within the Mauritian economy. But this process of continuous and self-sustaining improvement in production and in real standards of living can be achieved in Mauritius only if over the next five years or so there is a relentless effort to introduce all those economic reforms which are essential to set this process of economic growth at work.

CHAPTER 3

The Structure of the Economy

POPULATION[1]

3:1. The resident population of Mauritius at the end of 1958 was estimated to be nearly 614,000, and was increasing at a rate of some 3% per annum, one of the highest rates of natural increase in the world. This rate of increase is a fairly recent phenomenon. During the 83 years from 1961 to 1944, the population increased by some 35%; during the 14 years from 1944 to 1958 the population increased by 46%. The principal cause of this sudden upsurge was the elimination of malaria in the 1940s, with a resultant fall in the death-rate, which averaged 30·3 per thousand in 1931-3 and 27·7 per thousand in 1936-40, but had fallen to 11·8 in 1956, 13·0 in 1957 and 11·8 in 1958. This was accompanied by a rise in the birth-rate, which had averaged 31·1 per thousand in 1931-35 and 33·1 per thousand in 1936-40, and rose to a peak of 49·7 per thousand in 1950, falling after that date, but still remaining as high as 43·8 in 1956, 43·1 in 1957, and 40·8 in 1958.

3:2. As a result of these sudden changes, Mauritius has a predominantly young population. The following table, taken from the Titmuss Report, illustrates this:—

Table VIII. Age Structure of Population

Per cent

Age group	Mauritius, 1957	Countries of north-west and central Europe around 1950
Under 15 years	43·8	24·4
15-64 years	53·4	66·3
65 years and over	2·9	9·2
Total	100·0	100·0

3:3. Because there are so many young people in the population, the "economically active" members of the population, that is those who are either employed, self-employed, or are actively seeking

---

[1] Since the Titmuss Report discusses the population problem in such detail, we have done no more than state the facts in the broadest outline.

employment, form a comparatively small proportion of the total. In 1958, the Luce Report estimated the economically active population to be 201,000, or some 33% of the total population.

3:4. One other effect of the high proportion of children in the population is that the number of people of working age will increase rapidly during the next few years, and there will be an equivalent proportionate increase in the numbers of those seeking employment. In 1957 some 63% of the population between 15 and 64 were estimated to be economically active. According to the projections in the Titmuss Report, the population between the ages of 15 and 64 should reach 355,000 in 1962, about 417,000-418,000 in 1967, and between 488,000 and 494,000 in 1972. If the proportion of the economically active population to the total population of these ages remains constant, the economically active population should reach 224,000 in 1962, about 263,000 in 1967, and about 310,000 in 1972. In other words, the numbers seeking employment or some other occupation will be 60,000 more in 1967 than there were in 1958, and in 1972 will be nearly 110,000 higher—increases of 30% and 54% respectively over 1958. This is on the assumption that there is no emigration from the island, and immigration and emigration in recent years have been negligible.

THE NATIONAL ACCOUNTS

3:5. Mauritius is a most extreme form of a mono-crop economy. Sugar, with its by-products, accounts for 99% of the total value of exports and more than a third of the total output of goods and services. In describing the structure of the economy, we shall find it useful to show it in terms of the output, income, and the expenditure of the island. These three are different ways of analysing the same aggregate—the value of output consists of the income of those going to produce it, while the expenditure table shows the disposal of the national income. It is, however, useful to show the components of these three totals separately, since between them we can gain a clear picture of how the economy works.

OUTPUT

3:6. The gross national product at factor cost (that is the total value of output of goods and services, valued before any additions to their cost is made by indirect taxes, or any reductions are made by subsidies) was estimated to be about Rs. 658 million in 1958—or rather more than Rs. 1,000 (£80 sterling) per head of the population. This is a considerably higher average than is found in India or in the greater part of Africa, but is, of course, far lower than in most of Western Europe or the United States of America.

3:7. There was until 1958 a fairly steady rise in the value of the gross national product; the increase in 1958 was very small, reflecting the smaller sugar crop of that year. There was at the same time a rapid increase in the population, and the output per head of the population has not risen appreciably since 1953. On the other hand, there has been some increase in the gross national product per head of the "economically active" population. Since there has been a great increase in the birth-rate since the war, the proportion of children in the total population has been rising, and the proportion in the economically active age groups has been falling. The following table relates changes in the gross national product since 1953 to changes in the total population and to changes in the economically active population; this latter series, however, is a very rough estimate.

Table IX. Gross National Product, 1953-1958

Year	Gross National Product (Rs. million)	Population (thousand)	Gross national product per head (Rs.)	Economically active population (thousand)	Gross national product per head of economically active population (Rs.)
1953	566	525	1,078	187	3,027
1954	573	539	1,063	190	3,016
1955	591	560	1,055	193	3,062
1956	627	579	1,083	196	3,199
1957	655	597	1,097	199	3,292
1958	658	614	1,072	201	3,274

3:8. These figures show the value of output at current market prices, that is, before any allowance is made for changes in the value of money. If we allow for this and value the gross national product at constant (1953) prices, the result will show changes in "real" output. The following table gives a very approximate estimate of the gross national product at 1953 prices:—

Table X. Gross National Product at Factor Cost

Constant (1953) prices

Year	Total (Rs. million)	Per head of population (Rs.)	Per head of economically active population (Rs.)
1953	566	1,078	3,027
1954	559	1,037	2,942
1955	565	1,009	2,928
1956	571	986	2,913
1957	588	985	2,955
1958	587	956	2,920

3:9. These figures suggest that real gross national product per head of population fell by 11% between 1953 and 1958, and per head of the economically active population fell by about 3½%. These figures need to be interpreted with some caution; the gross national product is subject to annual fluctuations due to variations in the sugar crop and 1958 was a particularly unfavourable year. But even allowing for this, *we believe that there has been some downward tendency in the real output per head of the economically active population—that is, that the level of investment in Mauritius has been insufficient to provide employment for the increasing working population at a constant level of output.*

3:10. The following table shows the components of the gross national product in 1958.—

Table XI. Gross National Product at Factor Cost, 1958

Elements	Rs. million	%
Agriculture, forestry, hunting, and fishing:		
Sugar cane	147	22·3
All other	59	9·0
Mining and quarrying	1	0·2
Manufacture:		
Sugar	78	11·9
All other	43	6·5
Construction	30	4·6
Electricity, water, and sanitary services	11	1·7
Transport, storage, and communications	76	11·6
Wholesale and retail trade	67	10·2
Banking, insurance, and real estate	12	1·8
Ownership of dwellings	45	6·8
Public administration and defence	24	3·7
Other services	61	9·3
Gross domestic product	654	99·4
Plus Factor income from rest of the world	4	0·6
Gross national product	658	100·0

3:11. The growing and manufacture of sugar thus accounted for 34·2% of the gross national product. Moreover, the output of many other industries was part of the sugar industry's activities. Some of the construction was on behalf of the sugar industry; output of the transport industry includes the transport of sugar, and so on. We have not attempted to estimate the total direct and indirect contribution of the sugar industry to the gross national product, but it is certainly well over a half of Mauritius's output. The proportion of the national product directly accounted for by sugar during the period 1953-58 varied from year to year and there is no clear trend, but the proportion contributed by other agricultural and manufacturing industries has tended to decline.

Table XII. Some Major Elements in the Gross National Product, 1953-1958

Per cent

Elements	1953	1954	1955	1956	1957	1958
Sugar	35·0	33·2	34·0	37·3	35·4	34·2
Other agriculture ..	9·7	10·0	9·3	9·1	8·7	9·0
Other manufacturing ..	7·2	7·2	6·9	6·5	6·7	6·5
Transport and						
communications ..	11·3	12·4	12·4	11·6	11·8	11·6
Construction	4·8	4·9	4·4	4·3	4·6	4·6
Trade	11·0	9·6	10·0	9·6	9·9	10·2
Public administration ..						
and defence ..	2·8	3·1	3·2	3·2	3·4	3·6
Other	18·2	19·7	19·8	18·3	19·5	20·4
	100·0	100·0	100·0	100·0	100·0	100·0

3:12. As Table XII shows, the net value of all other agriculture and manufacturing is normally well under a half of the net value of sugar output, and whereas these amounted to 16·8% of the gross national product in 1953, by 1958 they had fallen to 15·5%, even though this was a comparatively unfavourable year for sugar output. In other words, it appears to us that, not only is Mauritius a mono-crop economy, but that it is becoming more so—that is, that the relative importance of sugar in the output of commodities, as apart from services, has been increasing.

INCOME

3:13. Table XIII, overleaf, shows the sources of income in the Mauritian economy in 1958.

3:14. Compensation of employees (wages, salaries, etc.) accounted for 52·3% of the total and income by self-employed persons (farmers, professional men, traders and so on) to a further 17·1%. Income from property (rent and dividends) accounted for 16%, savings of corporations (undistributed profits) to 10·3%, and direct taxes paid by corporations to 4·4%. Of total incomes derived from the sugar industry, 43·5% was compensation of employees, 19·9% was the income of sugar planters, 12·2% was dividends and rents, 15·4% was undistributed profits of the sugar companies, and 8·1% was paid in company tax.

3:15. Between 1953 and 1958, the sugar companies' undistributed profits have been consistently higher than the dividends paid by them, and over the six years totalled Rs. 207 million (including amounts set aside for depreciation) as compared with Rs. 137 million paid in

Table XIII. National Income and Depreciation, 1958

	Rs. million	%
Compensation of employees:—		
Sugar industry ..	96	14·6
Other	248	37·7
Income from farms, professions, and other unincorporated enterprises received by householders:—		
Sugar	44	6·7
Other	61	9·3
Income from property received by householders and private non-profit institutions:—		
Sugar	27	4·1
Other	81	12·3
Cyclone and Drought Insurance Fund* ..	2	0·3
Savings of Corporations:—		
Sugar	34	5·2
Other	32	4·8
Direct taxes on corporations:—		
Sugar	18	2·7
Other	11	1·7
Central government income from property and entrepreneurship	11	1·7
Less Interest on public debt	−4	−0·6
Less Interest on consumer's debt ..	−3	−0·5
Total ..	658	100·0

* Interest less expenses.

dividends. The greater part of the variations in incomes from sugar has been in the form of undistributed profits and planters' incomes as the following table shows.—

Table XIV. Sugar Industry Components in the National Income, 1953-1958*

Rs. Million

	1953	1954	1955	1956	1957	1958
Compensation of employees	88	88	90	92	94	96
Planters' incomes ..	38	36	37	45	49	44
Dividends, etc. ..	20	19	21	24	26	27
Undistributed profits ..	31	26	32	46	38	34
Cyclone and Drought Insurance Fund† ..	6	3	3	2	5	2
Direct Taxes ..	13	13	14	18	18	18

* These figures are on a "national accounting" basis and are not comparable with the estimates of costs submitted by the industry in the calculation of the negotiated price under the Commonwealth Sugar Agreement.
† Interest less expenses.

3:16. The following table shows the proportion of the national income accruing to the various sections of the community between 1953 and 1958.—

Table XV. Distribution of National Income and Depreciation,
1953-1958

Per cent

	1953	1954	1955	1956	1957	1958
Compensation of employees	54·1	55·5	53·8	51·0	51·0	52·3
Income received by householders from farms, professions, and other unincorporated enterprises	16·8	15·2	15·0	17·1	17·1	16·0
Income from property received by householders and private non-profit institutions	13·1	15·5	16·1	15·5	15·7	16·4
Savings of corporations*..	12·5	9·4	10·5	12·1	11·5	10·3
Direct taxes on corporations	3·2	3·7	3·9	3·7	4·1	4·4
Government income from property and entrepreneurship	1·1	1·4	1·7	1·8	1·7	1·7
Less Interest on debt	−0·7	−0·7	−1·0	−1·1	−1·1	−1·1
	100·0	100·0	100·0	100·0	100·0	100·0

* Including interest less expenses of the Cyclone and Drought Insurance Fund.

3:17. Compensation of employees (wages, salaries, and amenities provided by employers) thus normally accounts for a little over a half of the national income, incomes of self-employed persons (mainly farmers, professional persons, and traders) for a sixth, income from property (dividends and rents) to a further sixth, and undistributed company profits (including provision for depreciation) to a further 10-12%. There appears to have been some decline over this period in the share of the national income received by employees, and some increase in incomes from property, but the period is too short and fluctuations in the relative proportions are too pronounced for it to be possible for us to state with any certainty what the trend has been.

EXPENDITURE

3:18. The principal items in Mauritius' expenditure are private expenditure on the consumption of goods and services (such as food, clothing, rent, and transport), the consumption of goods and services by government (such as the services of teachers and doctors and civil servants), and the gross fixed capital formation of private and public enterprises (such as expenditure on new plant and machinery, public works, and development on sugar estates and in factories). The following table shows the gross domestic expenditure of Mauritius at market prices[1] in 1958.—

Table XVI. Gross Domestic Expenditure at Market Prices, 1958

	Rs. million	%
Private consumption	540	72·9
General government consumption	86	11·6
Gross domestic capital formation:—		
Government and public enterprise	23	3·1
Sugar industry	52	7·0
Other private enterprise	40	5·4
Total	741	100·0

3:19. Table XVII shows the proportion of the gross domestic expenditure accounted for by these items over the period 1953-58.

[1] This figure does not correspond with the value of income and output we have used in previous parts of this chapter. These were calculated "at factor cost"— that is in terms of the rewards paid to the factors of production concerned. Expenditure is valued at market prices, the principal differences being that valuation at market prices includes indirect taxes and excludes subsidies. The "gross domestic expenditure" of the nation may also differ from the value of output if there is a surplus or deficit on the nation's balance of payments on current account. Roughly speaking, if a country has a deficit in its balance of payments on current account (that is, if it spends more abroad than it earns abroad) its domestic expenditure will be greater than its domestic product. The following figures show the reconciliation between "gross domestic expenditure at market prices" and "gross national expenditure at factor cost" in 1958—the term "gross national expenditure" being an accounting device designed to balance the gross national product and the national income and depreciation.

	Rs. million
Gross domestic expenditure at market prices	741
Plus Exports of goods and services	294
Income received from abroad	15
Minus Imports of goods and services	−323
Income paid abroad	− 11
Plus Subsidies	3
Minus Indirect taxes..	− 61
Gross national expenditure at factor cost ..	658

Table XVII. Distribution of Gross Domestic Expenditure, 1953-1958

Per cent

	1953	1954	1955	1956	1957	1958
Private consumption ..	73·1	75·1	75·4	75·0	75·1	72·9
General government consumption	10·8	11·2	10·3	11·2	11·0	11·6
Gross domestic capital formation—						
Government and public enterprises	4·2	3·9	3·2	3·2	2·8	3·1
Sugar industry	4·3	4·6	3·7	4·5	5·1	7·0
Other private enterprises	7·6	5·3	7·3	6·2	6·0	5·4
Total	100·0	100·0	100·0	100·0	100·0	100·0

3:20. Private consumption expenditure over this period was about three-quarters of total expenditure, with little definite trend upwards or downwards. There seems to have been a slight increase in the proportion of government expenditure on consumption and a slight decline in the proportion taken by capital formation expenditure by government. The following table shows the main elements in gross capital formation and the proportion of gross capital formation to the gross national product between 1953 and 1958.—

Table XVIII. Gross Capital Formation 1953-1958

Year	Government Rs. million	Sugar industry Rs. million	Other Rs. million	Total Rs. million	Proportion of gross national product, %
1953 ..	24	25	44	93	16·4
1954 ..	22	26	30	78	14·0
1955 ..	20	23	45	88	14·9
1956 ..	19	27	37	83	13·2
1957 ..	19	34	40	93	14·2
1958 ..	23	52	40	115	17·5
Total ..	127	187	236	550	15·0

Thus, of Rs. 550 million spent on gross capital formation over this period Rs. 127 million, or 23·1%, was spent by government and other public bodies, Rs. 187 million, or 34%, was spent by the sugar industry and Rs. 236 million, or 42·9%, by all other industries, agriculture, services, and so on. Gross capital formation averaged 15% of the gross national product over the period.[1]

[1] As we suggest in Chapter 2 (paragraph 2:16) the proportion of *net* investment to *net* national income over this period has been possibly no more than some 12%.

3:21. The economy of Mauritius is a very open one—that is, a high proportion of its income is derived from exports and a large part of its expenditure is on imports. Exports in 1956-1958 were equivalent to 47·5% of the gross national product: imports in the same years were equivalent to 40·4% of gross domestic expenditure. (Exports in the United Kingdom—a moderately "open" economy—are equivalent to 16% of the gross national product.) We can put this another way: production of goods and services for the home market is of smaller importance in the total economy than in most countries. This has certain important consequences. First, the secondary effects on local incomes of any investment are fairly limited: in technical language, the value of the "multiplier" is low. This is because a large part of the additional income generated by any investment is spent on imports and does not go to increase home demand. In these circumstances, the high level of investment by, say, the sugar industry has little effect on encouraging expansion elsewhere in the economy. Secondly, it is not possible for Mauritius to generate its own internal inflation. An increase in internal demand is immediately reflected in an increase in imports, and (except where the import trade is under monopolistic control) it is impossible for local prices to be far different from world prices. In other words, Mauritius cannot, in present circumstances, use monetary and credit expansion to stimulate the local economy.[1]

VISIBLE TRADE

3:22. The following tables show the value of imports and exports between 1953 and 1959 and the structure of imports in 1958 and 1959.—

Table XIX. Visible Trade, 1953-1959

Year				Imports (c.i.f.)	Exports* (f.o.b.)	Rs. million Balance of visible trade
1953	..	..	..	..	251·1	276·5	+25·4
1954	..	..	..	..	214·4	268·4	+54·0
1955	..	..	..	..	254·5	252·5	− 1·9
1956	..	..	..	..	224·2	299·6	+75·4
1957	..	..	..	..	263·8	332·8	+69·0
1958	..	..	..	..	299·2	291·1	− 8·1
1959	..	..	..	..	286·9†	290·4†	+ 3·6†

* Including the value of Sugar Preference Certificates.
† Provisional.

[1] We are ignoring at this point the fact that, under the present currency arrangements such policies are in any case not possible. We consider that, by and large, these institutional arrangements reflect the economic facts of life in Mauritius.

Table XX. Structure of Imports, 1958 *and* 1959

	1958		1959	
	Rs. million	%	Rs. million	%
Food	88·3	29·5	76·8	26·8
Beverages and tobacco	7·2	2·4	7·0	2·4
Raw materials, except fuel ..	6·2	2·1	6·9	2·4
Mineral fuels, lubricants, etc. ..	13·2	4·4	13·5	4·7
Animal and vegetable oils and fats	7·7	2·6	7·6	2·6
Chemicals	29·3	9·8	32·8	11·4
Machinery and transport equipment	58·1	19·4	46·1	19·6
Other manufactures	88·8	29·7	85·6	29·8
Miscellaneous	0·5	0·2	0·5	0·2
Total	299·2	100·0	286·9	100·0

3:23. Food, drink, and tobacco thus account for some 30% of total imports, and manufactures (including machinery and transport equipment) for a little less than a half. Raw materials account for a very small proportion of total imports—a reflection of the general lack of manufacturing industry. The following table shows some of the principal individual imports in 1958 and 1959—.

Table XXI. Principal Imports, 1958 *and* 1959

	1958 Rs. million	1959 Rs. million
Rice	44·1	32·4
Wheat flour and meal	11·1	7·4
Live animals, chiefly for food..	1·9	1·3
Fresh, chilled, and frozen meat	1·2	2·2
Dairy products	7·3	7·9
Fish	3·9	4·9
Vegetables	6·8	7·3
Alcoholic beverages	3·9	4·7
Tobacco (including manufactures)	3·2	2·2
Lumber	3·0	4·5
Fertilisers, crude and manufactured	13·1	15·2
Petroleum products	11·7	12·5
Vegetable oils	7·5	7·4
Paints, enamels, etc.	2·3	2·7
Medicinal and pharmaceutical products	4·6	4·5
Soaps and other cleansers	4·1	4·3
Weed killers	1·4	2·1
Rubber tyres and tubes	3·9	3·7
Paper and paperboard	1·7	2·0
Cotton fabrics	10·7	11·0
Woollen and worsted fabrics	4·8	4·2
Gunny bags and sacks	2·5	1·0
Cement	6·7	7·1
Iron and steel	13·2	12·0

[continued over

Table XXI—continued

	1958 Rs. million	1959 Rs. million
Finished structural parts made of iron and steel ..	2·5	1·6
Tractors and parts	6·4	4·7
Mining, construction, and other industrial machines	13·1	10·8
Electric generators, motors, switchgear, etc. ..	2·6	5·3
Other electrical machines, apparatus, and appliances	14·5	14·9
Road motor vehicles	13·2	13·0
Clothing	5·2	5·7
Footwear	3·6	4·1
All other imports	61·2	60·5
Total	299·2	286·9

Imports thus include a wide variety of capital and consumption goods. The most important imports are rice, wheat flour, fertilisers, petroleum products, cotton and other fabrics, iron and steel, machinery, and road motor vehicles.

3:24. The structure of exports is far more simple, as is shown in the following table—

Table XXII. Domestic Exports 1958 *and* 1959

	1958 Rs. million	%	1959 Rs. million	%
Unrefined sugar*	275·0	96·4	277·7	97·0
Refined sugar	2·1	0·7	—	—
Molasses, inedible	4·9	1·7	4·8	1·7
Tea	2·3	0·8	2·7	0·9
Copra	0·5	0·2	0·7	0·2
All other exports	0·5	0·2	0·5	0·2
Total	285·3	100·0	286·4	100·0

* Including the value of Sugar Preference Certificates.

Sugar thus accounts for 97% of the total exports, and sugar by-products for a further 1·7%. Tea accounts for less than 1% and all other exports for less than half of 1%. In addition to these domestic exports, re-exports were valued at Rs. 3·6 million in 1958 and Rs. 4 million in 1959.

3:25. The following table shows the direction of visible trade in 1958 and 1959.—

Table XXIII. Direction of Visible Trade, 1958 and 1959

	Imports 1958	Imports 1959	Exports 1958	Exports 1959
United Kingdom	36·2	36·9	83·1	81·1
Other preferential tariff countries	33·4	35·7	11·3	16·5
Other countries	30·4	27·4	5·6	2·4
Total	100·0	100·0	100·0	100·0

The United Kingdom thus takes some four-fifths of Mauritian exports, but only supplies a little over a third of its imports: other preferential tariff countries (mainly Canada) are the next most important market, and this group of countries (mainly Australia, Burma, India, and the Union of South Africa) supply about a third of Mauritian imports. Non-preferential tariff countries take 5% or less of Mauritius' exports but supply 25-30% of its imports, most of these coming from France, W. Germany, Iran, Japan, Thailand, and the U.S.A.

THE INVISIBLE TRANSACTIONS

3:26. So far we have considered the visible trade component of the balance of payments—that is, the sum total of the transactions of Mauritius with the outside world. The principal other current-account items in the balance of payments (that is transactions which do not involve the increase or diminution of obligations between Mauritius and the rest of the world) are payments of dividends and interest by Mauritius to outside investors and to Mauritius in respect of Mauritian investments abroad: donations to and from Mauritius, and payment for other services (expenditure by tourists in Mauritius, travel abroad by Mauritians, airlines, etc.). Mauritius normally has a small deficit on these invisible items: this was about Rs. 4 million in 1956, Rs. 7 million in 1957 and Rs. 11 million in 1958, the rise partly reflecting increased expenditure on travel overseas by Mauritians.

THE BALANCE OF PAYMENTS

3:27. After allowance is made for invisible items, Mauritius had a surplus on current account each year between 1951 and 1957, but had a deficit in 1958, when a surplus of Rs. 71·1 million in 1956 and Rs. 60·3 million in 1957 was converted into a current account deficit of Rs. 19·2 million, principally as a result of a fall in the value of exports resulting from a poor sugar crop, which coincided with a rise in the value of imports following the record income from sugar exports in 1957. We have not yet seen any balance-of-payments estimates for 1959, but if the deficit on invisibles was roughly the same as in 1958, there was a small current account deficit.

3:28. If there is a surplus on current account, either Mauritians are on balance investing more abroad than people abroad are investing in Mauritius, or Mauritians (in which terms we include the government and the commercial banks) are increasing their overseas assets of other kinds (such as balances with banks abroad or with the Joint Colonial Fund). The available estimates suggest that both of these were happening during most of the period for which figures are available. Between 1955 and 1958 there was a steady flow abroad of direct private investment, amounting to between Rs. 5 million and Rs. 7½ million per annum. We understand, however, that the flow has greatly diminished in recent months, and may now be very small. We are informed that a large part of this overseas direct investment has been in sugar development in South and central Africa, and recent events have tended to discourage the flow of capital to these regions. Overseas direct investment in Mauritius has been very small. This is reflected in the structure of Mauritius industry, which, with the exception of one group of sugar estates, is almost all locally owned and controlled. During the greater part of this period, too, government and other public bodies (such as the Cyclone and Drought Insurance Fund) were increasing their external assets. In 1958, however, there was a great fall in the overseas assets of commercial banks, a fall which continued into 1959. In all, Mauritius' sterling assets rose from about Rs. 225 million at the end of 1952 to over Rs. 400 million at the end of 1957, but fell thereafter, totalling Rs. 360 million at the end of 1959. There will certainly be a further considerable fall in 1960 as a result of the cyclones (see paragraphs 7:46-48). The following table summarises the balance of payments on capital and current account in 1956-58.—

Table XXIV. Balance of Payments, 1956-1958

Rs. millions

	1956	1957	1958
Surplus on current account	+71·1	+60·3	−19·2
Private capital movements*	− 8·0	−20·4	− 7·0
Official and banking institutions*	−46·7	−49·5	+22·2
Balance (including miscellaneous transactions, errors and omissions)	+16·4	− 9·6	− 4·0

* A positive sign under these headings implies an *inward* movement of funds or a *decrease* in overseas assets: a negative sign implies an *outward* movement of funds or an *increase* in overseas assets.

3:29. The significance of the balance-of-payments estimates in Mauritius differs from their meaning in a country with a more autonomous monetary system. The monetary system of Mauritius is, in effect, centred on London. The currency system is that used in nearly all the colonial territories—the "sterling exchange" system. Under these arrangements, the local currency authority issues Mauritius currency in exchange for sterling at a fixed rate of exchange. The currency authority (which in Mauritius is in effect the government) thus automatically accumulates sterling equivalent to the amount of currency it issues; an increase in the local currency supply is thus automatically matched by an increase in the currency authority's overseas assets, although not necessarily in the assets of Mauritius as a whole. If the banks buy currency from the currency authority, they do so at the expense of their own overseas assets, so that there may in total be no change in the external assets of Mauritius. The accumulation of sterling is less automatic now than it was before 1954, since before that date colonial currency authorities were normally required to invest the whole of their currency backing in sterling securities. Since then, a part of their reserves may be invested in the stock of the issuing government, and in Mauritius some $12\frac{1}{2}\%$-15% of the currency backing is invested in obligations of the Governmen of Mauritius.

3:30. Just as the currency supply is closely linked with the territory's overseas assets, so the banking system is, for the greater part, an extension of an overseas banking system. Two of the three commercial banks operating in Mauritius are branches of banks with headquarters elsewhere; the third has close ties with one of the London clearing banks, and arranges overdraft facilities with this bank if necessary. Apart from the small local investment of currency funds, there are no means whereby the authority can use an increase in the supply of money to provide finance for its own investment programme, e.g. by selling securities to a central bank. In these circumstances balance-of-payments deficits tend to be self-correcting, since an excess of payments overseas over receipts from overseas causes an automatic decline in the domestic supply of money so long as the excess lasts. Of course, this is not the case if an excess of payments for imports over receipts from exports is matched by an inflow of capital—that is if there is direct private investment in Mauritius or if the London offices of the banks are willing to work on a smaller level of balances by the Mauritian banks with them or to offer larger overdraft facilities to the Mauritian banks, or if the government is using up its own balances of sterling to meet its financial requirements in Mauritius. But an excess of overseas payments which is not so matched by an inflow of capital will be accompanied by a decline in the monetary supplies available in Mauritius. The balance-of-payments deficit will be felt simply as a general lack of spending power in Mauritius, and the consequential reduction of demand in Mauritius will bring the excess of payments over receipts to an end without endangering the value or convertibility of the Mauritian currency. It could also mean that the Government of Mauritius was finding it difficult to meet its domestic needs by realising assets or by borrowing new funds in London. The currency system of Mauritius, implying as it does a lack of means whereby government can finance its operations by credit creation,[1] has as one effect the probability that a large fall in government's overseas assets will involve it in financial difficulties.

3:31. Thus one effect of the combination of a highly open economy with the type of monetary system which we have outlined is that the money supply is strongly dependent on external transactions—in particular the level of export earnings, expenditure on imports, and credit by banks with head offices overseas. As far as bank deposits are concerned, the chart in Chapter 7 (Figure III, paragraph 7:64) shows the wide seasonal fluctuations and the variations from year to year resulting from the seasonal nature of earnings from sugar and annual variations in the value of exports. The circulation of notes and coins is less subject to variations from year to year, although it is also subject to seasonal variations. The following table shows the money supply in Mauritius in June and December from 1956 to 1959.—

Table XXV. Money Supply—1956-1959

Rs. millions

		Bank deposits	Currency in* circulation	Total
1956 ..	.. June..	114·5	45·0	159·5
	December	114·3	54·4	168·7
1957 ..	.. June..	122·7	47·9	170·6
	December	159·5	58·7	218·2
1958 ..	.. June..	112·1	54·5	166·6
	December	124·6	65·1	189·7
1959 ..	.. June..	84·3	58·6	142·9
	December	120·1	70·6	190·7

* "Active" circulation—that is, total circulation less cash held by banks.

3:32. This table shows that bank deposits are far more important in the money supply than is currency in circulation; moreover,

[1] This, of course, is also a consequence of the narrowness of the local credit market.

whereas there seems to be some secular growth in the currency circulation which does not depend on variations in external earnings, bank deposits are sharply responsive to short-term fluctuations in the value of exports—that is, of sugar exports. This is what we should expect from our analysis of the distribution of the national income in paragraphs 3:13-17 above. We noted that the compensation of employees did not fluctuate with variations in export earnings; the greater part of the variations was absorbed by changes in savings by corporations and to a far smaller extent, by incomes of self-employed persons. Since the demand for currency depends largely on the incomes of employees, annual variations in export incomes have little short-run effect on the currency in circulation. If, however, there were a series of years with low export incomes, incomes of currency users would eventually fall and the demand for currency would drop. There is, however, an annual swing of more than Rs. 10 million between the maximum and minimum levels of currency held by the public—a swing which partly reflects the seasonality of employment, but also seems to owe a good deal to Christmas spending. The peak invariably comes in December, when currency in circulation usually increased by some Rs. 5 million over the November level.

SUMMARY

3:33. The main features of the Mauritian economy may be summarised as follows.—

(a) The population is increasing by 3 % per annum; during the next fifteen years the number of people seeking employment is expected to increase by some 54%.

(b) The gross national product per head of the population was rather over Rs. 1,000 (£80) in 1958 at current prices. The output per head of the population has not increased since 1953, although there has been some increase in output per head of the economically active population; real output per head of the total and economically active population have declined over the period.

(c) Sugar normally accounts for over a third of the gross national product; the relative importance of sugar in the total output of commodities appears to be increasing. The net value of output of all other agriculture and manufacturing is well under a half of the value of sugar output.

(d) Compensation of employees accounts for rather more than a half of the national income; income of self-employed people and income from property each account for a further sixth. Undistributed profits account for 10-12% and direct taxes on corporations to a further 3-4%.

(*e*) Private consumption accounts for some three-quarters of gross domestic expenditure, government consumption for a little over 10%, and gross capital formation for about 13-15%. Gross capital formation averaged 15% of the gross national product between 1953 and 1958. Of capital formation, about a third is in the sugar industry, a little under a quarter by government and other public bodies, and over 40% by all other industries, agriculture, and services.

(*f*) Exports are equivalent to not much less than a half of the gross national product: imports are equivalent to about 40% of gross domestic expenditure. The economy of Mauritius is thus highly "open".

(*g*) Imports cover a wide range of consumer and capital goods, food, drink, and tobacco account for a little under a third, and manufactures for nearly a half. Imports of raw materials are very small.

(*h*) Sugar with its by-products accounts for nearly 99% of total exports; tea accounts for nearly 1% and all other exports for less than one half of 1%.

(*i*) Mauritius has a very favourable balance of visible trade with the United Kingdom and Canada, and an unfavourable balance with other Commonwealth and foreign countries.

(*j*) Mauritius had a surplus on her current balance of payments between 1951 and 1957 but a small deficit in 1958 and, probably, in 1959.

(*k*) Direct investment abroad by Mauritius has averaged Rs. 5— Rs. 7 million per annum in recent years, but is believed to have declined lately; there has been very little external private investment in Mauritius, most Mauritian industries being locally owned and controlled.

(*l*) The greater part of the money supply consists of bank deposits; annual fluctuations in bank deposits are far more pronounced than variations in the currency in circulation, although both are subject to seasonal fluctuations.

Labour

INTRODUCTORY

4:1. The major objective of future economic planning must be to keep unemployment as low as possible. In Mauritius this implies three things:
(i) the alleviation of existing unemployment and under-employment;
(ii) the attack on the prevailing attitude, especially of young men, to manual work; and
(iii) the provision of productive employment for the annual increase in the labour force.
How great precisely are the problems that have to be faced?

PRESENT UNEMPLOYMENT

4:2. A number of different opinions have been expressed to us about the prevailing level of unemployment. The Luce Report suggested that in 1958 205,281 (or 61%) out of a total of 336,618 persons of working age were economically active. Of these 151,496 were males and 53,785 females. The survey showed that 31,001 persons (22,512 males and 8,489 females) or 15·1% of the economically active population were unemployed during the whole of the survey week in March 1958. Of this total 8,266 (or 26·7%) were under 21, and almost half of these had never worked in *any* industry or occupation. Another 4,256 persons were disabled in some degree or another. These figures would suggest an available unemployed adult labour force (aged 21 and over) in the inter-crop period of about 18,000, a total which would include a proportion of sick persons, unemployables and no doubt a number not genuinely in search of employment, the sex distribution being of the order of 13,000 males and 5,000 females.

4:3. It is to be noted that these estimates refer to the height of the inter-crop period. Nevertheless it is difficult to reconcile them with the recurrent shortage of labour for work on the sugar and tea estates and the difficulty experienced during March and April 1960, after Cyclone Carol, in obtaining labourers (and other grades) for repair and rebuilding work by private individuals, local authorities, and other employers of labour.

4:4. It is also difficult to reconcile them with the number of unemployed registered at the employment service offices and sub-offices which has seldom exceeded an average of about 2,000, the highest figure recorded during the past three years being 4,907 in January 1958, an exceptionally bad month. Moreover the total number of separate individuals who registered as unemployed at any time during the three years 1957-8-9 was 17,476 (during the same period 8,350 people were placed in employment). There is further evidence of a similar kind. At the time of the Luce Report for example, there were 29,623 applicants in receipt of poor relief, 30% of whom or just under 9,000 were men regarded as medical cases, yet only 3,702 men among the 31,000 unemployed declared they had not looked for work because of sickness. Similarly the Report indicates that 15,205 members of the economically active population rented, leased, or managed a small farm or holding. But in the sugar industry alone there were 21,000 freehold or tenant planters (metayers).

4:5. There is undoubtedly considerable unemployment and under-employment in the island, but it would seem unlikely on the evidence available that the extent of whole-time unemployment among adults genuinely seeking work—serious as it is—is quite as great as the Luce Report would suggest.

GROWTH IN THE WORKING POPULATION

4:6. Much graver is the unemployment threatened by the great population increase. The estimated annual increase in the working population up to 1972 (i.e. persons between 15 and 64 years of age who may be expected to seek employment) is about 7,500. All persons who will be of working age in 1972 have already been born, and the fact must therefore be faced that merely to maintain the existing low percentage of economically active persons rather more than 90,000 new jobs must be found over the next twelve years. Beyond 1972 the position will rapidly become even more serious unless a successful programme of family planning has in the meantime been adopted and carried into effect.

ATTITUDES TO MANUAL WORK

4:7. The whole position is further aggravated by the disinclination of many unemployed or under-employed persons to do manual work (see also paragraphs 8:8-9) which leads to the paradoxical existence side by side of unemployment and shortage of labour. A considerable proportion of people registering at the exchanges are in search of government employment only and are unwilling to take other work. Similarly, young men with no more qualification than a primary school education up to standard VI register as foremen or timekeepers, for instance, having neither qualifications for, nor claim to, such jobs. As mentioned above (paragraph 4:3), in March and April 1960 it proved difficult to find sufficient workers for reconstruction works and there is evidence that the sugar and tea estates could not get enough labour.

4:8. There is a danger that these difficulties will increase as more and more young men acquire basic, primary education. No figure is more significant than the estimate in the Luce Report that at March 1958 there were 4,200 young people under 21 who had never worked, of whom 50% were under 18. In 1958 8,977 children completed their primary education and 1,437 left the secondary schools. Yet in that year only 156 persons under 18 registered for work at the employment exchanges and only 40 juveniles were placed in employment by the exchanges. In 1959 almost 16,000 juveniles left school—including 1,500 from secondary schools. Each year will see a rising number of young people coming on the labour market with a smattering of education and a distaste for manual work, particularly in agriculture.

4:9. This attitude towards manual work stems largely from considerations of individual, family, and social prestige, and young people often prefer to live on the exiguous earnings of parents or other family workers rather than work with their hands. However their distaste is often strengthened—in the case of young Creoles and Indians at least—by the knowledge that advancement beyond field foreman or factory artisan is virtually impossible for them under present conditions.

RECRUITMENT AND CONDITIONS OF LABOUR IN THE SUGAR INDUSTRY

4:10. The average labour force in the industry is 55,000 divided, roughly, as follows.—

Table XXVI. Employment in the Sugar Industry

Type of worker	Millers, i.e. 24 factory estates	Small planters
Monthly paid	7,500	—
Other regular workers	1,500	—
Daily paid	28,000	18,000

There are in addition about 12,000 planters who cultivate two arpents or less and do not need to hire outside labour. These help to swell the labour force of the industry by hiring themselves out during the crop season. The figures for 1958 show an average figure for the whole industry of 49,629 employed in the period January to June and 61,263 in the crop season, July to December.

4:11. The workers employed on a daily basis are for the most part task workers and of the average labour force in 1958 of 55,446, no less than 46,359 or 82% were employed on this basis. The majority of these—in 1958 31,000 or 67%—are recruited by the "job contractors".

4:12. These "job contractors" are a unique feature of labour recruitment for the sugar industry. They are essentially recruiters of labour licensed by the Labour Commissioner under the provisions of the Labour Ordinance, who operate principally in the urban and semi-urban areas on behalf of the estates for which they are recognised. Having recruited the labour, they accompany the gang or group to the estates concerned in transport provided and paid for by the estates. The job contractors are paid by a number of methods, the commonest being either a percentage on the wages earned by the labour recruited by them or a fixed payment based on the job done (e.g. the weeding of a defined area). The worker receives his wages in full, the estate bearing the full cost of the job contractor's fee. The estate retains responsibility for workmen's compensation and for the payment of wages should there be any default on the part of the job contractor. Since labour provided in this way is generally employed on a task-work or piece-work basis, there is usually a certain amount of bargaining by the job contractor in the fixing of prices, partly for his own profit and partly also because of the need to keep his force of labourers contented. There is much chopping and changing of labour between individual job contractors according to the type of work available and the prices being quoted.

4:13. The job contractor's principal function is thus that of a recruiter, although it is clear that in many cases the relationship between the recruiter and his men is much closer than that which usually exists between worker and employer. Small advances of pay are often given during a period of sickness or unemployment and as mentioned earlier a considerable amount of day-to-day negotiation on task-work prices is undertaken by the contractor. Against this must be balanced the occasional cases of sharp practice by contractors not all of which are either detected or punished.

4:14. There are other drawbacks of which the most important is the extent to which the system contributes to the casualisation of the industry. In the period 1950-58 the difference between the labour force employed in the inter-crop and the crop season increased from 8,248 to 11,634 (in 1959 it increased further to 13,880) and the total regular labour force (including labourers employed on monthly contracts) fell from 12,270 to 9,087, that is from 18% to 16% of the whole. At the same time there has been a significant increase in the numbers recruited and paid by the job contractors, as the following table covering the years 1954-58 shows—

Table XXVII. Distribution of Daily Employed Labourers in the Sugar Industry, 1954-1958

	1954	1955	1956	1957	1958
Number of daily rate labour paid by estates	27,505	27,602	29,655	29,264	26,918
Number of daily rate labour paid by job contractors	15,845	17,050	17,088	18,959	19,441
Number of daily rate labour recruited by job contractors but paid by estate	16,927	17,315	18,689	14,347	12,363

4:15. From the estate point of view contract labour is cheaper than monthly paid or directly engaged regular labour, and this is no doubt a major reason for the increase. The worker recruited through the job contractor has little bargaining power and his conditions of service are ignored by the collective agreements covering terms and conditions of employment in the industry. Unlike the monthly-paid worker, he is not entitled to end-of-year bonus, allowance of half wages during sickness, free housing or an allowance in lieu or annual leave and payment for public holiday. The employer in short is not involved in any fringe benefits apart from his legal obligation to pay workmen's compensation.

4:16. Undoubtedly these conditions contribute markedly to the difficulties in the way of recruiting field labour and must contribute in some measure to the high absentee figures, particularly marked on Mondays and Saturdays.

Table XXVIII. Absenteeism in the Sugar Industry, 1957

	Inter-crop	Crop period	Crop period
	Numbers employed by estates		Tons of canes produced
Monday	25,397	29,094	19,699
Tuesday	28,031	34,298	25,933
Wednesday	29,497	36,210	27,522
Thursday	28,644	35,509	27,043
Friday	30,073	35,471	26,560
Saturday	26,302	30,907	19,416

A number of reasons have been put forward to explain these disturbing figures. Excessive drinking at week-ends and late cinemas on

Sundays with special showings on Mondays beginning usually at noon are among these. It has also been represented that the poor physical state of many of the labourers makes it impossible for them to work a full six day week, an argument which may be partly supported at least by the higher rate of Monday absenteeism in the crop season when work is harder and more exacting. The island habit of week-end visiting of relatives may be another contributory factor, but it is surprising that so little is known with certainty about a phenomenon which contributes so largely to the industry's labour shortages. The problem is not new. A quarter of a century ago the Protector of Immigrants (writing in 1936) had this to say: "Unfortunately day labourers are working four or five days a week—although agricultural work is available everywhere in the colony throughout the whole year—so that in cases of sickness they must needs apply for poor relief for themselves or for their dependents." It was not possible to make any detailed examination of the problem, but there was evidence in the attendance records of a medium-sized estate in the south of the island suggesting that job contracting contributes to high absentee rates and that payment of a regularity bonus appreciably reduces absenteeism.

4:17. The problem of absenteeism is not peculiar to Mauritius. In British Guiana, to take one example, the sugar producers and trade unions entered into an agreement (in 1951) designed to combat it by the payment to each worker of a special bonus of 30 cents (increased in 1952 to 35 cents) for every ton of cane cut and loaded by him on Saturdays and Mondays, provided he had worked at cutting and loading on both the Saturday and Monday and in addition had cut and loaded canes on the Friday previous to the Saturday and on one other day in the week. Similarly, field workers in a number of sugar-producing countries are entitled to annual paid holidays and/or bonus *pro rata* to the number of days worked, attendance being recorded, for example, on a card held by the worker. In Mauritius it would be difficult to introduce such schemes and to measure their possible effects until estate workers are paid by the estates and attendance records known. We recommend that, in order to test their efficiency in Mauritius, the industry should be encouraged to conduct a number of controlled and observed experiments involving the various forms of incentive and regularity bonuses etc., which have been adopted in other sugar producing countries. Some experiments on individual estates should be possible in advance of the full-implementation of the recommendation below concerning methods of payment (paragraphs 4:19 and 20). For example, there is nothing to prevent any employer from offering a bonus for all work done on a Monday or Saturday. An industry which has developed an intricate, well-balanced, and efficient organisation for receiving, evaluating, and paying for cane received from many thousands of cane producers ought not to find it beyond its capacity to improve on the existing methods of labour recruitment and payment. The conversion of the present large mass of drifting, semi-casual field labour into a more permanent and more regular labour force should now receive the same energetic attention as the production, marketing and agricultural problems of the industry have received in the past. In this connection we welcome the proposal that the Mauritius Sugar Producers Association should employ a suitably qualified personnel officer.

4:18. With improved regularity of employment and a more stable labour force, the present extraordinary total of 1,200 job contractors could be steadily reduced. It is a defect of the present law that the Labour Commissioner has no power to rescind a job contractor's license. We recommend that the Labour Ordinance should be amended to remedy this deficiency and that all job contractors should pay a fee for their licence.

4:19. We do not regard the abolition of the job contractors as at once practicable. No official organisation could at present replace their intensive personal recruiting activities. We have already commented on the difficulties in recruiting manual labour, and there is little evidence to support the suggestion that without improvements in the conditions and rewards, workers would be prepared to present themselves voluntarily at the labour offices for agricultural work if the job contractors were abolished. All that would happen would be that the industry itself would have to recruit labour through sirdars etc., perhaps even employing erstwhile job contractors for the purpose.

4:20. We believe, however, that much of the criticism of the present system would disappear if estates were to maintain records of labour employed and if all labour employed on the estates were to be paid direct by the estate management. Such a procedure could open the way to long-term improvements in the conditions of field labour. The present vicious circle requires to be broken. So long as conditions remain unattractive, recruiters will be needed and labour shortages are likely to continue. But if job contractors continue to be employed as at present, the basic records on which improvements for field labour must be based will be lacking and without improved conditions labour shortages must persist. We recommend that unless this principle is accepted by the industry and positive arrangements made to put into effect, within a reasonable period of time, the Labour Ordinance (Cap. 214) should be revised to prohibit the present practice of paying wages through job contractors.

4:21. The general organisation and coverage of the employment exchange service are satisfactory. The main centres of employment are covered by offices at Port Louis, Rosehill, and Curepipe, while a system of subcentres exists in the outlying districts which are visited regularly by an interviewing officer. In 1959 the average number registered as unemployed was 3,345, and the number placed in employment 2,173.

4:22. One unsatisfactory feature of the procedure in the exchanges, however, is the system of giving priority by date of registration when referring registered persons to employment. While such a procedure may be acceptable in respect of "relief work" or unskilled work provided by government, it must seriously undermine the confidence of private employers in the efficiency and impartiality of the employment service. The staff should be free to submit to any vacancy notified by a private employer the person they regard as best fitted to fill the vacancy.

4:23. It has been suggested to us that a system of compulsory notification of vacancies should be introduced, which would provide that all vacancies be filled through the employment service, but in our view this represents a misapprehension about the role of the service. Whilst saddling every employer (and the exchange service) with a heavy additional burden of reporting and recording, such a system would not create a single additional job. It was justified in the United Kingdom during war-time because of the serious shortage of labour and the overriding needs of national defence, but we do not support its introduction into Mauritius now.

THE RECRUITMENT AND EMPLOYMENT OF YOUNG PEOPLE

4:24. We believe that the next year or two will provide opportunities for an intensive drive on the part of the Department of Labour to register and place young persons. If the housing reconstruction programme gets into its stride before the end of the 1960 crop season there may be some shortage of certain types of labour, and the housing reconstruction programme itself should present opportunities of placing the better educated unemployed in work demanding literacy and ability to absorb instruction in new methods and processes. The Labour Department should regard the task of registering and placing young people during this period as a vital part of its responsibilities, particularly in relation to the hardcore of young men, numbering more than 4,000, who have never had any regular employment since leaving school.

4:25. In this connection, we strongly endorse the recommendation of the Luce Report that a new and specialised employment service should be established to help young people, of which an important element would be effective vocational guidance beginning in the schools at as early a stage as possible. For this purpose an experienced youth employment service officer should be recruited from overseas and suitably selected local personnel attached to him for initial training which would, if necessary, be completed in the United Kingdom.

4:26. In our view the transition from school to employment and the development of a sense of community responsibility would be further assisted for many young people if existing youth activities through youth clubs and other organisations were further developed with government assistance and encouragement. We recommend, therefore, that the government should do all in its power to assist existing youth movements. We were much impressed by the comparative success of the programme of youth work undertaken by the Department of Education and are of the opinion that the funds devoted to it might be increased. Whether Mauritius should dare to venture on something more ambitious than the present clubs is doubtful, but she would certainly find it worth while to study closely the work now done for example in Jamaica by the Jamaica Youth Corps. Neither the Jamaican pattern nor any other would lend itself to slavish copying by Mauritius, but it may well be that the underlying idea, namely of having large numbers of young men living together and working together on projects which are of value to the whole community and in so doing of breaking down the barriers which previously existed and of instilling a sense of devotion to the community, could be introduced into a Mauritian organisation.

4:27. Finally, we make a number of recommendations in Chapter 8 concerning ways in which we think the education system should be changed in order to produce employable rather than unemployable young people.

THE TRADE UNION MOVEMENT

4:28. We have referred earlier to the importance which we attach to the maintenance over the critical years immediately ahead of a policy of wage restraint as an essential element in the programme of economic development which we have recommended. Such a policy must necessarily impose heavy responsibilities on the trade union movement and its leaders. They cannot be expected to accept such responsibilities unless trade union leadership is given adequate opportunities for understanding and being consulted about the economic policies of the government. We recommend, therefore, that representatives of the trade union movement should wherever possible be given an opportunity to serve on advisory committees or other bodies which may be set up by the government as part of its economic development planning and that the government should regard the creation of an informed public opinion about the island's problems and their plan for dealing with them as an important part of their programme.

4:29. The trade union movement was until recently divided into two groups represented by the Mauritius Trade Unions Congress and the Mauritius Confederation of Free Trade Unions. The maintenance of realistic trade union policies under circumstances of trade union rivalry is clearly made more difficult and we commend, therefore, the recent formation of a Central Joint Council of Trade Unions through which concerted policies and opinions can be developed jointly by the two trade union groups.

EMIGRATION

4:30. Since the war there has been a great deal of talk of emigration as either an addition or an alternative to the kind of policies for economic development outlined in this report, and the 1955 Committee on Population urged that, despite past failures, emigration should not be "brushed aside". However, the results of the enquiries made since 1955—chiefly semi-official—have been as discouraging as the enquiries have been numerous, and, as we have already made clear, we cannot regard emigration as anything more than a minor mitigation of the immense population problem with which Mauritius is faced (see paragraph 2:12).

4:31. Foremost among the difficulties standing in the way of emigration on any appreciable scale are the restrictive immigration laws which many countries have adopted to protect their cultural and racial integrity. For instance, when an approach was made to the Australian Government in 1959 with a view to arranging the emigration of Rodriguans to Australia, the Australian Government replied that, since Rodriguans are not of entirely European descent, they would not be eligible, and declined to encourage a suggestion that a representative of the Government of Mauritius should visit Canberra. Similarly, restrictive policies on immigration may be found on every continent—Europe, Asia, North and South America, and Australasia, and, nearer to Mauritius, in both the non-self-governing and the independent territories of Africa. They are by no means confined to countries or continents in which the majority of inhabitants happen to have white skins.

4:32. A second major difficulty is that under-developed countries require immigrants who are technicians and skilled workers, that is, just the people of whom Mauritius itself stands most in need. The Japanese emigrating to Brazil, for instance, are chosen so that there are at least three competent agriculturalists in every family, and these are given a course of training before they leave Japan. In other countries it is industrial technicians that are in demand. Mauritius certainly cannot afford to export either competent agriculturalists or industrial technicians, and, as we have already said (paragraph 2:10), we are firmly opposed to a policy of "training for emigration".

4:33. A third difficulty is that those countries which need and have room for immigrants often lack the capital necessary to make their absorption possible. British Guiana, for instance, is thinly populated, and is peopled largely by Indians, and therefore superficially appears to offer good opportunities for emigration from Mauritius. However, it suffers at present from a high level of unemployment and, in common with Brazil and other under-developed countries, would need a large infusion of capital for any bold schemes for hinterland development by immigrant settlers.

4:34. The 1959 I.L.O. Report on International Migration clearly described the difficulties which face—*inter alia*—the South American countries:

"The productivity of the domestic labour force is low and must be offset by the immigration of highly skilled workers, i.e. technicians, skilled operatives, and farmers able to make a positive contribution to economic development. However, in most cases inadequate capital formation and the lack of foreign investment have meant that only a small fraction of the employment potential in these occupations could be fulfilled. Thus the kind of immigration most urgently needed for economic development has been reduced to small, not to say insignificant, proportions by the inadequacy of the development process itself. This vicious circle is common to most Latin American countries."

4:35. As the obverse of this there is, finally, the difficulty raised by the cost of the sponsoring country of any significant programme of emigration. Estimates of the cost of settling a family of five in a distant country vary greatly, the Downie Report on emigration to British Honduras giving a figure of £3,570 (Rs. 47,600). Assuming this estimate to be approximately correct, it is clear that the cost of any planned programme of Mauritian emigration would be prohibitive. The Downie Report proposes a total immigration into

British Honduras of 105,000 over 15 years, or 7,000 per annum, and assuming that all of these came from Mauritius, the total cost (at Rs. 47,600 for each family of 5) to Mauritius would be in the region of Rs. 70 million (£5·2 million), that is about twice the colony's recent average annual expenditure on development and over half its recurrent expenditure.

4:36. The United Kingdom is about the only country to which one or other of these difficulties—of legal bar, lack of skill, and cost—does not apply, though as we have already pointed out (paragraph 2:8) there are formidable difficulties of language and assimilation. Unskilled Mauritian immigrants would almost certainly find themselves in the lower income groups, and might well find the strain of living in a cold, strange, or urban community too much for them. In addition we feel bound to say that if immigration into the United Kingdom continues to rise, the United Kingdom Government might well be forced to limit it.

4:37. However, so long as United Kingdom policy remains unchanged, and there is free entry into the United Kingdom for Mauritians, we feel that the Government of Mauritius should examine the possibility of promoting emigration into the United Kingdom. Since 1955-6 the Government of Barbados, whose citizens enjoy the same privilege of free entry has actively encouraged such emigration through the provision of loans of up to Rs. 1,066 or £80. These loans are made only to selected immigrants, for whom work has already been found by a Barbadian Commissioner in London, and they are repaid in monthly instalments once he or she has arrived. Up to the middle of 1960 about 2,000 Barbadians had come to the United Kingdom under this scheme, and without suggesting that it should be copied in every detail, we recommend that the Government of Mauritius should study the possibility of introducing a similar scheme.[1]

4:38. In conclusion, we recommend that emigration should certainly not be "brushed aside" in 1960 any more than in 1955 and that particular consideration should be given to the possibility of emigration to the United Kingdom. At the same time we are convinced that the time has come to recognise, once and for all, the impossibility and implausibility of emigration as a solution of any significant importance to the economic difficulties of Mauritius. Answering a question about emigration in the House of Commons in February, 1959, the then Under Secretary of State for the Colonies,

[1] Some of the authors of this report are, in their official capacities, servants of the Government of the United Kingdom. We would like to emphasise that they make this recommendation as individual members of a mission set up by the Government of Mauritius to advise it, and not in their official United Kingdom capacities.

Mr. Julian Amery made the following reply. "During the last few years" he said "the Mauritius Government, and officials of my department have spent a very considerable amount of time and energy in trying to find outlets for organised emigration from Mauritius, but without success. Although such attempts will be continued, I am bound to say that I do not think emigration can provide an answer to the economic problems of the people of Mauritius. In my view all concerned would be wise to concentrate their energies in the future primarily on seeking other solutions." We cannot endorse this statement too strongly.

CHAPTER 5

Agriculture

INTRODUCTORY

Climate and Soil

5:1. Three climatic zones are commonly recognised in Mauritius. (1) The sub-humid zone, which is the coastal belt, has an annual rainfall of 35″-50″ with mean temperatures of 23°C. to 25°C. and mean maxima and minima of 30°C. (June) and 16°C. (August). About 10% of the cane lands are found in this belt.

(2) The humid zone or middle belt has an annual rainfall of 50″ to 100″. Mean temperatures vary from 21°C. to 23°C. with extreme means of 30°C. (January) to 15°C. (August). The bulk of the cane lands are found in this zone.

(3) The super-humid zone of the central plateau has a rainfall exceeding 100″ and may reach 200″. Mean temperatures are about 20°C. to 22°C. in January and drop to a mean minimum of 14·5°C. in August. Some 25% of the cane lands occur in this zone.

5:2. The soils were classified in 1946 by Halais into two main groups of laterite according to the age of the parent rock:—

(1) the mature or older soils being deep clays or clay loams; and

(2) the immature or younger soils being shallow and characterised by the presence of varying amount of stone and gravel.

The natural fertility status largely depends on the extent of leaching, this being severe in the high rainfall areas.

5:3. In the early days of settlement the boulder-strewn landscape must have presented a very uninviting picture to the would-be cultivator. Over the years, enterprise and faith in the future of the sugar industry, supported by an immense investment of capital and labour, have resulted in the characteristic and quite amazing present-day appearance of orderly cane fields, often quite small, surrounded or separated by "windrows" of great boulders and stones. As new and more powerful mechanical aids become available the process of reclamation continues; the faith and enterprise of the pioneers is undiminished today.

Land Utilisation

5:4. Present-day utilisation of land is shown on map opposite and in Table XXIX on page 73.

MAURITIUS - LAND USE

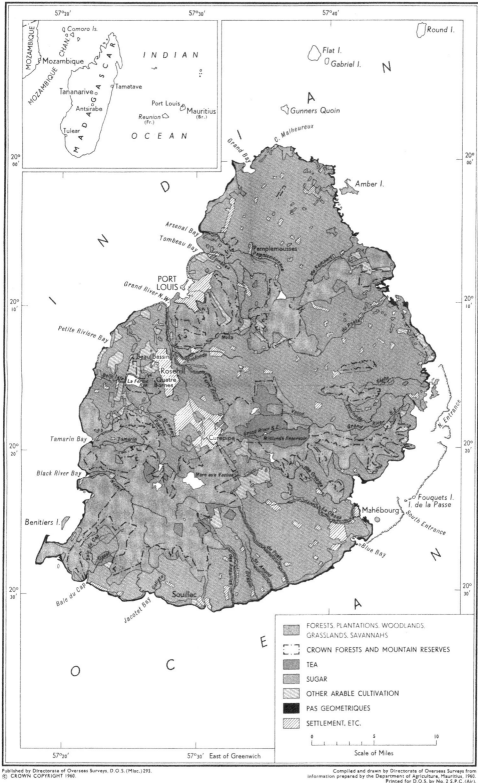

Inset map labels: INDIAN OCEAN, MOZAMBIQUE, MOZAMBIQUE CHAN., MADAGASCAR, Comoro Is., Mozambique, Tananarive, Tamatave, Antsirabe, Tulear, Port Louis, Mauritius (Br.), Reunion (Fr.)

Map labels: Round I., Flat I., Gabriel I., Gunners Quoin, Grand Bay, C. Malheureux, Amber I., Arsenal Bay, Tombeau Bay, Pamplemousses, PORT LOUIS, Grand River N.W., Petite Riviere Bay, Beau Bassin, Rosehill, Quatre Bornes, La Ferme, Belle Vue, Moka, Curepipe, Grand River S.E., Midlands Reservoir, Mare aux Vacoas, Tamarin Bay, Tamarin, Black River Bay, Beniters I., Bale du Cap, Souillac, Jacotet Bay, Mahébourg, Fouquets I., I. de la Passe, South Entrance, Blue Bay, N. Entrance

LEGEND:
- FORESTS, PLANTATIONS, WOODLANDS, GRASSLANDS, SAVANNAHS
- CROWN FORESTS AND MOUNTAIN RESERVES
- TEA
- SUGAR
- OTHER ARABLE CULTIVATION
- PAS GEOMETRIQUES
- SETTLEMENT, ETC.

0 .... 5 10
Scale of Miles

57°20'   57°30'   East of Greenwich

Published by Directorate of Overseas Surveys, D.O.S. (Misc.) 293.
© CROWN COPYRIGHT 1960.

Compiled and drawn by Directorate of Overseas Surveys from information prepared by the Department of Agriculture, Mauritius, 1960.
Printed for D.O.S. by No. 2 S.P.C. (Air).

4000/10/60

Agents for the sale of this map are :-
Edward Stanford Ltd., 12/14, Long Acre, London, W.C.2. Price 1/- net.
Copies can also be obtained from the Works and Surveys Department, Port Louis, Mauritius.

Table XXIX. Land Utilisation, 1958

	Acres	Acres	% of Total Island Area
Agriculture		213,600	46·3
Sugar	197,400		42·8
Aloe fibre (effective area)	3,700		0·8
Tea	3,600		0·8
Tobacco	1,000		0·2
Foodcrops	2,900		0·6
Vegetables	5,000		1·1
Arable land potentially productive ..		1,200	0·3
Private forest lands		5,800	1·3
Meadows, grassland, scrub, grazing grounds and waste lands		140,100	30·3
Crown forests		67,700	14·7
Natural reserves		15,500	3·4
Built-up areas		14,200	3·1
Inland water bodies		2,700	0·6
Total island area		460,800	100·0

Of the 140,100 acres described as "Meadows, grassland, scrub, grazing grounds, and waste lands" a good deal is of such a steep nature and so devoid of soil that no form of agriculture or forestry is possible, and much of the remainder is boulder-strewn and would, by normal standards, be classed as non-agricultural land, if recent experience had not shown that with modern equipment stretches in the higher rainfall areas can be reclaimed at great expense (upwards of Rs. 2,000 or £150 per acre) for sugar cane. An outstanding example of this is the reclamation work on the Plaine des Roches. The small remainder can more correctly be regarded as grazing land. It includes the Pas Geometriques (see the introductory explanation of terms used, and paragraph 5:104) but is mainly to be found in the north of the island and the Black River area, where rainfall is too low for cane cultivation and where, at least during certain seasons of the year, the Stomoxys-fly menace is not such as to prevent the daytime grazing of stock.

5:5. Leaving for the moment the question of providing water to the Black River District and the drier areas of the north, there are undoubtedly areas, possibly only a few hundred acres here and there, which could be cultivated and where the raising of stags is not the optimum use. We do not feel, however, that there is any substantial reserve of potential arable land as is sometimes suggested.

5:6. The Nature Reserves, classed at 15,500 acres, refer to mountain tops, whether in private ownership or not, and privately owned river reserves, represented by 50-foot-wide strips along the main water courses, the retention of which is considered necessary to prevent bank erosion. We suggest below (see paragraph 5:9) that there is urgent need to enact legislation to prevent the misuse of land, but provided this is accepted, we feel that once the water courses have left the gorges and reached the plains the restrictions on river bank reserves (which at present place an onerous and not very appropriate burden on the Forestry Department staff) should be removed (see paragraph 5:73). This would release some valuable land for the cultivation of fruit trees, vegetables, and food crops.

5:7. Forest Reserves, Crown and private, amount to 73,500 acres or some 16% of the total land area (see paragraphs 5:71 ff). Excisions from the forest estate have recently been made for tea planting, and sizeable additional areas are suitable for agricultural purposes.

5:8. It is not possible to say precisely how much new land can be released for agricultural purposes but we are convinced that the amount cannot make any significant contribution to the Mauritian need for more means of production and that more intensive production from the land already under use is the only answer. When the soil survey and land classification is completed—and we understand that the full results should be available in 1962—then will be the time to take stock of the resources. The survey will indicate the water, fertiliser, and cultivation treatments for the various soils, it will show the areas which are too steep for cultivation, it will suggest the crops best suited to the various soil types and make possible the preparation of a plan and a policy for the optimum use of every acre of Mauritian soil.

5:9. In pursuance of this policy it is in our view essential that legislation designed to prevent the misuse of land be enacted at the earliest possible date. We saw many examples of erosion and land destruction, particularly on steep slopes. In many cases adequate conservation measures could have been taken but in others the degree of slope was so great that cultivation should have been prevented. Land is a national heritage particularly precious perhaps in Mauritius and no man has the right to destroy it. Legislation, suitable for adaption to Mauritian needs, exists in many colonial territories.

5:10. We should add, in this connection, that there are certain areas at present reserved for the breeding of stags which are suitable either for cultivation or for the raising of beef. We recommend that if the owner is not prepared to carry out appropriate development he should be required, by sale or lease, to make such land available to those willing and able to undertake approved development.

5:11. In this policy of more intensive production the development and efficient employment of the country's water resources is in our view the most important single means available to Mauritius. The Black River district and the north of the island could undoubtedly make a very much greater contribution to the wealth of the island if water could be provided. Fortunately the high central plateau is blessed with a high rainfall and the topography suggests that from storage areas gravity feed to the less fortunate districts should be possible. Much capital has already been invested in schemes to provide water for agriculture and further schemes are under investigation, and we can think of no safer or more profitable form of investment. We therefore recommend the creation of a statutory Water Resources Authority empowered to assess the rival claims of agriculture, industry, and domestic need so that each new development can proceed along agreed lines with specific and understood objectives in mind. Since the exploration of underground water supplies is now showing promise we also recommend that the rights to and the use of such water should be regularised, and we suggest the Kenya 1951 Water Ordinance would provide a satisfactory model for use in Mauritius.

SUGAR

Area and Cultivation of Sugar Land

5:12. During the period 1929-1948 the average area under cane was 137,000 arpents with a high of 150,000 and a low of 117,000. Since 1949, when 156,000 arpents were under cultivation, the area has increased each year up to 1959 when the total area under cane was estimated at 190,000 arpents representing nearly 43% of the island area.

5:13. Of this total area of 190,000 arpents, 97,000 arpents (51%) are owned and cultivated by millers, 8,000 arpents (4%) are owned by millers but cultivated by tenant planters (metayers), and the remaining 85,000 arpents (45%) are owned and cultivated by freehold planters large and small. The distribution of the production area by category and size (arpents) is as follows.—

Table XXX. Distribution of Sugar Producing Land by Category and Size (arpents), 1959

Category	Under 10		10–99		100–199		200–499		500 and over		Total	
	No.	Aggregate area	No.	Aggregate area	No.	Aggregate area	No.	Aggregate area	No.	Aggregate area	No.	Aggregate area
Miller-Planter	—	—	—	—	—	—	—	—	25	97,000	25	97,000
Tenant Planter (Metayer)	2,622	6,000	92	2,000	—	—	4	1,000	—	—	2,718	9,000
Freehold Planter	17,829	31,000	903	23,000	73	11,000	37	12,000	9	7,000	18,851	84,000
Total	20,451	37,000	995	25,000	73	11,000	41	13,000	34	104,000	21,594	190,000

Sugar Production

5:14. Yields naturally vary according to season, variety, age of cane, nature of the land, management, etc., but, as the following average figures (1959) show, they also vary according to categories of production:—

> millers' land   ..   ..   32·4 tons;
> freehold planters' land   ..   21·0 tons; and
> tenant planters' land   ..   15·8 tons of cane per arpent.

Furthermore this difference between millers and planters remains fairly constant, despite the trend of increased production per unit of land, as the following table shows—

Table XXXI. Yield of Sugar per Arpent, Millers and Planters

Year	1954	1955	1956	1957	1958	1959	Average 1954–59
Millers ..	3·70	4·01	4·26	4·27	3·80	4·06	4·02
Planters ..	2·44	2·55	2·79	2·53	2·42	2·59	2·55
Percentage difference ..	51·6	57·3	52·7	68·8	57·0	56·8	57·7

The closing of this gap would result in increased production of about 100,000 tons of sugar or alternatively the release of some 25,000 acres for other purposes whilst maintaining the present total production level. We do not suggest that the gap can be closed, but it can undoubtedly be narrowed, *immediately* by the adequate and appropriate application of fertilisers based on information now available to the Mauritian Sugar Industry Research Institute, *in the very near future* by the use of new and improved varieties of cane (and a large source of such material is being developed for the benefit of planters), and *in the long term* by the use of irrigation.

5:15. The production of cane or of sugar is not in any way limited or controlled in Mauritius and the industry has so far been able to dispose of the full production without difficulty. Harvest and manufacture take place during the second half of the year and any sugar not shipped at the end of a calendar year is carried forward for adjustment in the following year (see paragraphs 2:36-37). The position of production, sales, and carry-overs for the past ten years is as follows—

		Metric tons		
Year	Production (crop year)	Exports (calendar year)	Local sales	Carry-overs
1950 ..	456,691	358,278	20,796	179,990
1951 ..	484,086	505,057	20,968	129,788
1952 ..	468,283	468,616	22,386	113,006
1953 ..	512,225	480,922	21,650	125,433
1954 ..	498,742	501,640	22,569	100,018
1955 ..	533,341	487,377	23,191	135,994
1956 ..	572,512	529,213	23,428	145,467
1957 ..	562,003	578,459	24,336	101,636
1958 ..	525,842	519,369	24,959	77,966
*1959 ..	579,880	507,086	25,000	125,760

* Provisional.

Sugar Mills

5:16. To reduce production costs and to improve efficiency the industry has followed a policy of centralisation in the milling of cane. A century ago there were some 260 mills in Mauritius with an average production of about 400 metric tons of sugar. At the end of the last war (1946) 33 mills with an average production of 8,800 metric tons were in operation but today the total production of close on 600,000 tons comes from 24 mills, each serving an area delimited by the Central Board (see paragraph 5:23). They are modern and highly efficient, and in terms of extraction and recovery Mauritius ranks very high among the principal cane sugar producing countries of the world.

Science and Sugar; the Sugar Industry Research Institute

5:17. The Mauritian sugar industry is highly and heavily mechanised. Ever more powerful units are being brought into use and with the establishment of the Mechanical Pool in 1951 these modern aids are brought within the means of even the small planter. The industry is served by a Research Institute of international repute, which it finances entirely itself. It has excellent facilities for its work and the breeding work, designed to provide ever-improving varieties of cane suited to the different ecological areas, fertiliser research (and the advisory service based on foliar diagnosis is a feature of the industry), and research on herbicides, pest and disease control, irrigation practices, sugar technology, etc., all appeared to be highly efficient.

5:18. A major activity of the Institute, and one of very great importance to agriculture in the island, is the soil survey which it is hoped will be available in report form by the end of this year, or early in 1961. We congratulate the industry on the initiative it has shown in organising it. It will provide maps on the scale one inch to the mile, show the distribution of soil types and nutrient status, suggest crops and cultivation methods suited to each class of soil, demarcate land of dangerous slope or otherwise unsuitable for cultivation, and in short provide the first scientific assessment of the agricultural potential of the island. This basic information will enable the government to take stock and it will provide valuable guidance on such problems as the optimum use of land—particularly land which is not beneficially used at present, the need for irrigation, the island's potential for tea development, and many other major matters of this kind. It must be followed by an era of field experimentation to test the findings of the laboratory, and for specific projects further and more detailed surveys may be required.

5:19. The Institute is also carrying out valuable work on the water requirements of sugar cane and the relative economics of flood and overhead spray irrigation. Present indications are that equal results are obtained from overhead irrigation using only one-sixth of the amount supplied by the flood method. The cost of capital installation for spray irrigation was given as Rs. 600 per acre. With the rapid development of irrigation and the many plans now under discussion we consider that it would be wise to add to the strength of the Institute of a soil physicist who we believe would greatly assist research and development.

5:20. We support the most stringent and uncompromising legislation covering the importation of planting material which could conceivably endanger the industry. During our stay we were informed that only by chance was a private importation of diseased cane from Reunion intercepted in time. Fiji disease (Madagascar) and gumming disease (Reunion) are near and constant threats; all possible safeguards must be taken against the introduction of these diseases.

5:21. The control of weeds in sugar cane by the use of chemicals began in 1952 and has quickly developed to the present stage where Rs. 2 million (£150,000) worth of herbicides are imported annually. Research at the Institute has resulted in standard formulations, application rates, etc., to the stage where chemical weeding of cane fields is standard practice on the larger estates. MCPA or 24-D derivatives in combination with TCA, Sodium Chlorate, or Pentachlorophenal, are commonly used. The more drastic pre-emergence spray is applied about a week after planting the cane sets, normally a hand weeding follows at about 10 weeks, and this is followed as necessary with MCPA or 24-D derivative sprays throughout the life of the cane. In the high rainfall areas as many as five sprays may be applied per annum. Application is by knapsack sprayers but power sprayers are now under trial.

5:22. This new development has the effect of considerably reducing the labour requirements of cane and from the estate angle it allows the release of considerable labour during the busy crop season. It also severely restricts the practice of inter-cropping[1] in the plant year particularly in the super-humid zone—experiments show that maize can be successfully grown in the other zones without adverse effect on the cane but that other crops would hamper the spray routine—and tends to deprive the small stock-keeper of his supply of grass which he formerly cut from dividing paths and verges. The use of herbicides as an aid to clean weeding does, however, considerably reduce the cost of the operation. Indeed, it would seem on the information supplied to us that in the super-humid and humid zones a reduction in wage rates of something like 25 to 30% would be necessary before a balance is struck with the cost of weeding when herbicides are employed.

The Organisation of the Sugar Industry

5:23. We were greatly impressed by the organisation, documentation, and general efficiency of the industry, for which a number of boards and institutions are responsible.

The Mauritius Chamber of Agriculture is an association of millers, planters, and other persons or firms connected with the sugar industry. Although the stated objects of the Chamber are to safeguard and promote the economic interests of the whole agricultural community attention is almost exclusively devoted to sugar and we felt that the interests of the small planter might not be adequately represented. Close contact is maintained with the United Kingdom Government through a representative of the Chamber in London. It is the main policy body for the industry and is charged with the implementation of Commonwealth and International agreements affecting the disposal of sugar.

The Mauritius Sugar Syndicate is exclusively a marketing organisation. It handles the whole crop of the colony and, jointly with the Chamber, is responsible for the discharge of obligations under the Commonwealth and International Sugar Agreements.

The Central Arbitration and Control Board is a semi-official body set up by statute and charged with the duty of determining the conditions under which canes are supplied to the factories and the terms on which cane is purchased.

[1] That is to say growing other crops between the lines of sugar cane.

The Mauritius Sugar Producers Association is an employers' union of all the sugar millers in the island. It is the negotiating body on wage matters and conditions of employment generally covering labour and staff employees and protects the interests of millers in negotiations with such bodies as the Central Board.

There are also a considerable number of other bodies concerned in one way or another with the sugar industry, such as the Agricultural Bank, the Société de Technologie Sucrière, co-operative credit societies, and associations of planters, employees, etc.

5:24. In view of its onerous task, we were not surprised to receive complaints about the operation of the Central Arbitration and Control Board. This is saddled with two main tasks.

(*a*) *Delimitation of factory areas.* Taking all economic factors into account, and particularly that of transport, the Board decides to which factory every planter must deliver his canes and the factory is under obligation to accept all such canes. Inevitably all factories do not operate with the same degree of efficiency and the Board was forced to fix a standard measure of efficiency for application to all factories. This was high and has acted as an incentive to factories. We now understand that consideration is being given to raising it still higher.

(*b*) *Purchase of planters canes.* The Mauritian planter is credited with two-thirds of the sugar recoverable from his canes on the basis of 98·5° polarisation and also two-thirds of the molasses and scums. The Board employs a large number of test chemists who are stationed at every factory during the crop season, but uncertainty over the methods they use to determine the recoverable sugar gives rise to disquiet. Every planter or group of planters who supplies a quantity of cane upwards of 1,000 tons may have individual tests applied. The tests comprise juice analysis and fibre determination but a difficulty arises in that the qualitative tests do not always agree with the figures obtained by the chemical control of the factory and a balance has to be struck so that the final figure agrees with the *actual* amount of sugar produced by the factory. A further complication arises from the need to arrange orderly delivery of cane throughout the crop season. If this were not done everyone would wish to deliver cane at the peak period of sucrose content. By a process of calculation, therefore, credit and payment is made as if all planters had supplied their canes *pro rata* from the first day to the last day of the milling period. The whole matter is highly technical and complicated and although we could detect no obvious flaws in the procedure it is easy to see that uncertainty may exist. Representations have been made for an enquiry by an outside authority. The Mauritius Sugar Industry Research Institute have put forward certain suggestions for modification of the method but we feel that if these suggestions do not satisfy the representatives of the planters an attempt should be made to improve confidence within the industry by obtaining the services of an outside expert to enquire into the machinery for ensuring an equitable return to the planter for the cane he produces.

The Sale of Sugar and the Sugar Industry Funds

5:25. As stated above (paragraph 2:39) the whole of the sugar production of the island is marketed by the Mauritius Sugar Syndicate, the net proceeds from the sale of the whole crop being made up of sugar sold under the Commonwealth Sugar Agreement at the United Kingdom negotiated price, sugar sold on preferential markets, sugar sold on the free world market, sugar sold locally, and the value of Colonial Preference Certificates. The proceeds of each crop are averaged out per ton of total sugar produced and paid to each estate and planter *pro rata* to their production. Thus each producer gets a *pro-rata* share of the various prices at which the sugar was sold to different buyers.

5:26. The level of the various prices received for sugar sold in the different markets and of the average price received by the Mauritian producers for the last five years have been shown in Table VII (paragraph 2:39). The Mauritius Sugar Syndicate, which sells the sugar, pays to the producer the average price shown in column 6 of Table VIII, less various cesses and other payments which are made on the production of sugar. The most important of these are a payment of about 5% of the value of the crop into the Sugar Industry Cyclone and Drought Insurance Fund, payments on the negotiated price of sugar sold under the Commonwealth Sugar agreement of one shilling per hundredweight (about 13 rupees per metric ton) to the Sugar Industry Rehabilitation Fund, and of sixpence per hundredweight (about 6·5 rupees per metric ton) to the Sugar Industry Labour Welfare Fund. There are also payments of 30 cents per 100 kilos for the Sugar Industry Research Institute, and of 10 cents per 100 kilos for the Sugar Industry Reserve Fund; these payments are effected on all sugar exports.

5:27. The value of receipts for sugar between 1953 and 1958 is shown in Table XXXIII overleaf.

5:28. Payments for the foregoing purposes (excluding premiums to the Cyclone and Drought Insurance Fund) and for the expenses of the Syndicate and the Central Board usually account in all to some 4% of the proceeds of sugar sales, and the industry therefore

Table XXXIII. Gross Sale Proceeds of Sugar, 1953-1958

Million rupees

Crop year				Exports	Local sales	Total proceeds
1953	..	..	..	..	265·6	8·1	273·7
1954	..	..	..	..	250·8	8·3	259·1
1955	..	..	..	..	263·0	8·6	271·6
1956	..	..	..	..	299·8	9·1	308·9
1957	..	..	..	..	290·7	8·9	299·6
1958*	..	..	..	..	265·5	8·5	274·0

* Estimated.

receives about 96% of the value of all sugar sales. By-products usually yield a further Rs. 5 million.

5:29. Of the total amount received by the estates for sugar, wages, salaries, and other payments connected with direct employment normally account for about 22%, and purchase of canes for another 28%. The cost of transport, bags, fertilisers, and fuel and lubrication amount to a further 10% and Cyclone and Drought Insurance premiums for about 5%. If other costs are included, total payments amount to rather less than three-quarters of total receipts, including receipts from sales of by-products, leaving rather more than a quarter in profits, including depreciation and interest. Of the profits, provision for depreciation accounts for about a sixth, and interest for a further 5%. About a fifth of profits is paid in income tax, and the remainder is divided between dividends and undistributed profits, with dividends accounting for rather more than a quarter of total profits, and undistributed profits for a little over 30%. All the evidence we have seen goes to suggest that the sugar companies have followed an extremely conservative policy in respect of dividends over the past few years and have ploughed back large amounts into the industry; roughly a half of total profits has been retained for capital expenditure or depreciation, and less than a third has been distributed. It is estimated that, in the period 1946-1959, the estates spent some Rs. 328 million (£24·6 million) on factory and estate modernisation, expenditure between 1957 and 1959 averaging Rs. 37 million (£2·775 million) per annum.

5:30. The following estimates apply to the estates only: on information available it appears that planters' capital expenditure has been only a fraction of that of the estates—a factor which may be partly responsible for the lower level of yield on planters' land.

5:31. Because of the ever-present danger of cyclones, the Cyclone and Drought Insurance Fund is an important element in the sugar industry's financing. The Fund was established in 1946. Its main source of income is the levy on sugar production mentioned above, but it also has some other sources of revenue, including 70% of the interest paid by the sugar industry on the loans made to them by government after the 1945 cyclone. There have been various changes in the working of the Fund over recent years, the most recent being in 1960. Under the current arrangements, if any sugar-growing area is declared an area in which an "event" took place in a particular year—an event being defined as a cyclone or a drought—compensation is paid on the difference between the actual yield per arpent and the yield in a "normal" year. The balance of the Fund at the end of May 1959 was Rs. 108·5 million. In April 1960, it was estimated that, after allowing for immediate liabilities and estimated claims, net funds available to meet future claims totalled Rs. 104·6 million. It is estimated that, if there is a 50% loss of crops as a result of the 1960 cyclones, the Fund will have to provide some Rs. 76 million in compensation over and above an amount of about Rs. 35 million which has been re-insured.

5:32. We have heard several complaints about the working of the Fund. First, it has been argued that the Fund would be insufficient to meet two successive cyclone years, and that the premiums should therefore be increased. As against this, we are informed that the level of the premiums is based on a careful actuarial calculation of the risk involved. Secondly, we have been told that excessive claims have been made against the Fund, including some claims which were actually fraudulent. (Compensation payable by the Fund was Rs. 9 million in respect of the 1957 crop, Rs. 20 million in respect of the 1958 crop, and some Rs. 10 million for the 1959 crop.) We were informed that the fraudulent claims were mainly by planters, who, because of the lack of a detailed survey of sugar land, were able to represent themselves as having had losses which had not, in fact, occurred. We understand that a complete survey of land under sugar is now to be undertaken by the Fund, and when it is completed this type of fraud should be more difficult.

5:33. It has, however, been argued that there is an inherent bias in the system in favour of paying out claims. This arises from the definition of a "normal" year, which is not a true average year in respect of yield, but is the average of the three preceding years in which there was neither a cyclone nor a drought. In other words, the yield of a "normal" year is higher than the yield of an average year. In certain parts of the island, where droughts are common, this could give a strong bias in the direction of increasing claims on the Fund. We appreciate that the present arrangements are the result of a good deal of experience and thought, and we would not wish to made any specific proposals to meet this difficulty. We would suggest, however, that the Board of the Cyclone and Drought Insurance Fund consider the following questions,

(*a*) Is it necessary for compulsory insurance to cover such a high proportion of losses incurred as a result of cyclone or drought? Would there be any advantage in having compulsory insurance to cover, say, a half of such loss, or in making the planter or estate concerned meet the first 20% or 30% of any loss, leaving any insurance in excess of this to the decision of the grower? The present system ties up very large sums in sterling balances, and, although we fully agree with the necessity for an insurance scheme, it does not appear to us to be essential that such a high proportion of loss be met by a compulsory scheme, especially if this involves any considerable increase in premiums.

(*b*) Is the definition of a "normal" year entirely satisfactory? Would there be any advantage in re-defining it in such a way as to cover, say, the previous seven years, whatever they may have been? We understand that sufficient data are not available to go back seven years in respect of a good deal of planters' land, but, as information is built up, this should become possible.

5:34. In raising these questions, we have no wish to criticise the administration of the Fund. We are fully agreed on the need for large-scale sugar crop insurance in Mauritius; indeed, the lack of such insurance in 1960 would have involved a major disaster. We are, however, impressed by the fact that, in the years 1957-59, nearly Rs. 40 millions of claims were admitted, and that these were years in which there was no major disaster. Since premium income is of the order of Rs. 13-14 million per annum, this means that claims in three not very bad years were about equivalent to premium income. If this were to continue, the Fund would not be in a position to meet another cyclone year. We believe that the purpose of the Fund should be to meet serious loss, and that it should be ready to do so. We therefore hope that the Board will give some consideration to these questions, so as to avoid what might otherwise be a need to raise premiums to an excessive level.

OTHER NON-PASTORAL AGRICULTURE

Tea

5:35. Tea has been grown for local consumption in Mauritius for many years but it is only recently that serious efforts have been made to establish the crop as an industry of importance. In 1947 a small Tea Division of the Department of Agriculture was created, this interest by government led to some sporadic and uncontrolled development by small planters, and by 1954 the industry was faced with a surplus over local needs of some 250,000 lbs. This surplus was successfully presented on the London market and export sales, after meeting local needs, have shown a gradual increase up to just over 1,000,000 lbs. in 1959. In this year (1959) total production was 2,000,000 lbs. and the total planted area around 4,000 acres.

5:36. Whilst there are five manufacturing planters in Mauritius, the industry has so far lacked leadership from any large and experienced tea company. Recognising that leadership and encouragement were needed, Legislative Council in 1955 approved government-sponsored expansion up to an acreage of 15,000 acres under tea. The first or pilot phase of this development aims at opening up 3,000 acres of new land (mainly from the Crown Forest estate) to tea by mid-1962, when there should be 6,000 acres under tea. Planters selected for this project develop their gardens according to their resources but receive government assistance in the form of easy rental terms, free seed and subsidies for land clearance, use of machinery, buildings, fertilisers, and roads. At the same time the government is itself developing 400 acres until the tea is three years old, when tenants will take over. On the same policy lines government has engaged the Nuwara Eliya Tea Estates Co. Ltd. as agents to manage the government-owned Midlands Estate (some 500 acres of planted tea) and to construct and operate a modern tea factory which went into limited production in 1959.

5:37. At the end of 1959 the distribution of the tea area between the various producers was as follows—

Table XXXIV. Distribution of Tea Area, 1959

Producers				Area in arpents
5 Manufacturing planters	..	..	..	1,207
279 Non-manufacturing planters		..	..	926
66—less than 1 arpent	..	..	.. 36	
189—1-5 arpents each	..	..	.. 345	
11—5-10 arpents each	..	..	.. 77	
13—over 10 arpents	..	..	.. 468	
Government plantations ..	..	..	..	550
Project plantations (immature) ..	..	..		1,111
		Total area		3,794

Since the recent cyclones had stripped the tea bushes of their leaves, it was not possible to obtain a fair appreciation of the quality of the planted tea but it is believed that a good proportion of the mature tea is of inferior China-hybrid variety. Planting distances were variable and in many of the small gardens tea had originally been planted between rows of sugar cane, with the result that the stand of tea bushes and the canopy were unsatisfactory. Nevertheless, we were reliably informed that yields of 1,000 lbs. of made tea per arpent can readily be obtained from mature gardens and the prices obtained on the London market show that the quality of Mauritian tea compares favourably with that produced in East and Central Africa. Rainfall is adequate and well distributed and, although temperatures may be a little on the low side, the natural conditions for tea cultivation appear generally favourable.

5:38. The cost of land preparation, planting, and caring for tea up to the age of three years was estimated to be Rs. 3,000 per arpent and this will be increased by a further Rs. 400-500 if seedlings raised in nurseries or clonal material is used, instead of the present doubtful practice of planting seed at stake. Comparable figures for Nyasaland would be in the region of Rs. 2,000 and in East Africa comparable figures would be Rs. 2,400 for estate plantings and Rs. 1,100 for smallholding tea. These differences in initial establishment costs are not so vitally important but on recurrent costs it is generally accepted that tea requires on average one man per arpent throughout the year and on this basis, using current wage rates, the annual cost per arpent in Mauritius is Rs. 1,530 compared with approximately Rs. 400 in Nyasaland and Rs. 600 in East Africa. These figures are sufficiently reliable to show that Mauritian teas are at a considerable disadvantage on production costs and for this reason we are of the opinion that an industry based on smallholder production, using family labour, is the most promising line of development. We would, however, emphasise that the success of this form of development depends on the extent to which the organisation and standard uniform practices of estate cultivation can be imposed on the participants.

5:39. If the tea industry is to expand and prosper, generous but firm guidance and assistance must be given to it. It must be recognised that experimental results and techniques which suit conditions in Ceylon or Africa do not necessarily apply to Mauritius. The first and most important function of government is to make available to the planters reliable information on all aspects of tea culture and this reliable guidance must be based on experimental work carried out in Mauritius. After all, the tea bush has a life of fifty years or more and it is clearly wise to try and ensure that quality material only is planted and that it is given a favourable start in life. The highly leached soils of the tea area will be demanding in fertilisers and the economics of fertiliser application must be worked out by experiment. We stress the need for research because we believe that there is no short cut to successful tea culture, and also particularly on account of the comparatively high labour costs in Mauritius, because there is no margin for inefficiency if the industry is to succeed.

5:40. We therefore recommend that at least one fully qualified officer with supporting staff should be appointed as soon as possible for research work on tea. We also recommend that the Tea Board of Mauritius should try to establish formal relations with either the Tea Research Institute of East Africa or the Tea Research Station in Nyasaland, so that exchange visits of specialist officers can take place.

5:41. Prior to the recent cyclones the need for adequate soil conservation measures, arrangements for water disposal, and the need for shelter belts had not been appreciated. As a result newly cleared land and newly planted land suffered very severely from erosion and gullying. Valiant efforts are now being made by government to repair the damage and the lesson for the future is that no tea should be planted before adequate protection works have been provided. Guidance for the staff employed on this highly skilled work should be obtained at the earliest possible moment and we recommend that an approach be made to the Government of Kenya for the loan of an officer experienced in this type of work.

5:42. Based on experience to date and on the happenings during recent cyclones, the Department of Agriculture is of the opinion that the government should, as for smallholders, take over the development of new project planters' land up to the stage when two- or three-year-old tea can be handed back to the owners. We certainly agree that much firmer control over the activities of individual planters is essential and the Department's proposal may be the most practical means of doing this. Present subsidies, which are generous, could be used to offset the establishment costs which the planter would be required to take over. Should this form of development be accepted (and we think it has much to recommend it) then, the agreement of planters having been obtained, we would recommend that the Department should consider employing, where possible, contractors for specific jobs and operations rather than that the work should be carried out by direct government labour.

5:43. As an alternative method, we recommend that consideration be given to the setting up of a Tea Development Authority. This would be a non-profit making organisation financed by government and charged with the task of preparing land for tea and of planting and developing it to the two- to three-year stage. The Authority should function on commercial lines and have greater financial latitude and freedom than is normally given to government departments. It would have the added advantage of relieving the Department of Agriculture of a task for which it is not designed. Agronomic and other research work on tea should remain with the Department of Agriculture and clearly it should work closely with the Authority.

5:44. We further recommend that consideration be given to some method of insuring tea against possible loss from cyclone damage. Damage to tea factories and installations can, we suggest, be covered by normal commercial insurance, but it seems doubtful whether this form of insurance would be available to cover damage to young tea plants or to loss of leaf. The premium for established plantations could be collected as a cess on made tea, but for the beginner, tea is at its most vulnerable stage during its first years of life when no return is being obtained. Individual new planters may be prepared to pay a premium at this early stage, but, if not, insurance cover may only be obtainable after the tea has started to produce. We find ourselves unable to make any clear recommendation on this point and merely suggest that the Tea Board should give thought to ways and means of obtaining a satisfactory solution.

5:45. Finally, we would emphasise that if the tea industry is to develop satisfactorily the participants must be prepared to accept a considerable degree of regimentation and control. This control can only be exercised with the aid of legislation and we recommend that a study be made of the form of development and the supporting legislation for smallholding tea in Ceylon and Kenya.

Tobacco

5:46. It is estimated that some 5,000 people earn their livelihood in this industry, engaged in the cultivation of three types of tobacco— Virginia flue-cured, Amarello flue-cured, and Amarello air-cured— and in processing and manufacture. There are 87 producers of flue-cured tobacco compared with 378 of air-cured tobacco which is mainly a family concern. For the three types the 1959-60 production position is as follows.—

Table XXXV. Tobacco Production by Type and Area, 1959 and 1960

Type	Arpents	Kilos	Yield per arpent (kilos)	Average gross return per arpent (rupees)	Average gross value per kilo (rupees and cents)
Virginia flue-cured ..	724	296,174	409	2,492	6:09
Amarello flue-cured ..	143	125,075	875	4,542	5:19
Amarello air-cured ..	162	145,691	899	2,085	2:32

Production is geared to local requirements, and in accordance with the policy of the Tobacco Board, which controls by licence the area and type of tobacco to be grown, there has been a gradual but marked switch-over to Virginia flue-cured tobacco over the last ten years. The trend of consumer demand is away from Amarello and towards the more expensive Virginia cigarette, and the Board's policy is to encourage the production of a quality leaf capable of replacing imported cigarettes and leaf tobacco as much as possible. At present, each of the two companies in Mauritius make one brand of cigarette manufactured wholly from imported leaf, other brands having a varying percentage of imported Virginian leaf, and some cheap brands made entirely from local leaf.

5:47. The total consumption of leaf in local manufacture is just over one million pounds and of this some 20%, valued at Rs. $1\frac{1}{4}$ million (£94,000), is imported. In addition, cigarettes to the value of about Rs. 1 million (£75,000) are imported annually. There is, therefore, still a margin for increased consumption of locally produced leaf and the extent to which this can be taken up will largely depend on the improvement of the quality of local leaf, which is now taking place. (In 1953 the percentage of bright and medium grades was 42; in 1958 and 1959 the percentages were 78 and 75 respectively.) At the same time the low price of imported cigarettes (Rs. 8 per 100) makes it difficult to foster local production with local leaf. The degree of protection given to local production can be adjusted by raising the import duty on imported cigarettes and leaf relatively to the excise duty on home produced cigarettes and leaf; and the general level of cigarette prices and of revenue from tobacco duties can be adjusted by raising or lowering the import and excise duties together. By judicious adjustment of import and excise duties, it is therefore possible to combine any desired degree of protection of domestic production with any desired average level of cigarette prices and of revenue from tobacco duties. We recommend that the government should be prepared by means of such an adjustment to give greater protection to the domestic production of tobacco leaf without any sacrifice of revenue from tobacco duties.

5:48. We do not feel that the industry can count greatly on further increases in the total local consumption of cigarettes. The consumption of cigarettes in Mauritius has reached close on 700 million per annum or some 1,100 per head of population. This is very high and it would seem unwise to count on more than a modest 2% or 3% increase per annum.

5:49. There remains the export market as the only outlet for any marked expansion of the industry. Amarello has gone out of favour and although occasional parcels of air-cured leaf may be sold on the continent of Europe we see little prospect of a steady market for this type. With a small industry the emphasis must be on quality Virginian leaf. Reasonably satisfactory quality is now being produced but we understand that the price at which it can be offered is some 50% higher than the average price of equivalent Rhodesian grades. In addition, buyers show little interest in the small consignments that Mauritius could produce, and if they do the demand is for specific grades and not the "run of the crop", thus saddling the Board with unwanted grades.

5:50. We feel that if Mauritius is to continue to explore the export market the first step should be to consider whether and in what ways the price of their leaf can be reduced to a competitive level. It is a closed industry and, we feel, a "cosy" one for the lucky few who are in it. Production costs are variable and difficult to obtain; land values and land rents are high and labour expensive but the Tobacco Board restricts the production of leaf by a quota system, producer prices are based not on costs but on the price at which cigarettes can sell in Mauritius, and we were told that "it is generally agreed that the net profit of the planters is about 30% to 40% of the gross return". We therefore recommend that so long as the quota system persists, the guaranteed price offered to the producers of leaf should be gradually reduced. Steps should be taken to ensure that any such reduction in price is passed on to the final consumer of Mauritian tobacco, whether it be in the form of cigarettes or the export of Mauritian leaf; or alternatively in the case of the domestic consumption of Mauritian tobacco, the reduction in the price offered to the producer could be absorbed by a higher rate of excise duty.

5:51. To summarise, it is our view that expansion of the industry should be encouraged, that certain steps can be taken to increase the consumption of locally produced leaf, that the whole price structure be critically examined to determine whether quality leaf can be placed on the world market at a competitive price, and that agronomic research be continued towards this end.

Ginger

5:52. Green ginger of good quality is a cash crop of some importance. Production is estimated at 700-800 tons per annum of which some 250 tons is consumed locally and 300 tons exported. This crop has recently been the subject of study by a local committee which, in brief, recommended development of the crop by the establishment of a producers' organisation with statutory powers to control planting and export. Whilst we do not dissent from this recommendation, on the assumption that control over planting is directed to ensuring that correct methods and soils are used and that

90

control over export is designed to ensure quality, we would not support any major expansion of the crop for the reasons that carelessly-cultivated ginger creates conditions which favour soil erosion. We understand that all the preserved ginger entering world trade is prepared in Hong Kong. From outward appearance it seems possible that Mauritian ginger would be suitable for this trade and we have already initiated arrangements for the supply of samples to the Tropical Products Institute in order that the intrinsic value for this purpose may be determined. If the results are promising only modest capital would be required to establish a local industry for the preparation of the preserved forms for commerce.

Food Crops

5:53. We have already referred to the dependence of Mauritius on imported food supplies and to the economic, physical, and psychological difficulties of alleviating the position (paragraphs 2:41 ff). During the Second World War compulsory planting of food crops by estates and large planters was introduced but results fell far short of the targets set, partly because of drought, cyclone, and lack of "know-how", and partly because compulsion does not induce human beings to give of their best in skill and drive. After the war (1947) food supplies were still difficult and a system of subsidies and guaranteed prices was introduced and the following table shows the effect of those measures.—

Table XXXVI. Area of Foodcrops Harvested, 1946-1949

Arpents

Year	Maize	Cassava	Eddoes	S/Potato	G/nuts	Potatoes	Rice	Total
1946–47	2,973	507	160	180	356	—	—	4,176
1947–48	10,000	1,600	425	625	2,200	800	1,875	17,525
1948–49	9,862	2,405	587	621	2,006	955	856	17,292
1949–50	8,078	1,382	420	215	1,291	1,120	649	13,155
1950–51	4,874	862	316	301	1,120	977	379	8,879
1951–52	4,429	865	353	413	1,654	1,181	71	8,966
1952–53	4,244	752	308	409	1,188	1,366	66	8,333
1954	*	*	*	*	*	*	*	8,191
1955	3,345	504	108	259	546	785	37	5,584
1956	2,405	272	168	191	394	933	—	4,363
1957	1,597	305	183	345	1,052	571	—	4,053
1958	883	72	85	340	371	1,043	—	2,794
1959	908	86	99	218	289	1,117	—	2,717

* Not available.

When the subsidies were withdrawn after 1948-49 the decline was immediate. A mechanical unit set up in April 1951 which cleared new land on condition that food crops were planted for at least one year, maintained the level of the area under food crops for a time but since 1954 when imported food became more freely available and local production costs rose the decline has continued.

5:54. The area devoted in 1959 to vegetables other than those listed in Table XXXVI is estimated at close on 7,000 arpents.

5:55. The following figures for 1959 indicate the extent of the Mauritius import trade in the more important food crops and crop products.—

Table XXXVII. Import of Major Foodstuffs, 1959, by Weight and Value

Commodity	Weight (Metric tons)	Value (1000s. of Rupees)
Rice	70,500	44,114
Maize	3,471	1,130
Potatoes (including seed)..	4,019	1,803
Beans, peas, lentils	5,491	4,374
Other vegetables	1,297	668
Peppers and spices	648	830
Groundnuts	38	41
Cotton seed oil	3,337	5,011
Other vegetable oils, coconut, groundnut, sunflower, etc.	1,300	2,000

5:56. There is therefore a considerable margin which could be taken up by home-produced foodstuffs and, indeed, should be if the health of the population is to be safeguarded. The area devoted to protective food crops is already at the danger limit.

5:57. There is no reason why it should not be profitable for planters to respond. Where instances of poor success with food crops are quoted it must be remembered that all the best land and skill go to the growing of sugar. On settlements we visited, and these are not isolated examples, it is readily possible to obtain say a crop of groundnuts and a crop of potatoes within the year bringing in a gross return of Rs. 2,333 (£175) per arpent as opposed to sugar cane with an annual return of say Rs. 800 (£60) per arpent.

5:58. Yet the estates and larger planters grow virtually no food crops, and the small planters on settlements are continually requesting to be allowed to plant all their land with cane. The only regular producers of food crops and vegetables apart from a few specialised market gardens near the larger towns are small planters with 10 arpents or less who rotate food crops with cane and whenever possible take a catch crop between cane rows. The reasons for this situation are primarily the uncertainty of the market for foodstuffs, shortage of field labour, the use of herbicides in the cane fields (see paragraph 5:21), and the prevalence of praedial larceny. We appreciate these difficulties, but we do not feel that they are insurmountable, and, indeed, we believe that it should be possible to make food crops as attractive and secure as cane.

5:59. The first and central requirement is an improvement in marketing organisation and the establishment of a central Agricultural Marketing Board (see paragraphs 5:144-151). Given the establishment of such an organisation there are a number of other conditions which we recommend the government should take steps to meet.

(1) The fixing and publication in advance of the various sowing or planting times of a remunerative, guaranteed price for the producer.

(2) The provision of adequate storage and, if required, processing facilities for the Board to enable it to spread sales and cope with gluts.

(3) An improvement of the agricultural advisory services and extension of research.

(4) A review of legislation aimed at giving improved security of tenure to the small planter and the prevention of subdivision of land below economic limits.

(5) A tightening of the law against praedial larceny.

5:60. If these conditions are met, it is not unreasonable to expect that estates and large planters will be interested in cropping during the fallow period between the cutting of the last ratoon and replanting. It is estimated that normally some 3,700 arpents would be free for such cropping during the growing season, November-June, and 1,300 arpents during the season July-October, or 5,000 arpents in all. This area could well produce the current import requirements of potatoes and maize, though estates and large planters may more readily be encouraged to grow oilseeds like groundnuts, sunflower, and soya. These would not only relieve import requirements but would assist the existing oil expressing industry and provide by-products valuable for cattle feed.

5:61. In general we recommend that in the early stages of the Board great care should be exercised in entering into commitments for the more perishable vegetables and without neglecting them we suggest that crops such as maize, potatoes, beans and pulses, groundnuts, sunflowers, and yams should first receive attention until experience is gained. We also feel that propaganda should be directed towards individuals, estates, and employers, for the growing of fruits, particularly citrus fruits, like limes and oranges, which could be so valuable a contribution to better health. Even making due allowance for the hazards of cyclone, theft, and disease we were disappointed in the present lack of interest in fruit cultivation.

The Aloe Fibre Industry and the Sack Factory

5:62. Plants yielding fibres suitable for making sacks, ropes, etc. have been grown in the colony for a long time, but of late years it is the aloe (*Purcraea gigantea* or Mauritian hemp) that has received most attention. Originally most of this fibre was exported, but in 1932 a factory was established by private enterprise for the local manufacture of sacks. This plant was forced to close down in 1935 on account of lack of capital, technical deficiencies, and competition from jute, and it remained closed until 1941 when the government bought it up, installed new machinery, and re-started production. During the war and afterwards, until jute again began to compete, it made good profits, and, indeed, in 1951, somewhat inadvisedly, the capacity was doubled up to 3,000,000 sacks a year. Since then, competition from jute has become stronger, the sugar industry has reduced its requirements, and there have been numerous labour troubles. In consequence the factory has been working at a loss for some years and, if it were still a commercial concern, by this time it would probably have been shut down again.

5:63. In fact however it does not work as a commercial concern. A tripartite agreement between the factory, the sugar industry, and the Hemp Producers' Syndicate provides that the price of fibre and sacks be tied to that of imported jute. In the event of an operating loss, the sugar industry pays a subsidy up to a maximum of 17 cents a sack and the hemp producers 2% on the value of the fibre purchased. In 1958 these subsidies amounted respectively to Rs. 247,000 (£18,525) and Rs. 31,000 (£2,325), thereby helping to reduce the gross loss from Rs. 403,000 to Rs. 68,000 (on sales of 1,453,750 sacks). The result is that both the hemp producers and the sugar producers are dissatisfied. The hemp producers maintain that prices are not remunerative, and consequently the production of fibre is steadily falling off. In 1960 there may not be enough to supply the factory's commitments which would then have to be met by imported jute. Meanwhile, despite reorganisation, the factory continues to run at a loss and the sugar industry expresses unwillingness indefinitely to subsidise an industry which they claim is uneconomic and adding directly to their own costs.

5:64. The question whether or not it has a permanent commercial future in the economy of Mauritius depends on three main factors:—

(*a*) whether the cost of sacks could be reduced enough to be competitive with jute and, if so how much capital would be required;

(*b*) what the eventual requirements of the sugar industry will be; and

(*c*) whether the land now devoted to Furcraea production (or that might be given up to it) could be put to better use.

5:65. So far as the factory costs are concerned it is clear that the cost of fibre accounts for too high a proportion of the total (about 70%) and that, if the factory is to break even, this item must be reduced by about 30%, that is, from about one rupee per kilo to 73 cents, and rather more if the hemp producers are to get a higher profit as well. Probably not much more can be done towards bringing down the other factory costs although we think the Hemp Producers' Syndicate should endeavour to produce calculations which would enable a more authoritative judgement to be made. We consider that the factory should be under the supervision of a full-time manager who should be a qualified engineer and have special experience in fibre industry in other countries. Without continuous expert supervision the factory cannot be expected to operate at maximum efficiency.

5:66. The requirements of the sugar industry obviously depend on the method of handling sugar. However, based on the present method, the Sugar Syndicate has given the following estimate—

(*a*) for local handling 600,000 heavy type aloe bags;

(*b*) for export sales 600,000 light type aloe bags; and

(*c*) for local sales 300,000 mixed aloe and jute bags.

The total of 1,500,000 would just about provide an economic output for the factory. Naturally, it would be better if production could approach more nearly to the maximum capacity of 3,000,000 but in fact so much of the unit cost, including labour, is independent of output that above a certain limit the effect of higher production is not very great. If full bulk loading of sugar were introduced, requirements would fall to below 1,000,000. Against this there is a possibility that rice may be imported in Mauritian hemp bags, though this is not a factor to be permanently relied on. All things considered, it would seem that for some years to come the demand for sacks should enable the factory to operate at an economic level.

5:67. The problem, therefore, resolves into the supply and cost of the raw material. Fibre production amounts to some 1,500 tons per annum and is obtained mainly by the exploitation of wild, or semi-wild, stands of Furcraea. The decline of the industry is illustrated by the facts that in 1953 40 factories operated on 12,000 arpents of wild Furcraea and 3,000 arpents of planted Furcraea, as compared with 19 factories operating on 6,000 arpents of wild and 800 arpents of planted material at the present time. The factory cost of producing one ton of fibre was estimated at Rs. 930-Rs. 1,100 (£70-£80) and this very high cost reflects the relative inefficiency of the industry at both field and factory level, as compared with modern estate production of fibre in other countries.

5:68. The research required and the steps needed to put the industry on a modern and efficient plantation basis are described in "Reports on the Mauritius Fibre Industry" by G. W. Lock and P. W. Lees (1947), and the position is unchanged today. We are convinced that through land clearance (boulders and stones), cultivation, correct spacing, the use of selected planting material, the use of fertilisers, the adaptation of suitable cutting cycles, etc., the yield of fibre per unit of land *could* be very greatly increased. Under such intensive conditions it would not be unreasonable to expect that the present production of 1,500 tons could readily be obtained from 3,000 arpents. However, at present prices, even this would represent a gross income of only Rs. 500 per arpent, which compares very unfavourably with sugar. It is understandable, therefore, that the owners are not prepared to face the formidable and expensive task of land clearance unless a more remunerative crop than hemp can be planted. As and when irrigation becomes available, capital will no doubt be found for land clearing but other crops will be planted. Whilst, therefore, we think the government might give moderate financial assistance towards an assessment of the value of more intensive methods of cultivation, we do not think that any revolutionary changes in the present method of growing the crop are possible.

5:69. We think some assistance and encouragement should be given on the processing side, and we support the recent suggestions of Dr. Kirby of the Tropical Products Institute that (a) the prototype mechanical feeder, designed by the Department of Agriculture, should be followed up to the stage of practical field tests, and (b) that a mobile decortinator should be tried out. The performance of both innovations should be carefully checked against existing practices, with a view to reducing costs of the raw material. We suggest that, in addition, an approach might be made to the sisal research station in Tanganyika or to the sisal research station in Kenya to examine the possibility of processing for the whole industry at a central factory. By arrangement these stations might, if sources of leaf do not already exist, grow a small area of Furcraea in order to test the suitability of the modern sisal decorticator for the extraction of Furcraea fibre.

5:70. The long-term future of the sack factory is clearly still in doubt. We think that it is not inconceivable that, if a real effort is made to reduce costs along the lines indicated, not only might the factory be enabled to pay its way but the export trade on which it was originally founded might be revived. Meanwhile, unless the situation deteriorates rapidly we cannot advise the closing of the factory and we hope that the present or similar arrangements for subsidisation will continue. The extra cost to the sugar industry is small compared to the assistance rendered through Commonwealth preferences and we think that particularly over the next few years the paramount consideration should be the continued employment of the 2,500 workers in the field and the 250-300 in the factory itself.

Forestry

5:71. Table XXIX at the beginning of this chapter shows that Crown Forests amount to 67,700 acres but the simple figure is misleading since much of the area can never be productive and much again has been allocated to tea development or otherwise leased. It is estimated that the effective *productive* area is 25,000 acres and of this some 10,000 acres have been planted to fast-growing species which unfortunately suffered very severe cyclone damage. The current local annual production of timber is 520,000 cubic feet and annual imports run at 1,280,000 cubic feet valued at Rs. 4 million. The requirement of Mauritius in 30 years time is estimated to be 2,700,000 cubic feet, which could be met from 13,500 acres of fully stocked productive forest.

5:72. Mr. Swabey, the Secretary of State's Adviser on Forestry, visited Mauritius in October, 1959, and we attach as an appendix an extract from his Report, the whole of which we commend to the Government of Mauritius. We support his reasoning on the need for a firm and formally approved forest policy and his request for adequate legislation, particularly the legal gazetting of the main productive state forests. Using the results of the soil survey of the island it should be possible firmly to dedicate specific areas to meet the forest-products requirements and the water-conservation needs of Mauritius and we are of the opinion that with a settled and expanded planting programme a much more substantial contribution could be made from local sources to the timber requirements of the island.

5:73. To facilitate an increase in development of forest without increasing direct government expenditure we support Mr. Swabey's recommendation that consideration should be given to relieving the Forestry Department of certain abnormal burdens which it now carries. We have the following in mind.

(1) At present all forest produce is felled, extracted, transported, and retailed by the Department under cumbersome and costly

government procedure. This is one of several instances where direct government activities could with economy be replaced by private enterprise. Fees and royalties should be prescribed and the Department empowered to issue licences to cut timber, etc.

(2) As we suggest later (paragraphs 5:103-106), a review of the status of the Pas Geometriques should result in reliefs for the Department from tiresome and costly supervision and administration.

(3) Supervisory work over river reserves will be considerably reduced if the recommendation in paragraph 5:6 is accepted.

5:74. If the forests are to make a greater contribution to Mauritian needs it is essential that a modern sawmill and seasoning and preservative treatment facilities be provided. Ideally the operation of this commercial enterprise should not be the direct responsibility of the Forestry Department. If, however, as seems probable, the capital has to be found from government sources, although the possible participation of the Colonial Development Corporation should not be overlooked, an experienced manager should be appointed and be given freedom to operate on commercial lines and the plant would be run as a self-accounting unit of the Forestry Department (see also paragraphs 6:49-50).

LIVESTOCK

General Considerations

5:75. The gross annual value of production from livestock in Mauritius has been estimated for us as approximately Rs. 20 million (£1·5 million). The value of imports of live animals (mainly for food),

Table XXXVIII. Cattle and Foodstuffs Imported into Mauritius,
1955-1958

	Unit	1955	1956	1957	1958
1. *Live animals*					
Bovine cattle	Head	5,588	6,183	1,823	4,256
Sheep and lambs	,,	450	100	1,180	7,050
Poultry	No.	—	13,364	9,800	1,100
2. *Meat and meat preparations*					
Frozen meat	M/ton	369	374	361	607
Bacon and ham	,,	32	32	30	41
Preserved and canned meat, including sausages	,,	257	261	223	286
3. *Dairy products*					
All milk and milk foods ..	M/ton	2,044	1,788	1,938	2,108
Butter and ghee (animal) ..	,,	294	263	271	341
Cheese	,,	108	94	95	123
Eggs with shell	000	970	1,037	1,195	719
Other dairy products	M/ton	40	27	31	68

meat and meat preparations, dairy products and eggs was Rs. 11,767,572 (£882,568) in 1958, showing an increase of Rs. 1,588,540 (£119,140) over that for 1957 (neither total taking into account imports from Rodrigues). The foregoing table shows the import trends during the past four years.

5:76. The most important types of livestock are milk cattle and goats. A livestock census was carried out in 1950 when milk cattle, herd cattle, draught cattle, goats, sheep, and pigs were enumerated. A check count of dairy cattle and herd cattle only was carried out in 1956 but, unfortunately, owing to staff shortage the other types were not enumerated. Cattle figures are, however, available from earlier census years and it is possible to make the following comparison.—

Table XXXIX. Milk and Herd Cattle,
1939-1956

				1939	1943	1950	1956
Milk cattle	..	..	..	..	19,891	28,620	32,143	38,039
Herd cattle	..	..	..	..	6,035	5,823	5,070	2,495
			Total	25,926	34,443	37,213	40,514

5:77. Between 1950 and 1956 draught cattle are reported to have dropped from 3,069 to 1,904; herd cattle have also been further reduced to 2,225 in 1958, and are still going down in number, while milk cattle are reported to be in the region of 39,500 at the end of 1959. These figures can be assumed to be fairly reliable, but as regards other forms of livestock the estimates are merely informed guesses as follows:—

goats—about 50,000;

pigs—about 7,000; and

sheep—"a small number".

No attempt has been made to enumerate poultry.

5:78. Exports of livestock and livestock products from Mauritius are negligible and the entire industry is designed to meet local demands. The fact that imports are rising suggests that local requirements are not being met at present, and with a rising population, the need for imports will grow rapidly unless active steps are taken to reorganise the industry and encourage its further development.

5:79. Before dealing with the individual types of livestock in greater detail, reference might be made to a few general considerations in relation to livestock development in Mauritius. In the first place, the island is most fortunate in having no serious epizootic disease of cattle, none of the common bacterial diseases other than tuberculosis and, indeed, none of those diseases caused by protozoa transmitted by ticks or flies. From the cattle point of view, therefore, the disease position could not be more favourable although strict precautions against the introduction of new diseases must be strictly maintained.

5:80. Another item on the credit side of future livestock development is that Mauritius possesses in the Creole breed a dairy-type animal which is well adapted to a tropical environment. Many of these animals have in their genetical make-up a varying proportion of Friesian blood, and are potentially high-yielding animals. The current policy of breeding to an approved Creole phenotype is sound and in course of time a valuable national herd of tropical dairy cattle could be built up. There is a growing demand for such animals in many tropical territories throughout the world.

5:81. The debit side of the picture is, however, quite gloomy. There is an almost complete lack of suitable land which owners would be prepared to develop along modern lines for livestock production. Sugar, as we have seen, is the crop of choice even for the most marginal agricultural land, and improved pastures, as such, are almost non-existent. Stall feeding of fodder on a "cut and carry" basis is expensive, particularly if labour has to be employed for this purpose, and all food concentrates, apart from molasses, must be imported and absorb an excessive proportion of production costs. The small owner-producer is almost completely ignorant of modern management practices and of the hygienic production of milk. The marketing facilities for milk are unsatisfactory and adulteration is rife.

The Dairy Industry

(i) *Present position*

5:82. As can be seen from Table XXXIX, the milk-cattle population in Mauritius has increased 100% since 1930 and approximately half of the total consists of animals of Creole type. Some 500 only are owned by a few sugar estates, the remaining 39,000 being in the hands of 19,000 small peasants owning virtually no land at all. Thus, the average number of cattle per owner is about two. In the 1956 Dairy Cattle census the ownership distribution was as follows.—

Table XL. Ownership of Dairy Cattle, 1956

No. of head of cattle	1	2	3	4	5	6–10	11–20	21–30	31–50	51–100
No. of owners	7,214	7,958	2,896	881	230	145	9	3	4	2

100

5:83. The animals of the estate owners are housed in buildings which can be classed as fair to good, feeding is carried out by some on a production basis using concentrates, and an attempt is made to control hygiene. We were informed, however, that milk production did not pay because of the high labour cost of cutting and transporting fodder and the high cost of concentrates. This almost certainly explains why the larger owner is gradually disappearing.

5:84. Most small owners keep their animals in primitive, ill-designed sheds in semi- or complete darkness and hygiene is non-existent. It should be recorded, however, that one or two cowsheds of modern design have been built, e.g. at Phoenix, but this type of construction is probably too expensive for most producers without considerable financial assistance. Fodder is collected by the owner and his family from wayside grasses, scrub, or crown lands during the inter-crop season. During the crop season the fodder consists principally of cane tops. A number of the small owners buy and feed concentrates and/or cheap cattle food and sales of both are increasing.

5:85. The average daily production of milk per cow in a well-managed estate dairy is about 7·2 kgs. (range 4·5 kgs. to 13·0 kgs.), the cows being fairly high-grade Friesian. In 1958 the average production per cow of the Creole type was 6·77 kgs. at the government Livestock Breeding Station, Curepipe. The average yield of cows in the hands of the small producer is not accurately known. The figure given to us officially was 3·5 litres (3·1 kgs.) over 300 days, but in discussion with producers, who kept sales records, it was apparent that yields fell off rapidly after three months, and the average cannot be much more than 2 litres (1·8 kgs.). In spite of these very low yields from cows owned by the vast majority of producers, the total daily production of milk for sale has been given as 48,000 litres (approximately 10,500 gallons) which is considerably below the current demand.

5:86. The milk from the estates and from government farms is purchased by two main contractors, at 40 cents per litre, who retail it in bottles at 60 cents per litre or 50 cents in other containers. The retailing of the milk of the small producer is carried out by itinerant milkmen who collect and carry in locally made "saddle tanks" on bicycles and distribute to a fixed round of customers. The reports of prices paid to the small producer vary from 27 to 37 cents per litre, retailing at 40 to 45 cents per litre. In spite of the poor quality and frequent adulteration there is apparently a ready sale for this product. In equivalent liquid form the retail price of dry powdered milk is 66 cents per litre. Condensed milk costs Rs. 1·66 per litre but although expensive it is very popular with the consuming public.

5:87. The government is at the moment assisting the dairy industry in several ways. The breeding stations at Curepipe and Palmar are producing and rearing Creole cattle of an improved and more standardised type of selective breeding. Progeny-tested sires from the stations are used in artificial insemination work throughout the island. In 1959, 5,235 cows were inseminated with semen from 14 bulls and 2,738 re-inseminations were necessary. In course of time this service must lead to an all-round improvement in the quality of the national dairy herd. Secondly, the Richelieu Livestock Feed Factory manufactures specially balanced concentrates and a cheap cow feed prepared from bagasse, molasses, and urea. Over 1,000 tons of the latter were sold in 1958. Thirdly, the Department of Agriculture operates an advisory extension service. Apart from the specific service of artificial insemination, however, it is abundantly clear that a much greater effort by extension service is required if the dairy industry is going to develop along proper lines.

(ii) *Future development*

5:88. *Estates.* As mentioned earlier the production of milk by estates, from 20 or more cow units, has not been a paying proposition in Mauritius, owing to the high cost of labour and concentrate food. As a result, this source of milk is gradually disappearing entirely, and it is a matter for decision whether this type of production should be encouraged in future. Elsewhere economic milk production is based on efficiently utilised productive pastures, and not on forage crops. There is also in Mauritius the problem of the Stomoxys fly, but this can be overcome by night grazing when this fly is inactive and other means of control are being investigated. It is possible that the cost of concentrates might be reduced but not to any significant extent. Therefore, unless estates are prepared to allocate suitable land for establishment of pasture grasses of the sward type, e.g. *Digitaria* spp., and to fence these pastures for the most efficient utilisation, future prospects are not very bright. In our view such production methods, on an accurate accounting basis, should, first of all, be demonstrated on a government farm and the difficulties overcome before advocating their adoption by estates, even making allowances for the fact that other milk production techniques are carried out more effectively with the larger unit.

5:89. *Small producers.* It is possible that control of slaughter of dairy-type female stock has been responsible for the increase in milk cattle recorded. It is more likely, however, that the popularity of the dairy cow with the small peasant is due to the fact that she provides him with a fairly steady supplementary income in spite of all the difficulties with which he has to contend. Although his production methods may be inefficient and his product extremely poor in quality, he, apparently, can still sell it profitably. The fodder costs him nothing, his family provides the labour free of charge, and the only financial outlay, with the exception of his foundation cow or replacements, is stock feed or concentrates. On several occasions we were supplied with evidence that the income from a cow represented the difference between solvency and insolvency. For this reason alone we consider that this type of milk production deserves every encouragement and assistance, and this has been minimal up till now.

5:90. In this connection we were most interested to observe the outcome of the government land settlement experiment at Palmar, which was supposed to have a primary emphasis on milk production. The land was prepared by government for cultivation and houses for the settlers were built. The cropping side of the programme was efficiently carried out, but in our view the Livestock Division of the Department of Agriculture missed a golden opportunity of demonstrating to all small milk producers on the island efficient and up-to-date methods of production on a small scale. Simple cowsheds could have been erected for assessment of suitability, management and production methods demonstrated by close and constant supervision, and marketing problems examined and tested out. Not one of these things was done and yet this is the most effective form of extension service. We recommend that this aspect of the Palmar settlement scheme be completely reorganised and that all aspects of dairy husbandry, within the capacity of the small producer, should be dealt with, management, feeding, calf-rearing, milk hygiene, and marketing. Milk records could be kept and accurate production costs. Assistance by government staff should be considerable, particularly in the early stages, but expenditure of funds should be low in relation to the experience gained which can by demonstration be passed on to other producers, and the experiment can be repeated in other areas.

5:91. During the recent cyclone many cowsheds were destroyed and the opportunity should not be lost of rebuilding and equipping for more efficient and hygienic production in the future. Propaganda, discussions, and information leaflets may all be useful, but some financial assistance in the form of a long-term loan or directly by government is essential to provide the small producer with minimal facilities for achieving reasonable standards of hygiene, and sufficient supervisory staff should be available to assist him in maintaining these standards.

5:92. As mentioned earlier, the breeding of good dairy animals is being achieved through the existing artificial insemination service, using semen from progeny-tested bulls of the Creole type. It has not been possible to assess so far the effect of this in raising the general level of productivity although we were informed that some data was being collected. It appears to us that the cost of this service is high, particularly with regard to the official mileage involved, when operating from a single centre. We were unable to obtain an accurate cost figure per insemination, but steps should be taken to reduce costs by operating from district centres.

5:93. Of much greater importance than breeding is the feeding of the dairy animal. The Livestock Feed Factory has done a great deal here, but a much greater effort is required to reduce the cost to the producer of the various stock feeds. The Livestock Division of the Department of Agriculture, as at present organised, has not given sufficient encouragement to the carrying out of properly designed trials of new ration formulae. Although much has been done, greater effort is required in the investigation of better pasture grasses, other forage crops, and silage preparation in small units. More land at the breeding stations, at present under cane, should be devoted to this important work. The possibility of production under irrigation should also be considered.

5:94. It was represented to us that under present conditions an owner of a single cow can make a profit of Rs. 10 per month, and that if the same animal was properly fed that profit could be trebled. Whether this is a reasonable estimate or not we cannot say, but the rapid fall in production from the third month of lactation is certainly due to inadequate feeding, and if this can be ameliorated yields will increase and loans repaid more rapidly. A co-operative system might be introduced to facilitate the greater use of stock feed and concentrates by small producers.

(iii) *Milk marketing*

5:95. The marketing of the milk of the small producer is most unsatisfactory and, coupled with the more efficient production methods which we have proposed, a new system should be introduced. We were informed that milk producers formed a co-operative some years ago, and that the project failed principally owing to the existence of a multiplicity of small competing retailers. We consider that the existing total daily production, the potential for increased production in future, and the relatively good communications justify the establishment of a centralised milk processing plant to ensure to the consuming public better quality milk of recognised standard. We had the opportunity of discussing with a local entrepreneur proposals for such a plant financed by local and outside capital. We believe that the scheme is sound and based on modern developments in this field. Local enterprise of this sort is worthy of every encouragement

104

by government, by appropriate assistance as outlined below (paragraphs 6:99ff). An interesting feature of the proposals is that some at least of the existing milk collectors will continue to operate on behalf of the undertaking, and that the milk after processing will be sold in sealed containers for retailing, through existing channels. As and when the plant is established we recommend that the producers form new co-operatives delivering milk at a fixed wholesale price to rural collecting centres which will be established as part of the scheme. We believe that milk can be marketed more successfully and economically by a privately operated scheme of this sort than by the official Agricultural Marketing Board discussed below (paragraphs 5:59-61 and 5:144-151.)

5:96. The consumption of fresh milk *of good quality* should be encouraged and increased in Mauritius, reducing the importation of processed milk, valued at Rs. 4,164,000 (£314,800) in 1958. The present daily consumption of fresh milk per head of population is $2\frac{1}{4}$ ozs. which compared unfavourably with India, 4 ozs., South Africa 7 ozs., United Kingdom 18 ozs., and New Zealand 24 ozs.

Beef Production

(i) *Present position*

5:97. Cattle slaughtered for human consumption in Mauritius during the years 1949 and 1955 to 1958 were as follows.—

Table XLI. Cattle Slaughtered for Human Consumption, 1949 and 1955-1958

Year	Local					Imported		Grand total
	Bull calves	Milch heifers	Breed: cows	Other than milch breed	Total	Rodrigues	Madagascar	
1949	5,287	212	2,072	815	8,386	352	2,686	11,424
1955	2,833	50	1,551	871	5,305	850	5,575	11,730
1956	3,350	144	1,571	820	5,885	354	6,584	12,823
1957	4,418	46	1,431	804	6,699	885	5,763	13,347
1958	5,139	91	2,569	519	8,318	703	4,319	13,340

5:98. The average current price for bull calves of the milch breed, and for discarded cows unfit for economical milk production, is Rs. 1·50 per kilo, live weight. Herd cattle and old draught animals are sold at a slightly lower price, usually Rs. 1·40 per kilo, live weight. The Madagascar and Rodrigues cattle sell at Rs. 2·90 per kilo, dead weight (i.e. less skin and offals), the killing out percentage varying from 47% to 55% of the live weight. The average retail price of local meat is Rs. 5·20 per kilo.

5:99. In 1958, 607 metric tons of frozen meat were imported valued at Rs. 1,195,000 (£89,625). The controlled maximum retail prices of imported frozen meat are as follows:—

fillet—Rs. 5·50 per kilo;
beef without bones—Rs. 3·60 per kilo; and
beef with bones—Rs. 2·40 per kilo.

Thus, local beef of poorer quality appears to be much more expensive than the second two categories of imported meat.

5:100. As can be seen from Table XLI the main source of local beef is from the milch breed. Heifers and cows are only slaughtered under permit. It was reported to us that the slaughtering of such a large number of immature bull calves was due to the fact that owners are unable to feed them, and also because they need the cash. Herd cattle only supply about 7% of the local beef. We were informed that the gradual reduction in herd cattle numbers is due in some cases to tuberculosis, but mainly to government policy regarding Pas Geometrique lands (see paragraphs 5:103-106).

(ii) *Future development*

5:101. In most other countries of the world it is generally agreed that the slaughter of immature calves at, for example, nine months of age is a most wasteful and uneconomic way of producing beef, except for a high-class luxury trade in countries where supplies of mature beef are adequate. In the past, attention has been drawn to this wasteful practice with a recommendation that it should cease. Some members of the Livestock Division of the Department of Agriculture stated categorically that it would be uneconomic in Mauritius to "grow out" these immatures, without producing any specific evidence in support of this opinion. It is doubtless true that the small cow owner without land and with only limited facilities could not do this himself, but there is no reason why he should not sell as stores to others with land and facilities, and not to butchers for slaughter. Four to five thousand calves, possibly more in future, reared as bullocks could and should contribute a great deal more to the meat supplies of the island.

5:102. Tuberculosis has been virtually eliminated from the milch cattle of the island, an occasional case occurring as a result of housing the cow with an infected draught bullock. The incidence in the herds has been greatly reduced in recent years to a reported 2% to 3%. There has been some difficulty in interpreting some of the tuberculin tests, using standard tuberculin, but in spite of this it is recommended that a concentrated effort be made by the veterinary staff to eradicate the disease from the island.

5:103. A satisfactory solution to the vexatious question of the Pas Geometriques is now long overdue. There is no serious problem connected with the area allocated to campement leases, building sites, agricultural use, salt pans, and lime kilns. The main controversy concerns the 3,388 arpents leased on a basis of maximum forestry exploitation. It appears to us that the existing form of tree planting lease has been a comparative failure. Some areas consisting of coral rock with little soil cover are unproductive, "wilt" disease has caused problems in certain areas, although in others the casuarina has established itself well enough.

5:104. The primary function of the trees on Pas Geometriques land is to protect inland cultivation and provided government ensures that this is done the secondary use of the land should be left to the lessee, e.g. for grazing. The natural grass sward of the Pas Geometriques is *Stenotaphrum dimidiatum* which is a very poor fodder grass. As a supplementary fodder for a short period of the year Acacia grows well in some areas. In our view, owing to the poor quality of the soil and close proximity to the sea, it will be an extremely expensive exercise, even with wider tree spacing, to establish improved grasses, using fertilisers, with the object of providing maintenance and production rations for a dairy cow, without supplements. If there is any doubt about this a small experiment could be carried out by the Department of Agriculture on Pas Geometriques land on an accurate accounting basis.

5:105. It appeared to us that the most economic use of the Pas Geometriques land under discussion would be as grazing land for beef production, bearing in mind the primary function of the land mentioned earlier. We were also convinced that, as many of the areas cannot be self-supporting for livestock, owners of adjacent land are more conveniently placed to utilise the land effectively.

5:106. To bring the diminution of the number of herd cattle to a halt, to encourage their increase in future, and to provide facilities for the growing out of store bullocks of the milk breed, we strongly recommend, as a matter of urgency, that an early decision be taken by government, certainly before 1964, regarding the future of the Pas Geometriques land. We were impressed with the proposed grazing lease agreement drawn up by the Director of Agriculture which can be used as a basis for discussion, and we would stress the importance of having the leases long-term in character, with security to the lessee and safeguards for renewal. Provided these conditions are fulfilled we consider that the present system of auctioning should be continued.

5:107. Under the development plan proposals have been made to import beef cattle of improved type to grade up the existing herd cattle. We support this. It is always a controversial question with breeders which breed to select, but we would wish to emphasise the importance of stamina as well as conformation. The economic nutritional level available in Mauritius is such that early maturing breeds cannot be supported, and we suggest that improved Zebu cattle of, e.g., the Boran type from East Africa, might be suitable. No matter what breed is chosen, care should be taken in selection and adequate quarantine precautions applied at the time of introduction.

5:108. Consideration might also be given to the limited use of beef-type bull semen on milk cows at a later date. The female progeny of all the milch cows will not be required for dairy stock replacements, and beef/dairy cross-animals are nowadays contributing substantially to the beef supplies of other countries. In Mauritius the need is great and a pilot experiment along these lines should be carried out by the Department of Agriculture in the first instance.

5:109. The research work on pastures and fodder recommended for the dairy industry is of equal importance in beef production. It is perhaps of greater importance as far as pasture is concerned since the herd cattle will not be stall fed. If productive pasture of the sward type can be established, and *Digitaria decumbens* looks most promising, a much greater proportion of the meat requirements of the island could be met by local production.

(iii) *Beef marketing*

5:110. We did not encounter any marked criticism of the existing arrangements for beef marketing. Slaughter of local female stock is only allowed on permit. Butchers or other middlemen purchasers buy from producers at an agreed live-weight price. The live weight is estimated by eye examination and not by weighbridge. While we would not doubt the stated efficiency of the local experts in such matters most other countries in the world now accept the fact that an efficient weighing machine is the most reliable method of determining live weight. As a safeguard to the producer we suggest that consideration be given to the installation of weighbridges at abattoirs. There is no price differential according to whether the beef is derived from milk, herd, or Madagascar cattle and the slaughter of local cattle on quota is not permitted when Madagascar cattle are available.

5:111. We were informed that there is a consumer preference for beef from local milk cattle and, since we believe that better finished animals can be produced by the better feeding standards we recommend, consideration should be given to arranging prices on a quality basis. At the moment there is no incentive to better production when the price to the producer is the same for the good, bad, or indifferent animal apart from its actual live weight.

5:112. We were not greatly impressed with the arrangements for meat inspection and standards appeared lax. There is a shortage of veterinary staff who have a wide range of other duties to perform, and the initial inspection is the responsibility of municipal abattoir personnel who have had some training.

5:113. Under the development plan, proposals have been made for the construction of a new abattoir and quarantine station at Fort George. This is certainly urgent and abattoir improvements are required elsewhere. Adequate cold storage should be made available at Fort George so that slaughtering of animals imported on the hoof can be expedited and meat released as required. Smaller cold storage units at markets would also be useful for storage of unsold meat, as is now done in many tropical countries. Experience elsewhere has shown that the capital expenditure and running costs of such market units can be quickly met by low rates of rental, and they soon become popular with butchers. We recommend installation by the market authorities.

(iv) *By-products*

5:114. We were surprised when we were informed that no by-products other than hides and skins were available from Mauritius abattoirs, since condemnation of meat unfit for human consumption, e.g. tuberculous carcases, occurs from time to time. Material of this nature and blood, etc. can be converted into valuable stock-feed, contributing considerably to the revenue of the abattoir. At the moment Mauritius imports all the meat and bone-meal incorporated in rations of the Livestock Feed Factory. At least some of this could be produced locally and we recommend the installation of a plant to salvage abattoir material and condemned material from the fishing industry. If necessary, government should furnish a loan for this specific purpose.

5:115. All Mauritius hides and skins are processed locally and not exported. The standards of flay and preparation could be improved considerably increasing the value of the finished leather.

Venison

5:116. Under the heading of meat production reference must be made to the contribution which the deer population makes to the diet. The total number of stags and hinds on the island is not known accurately. The actual annual off-take is likewise not known, but we were supplied with a figure between 4,000 and 5,000. Others we consulted took the view that this estimate was probably on the high side. An interesting figure we were given was a yield of 750 stags per annum from 2,000 acres, which means one stag from a little over 2⅔ arpents. Stags will sell from Rs. 80 to 100 each, the skin not being salvaged for processing, and we understand that the price of the venison is beyond the pockets of others than the well-to-do.

5:117. We had the opportunity of seeing stags occupying land capable of growing a wide range of agricultural crops, and which certainly could be converted into good pasture for herd cattle or to the production of fodder for milk cattle. We believe that stag rearing should be confined to land which cannot be used for any other purpose, and that this matter should be considered during the land and soil survey considered above (paragraph 5:18).

Goats

5:118. The number of goats slaughtered for meat is shown in the following table—

Table XLII. Goats slaughtered for Meat, 1949-58

Year					Rodrigues	Mauritius	Total
1949	..	..	..	..	..	2,240	14,130	16,370
1955	..	..	..	..	..	4,472	16,424	20,896
1956	..	..	..	..	..	2,401	18,993	21,394
1957	..	..	..	..	..	3,076	13,142	16,218
1958	..	..	..	..	..	3,242	10,484	13,626

5:119. The goat thus contributes a considerable amount to the consumption of meat on the island. It could not be determined why there had been a marked reduction in the number from Mauritius slaughtered in 1957 and, again, in 1958. If, in fact, the estimated census figure of 50,000 goats is correct, the off-take figure of 10,000 for 1958 should be greater.

5:120. There is no doubt that goat rearing can be a very suitable and profitable undertaking for the small peasant farmer. We had direct evidence of this at the Palmar Settlement Scheme where the goat had multiplied rapidly under housed conditions, providing meat for the family and animals for sale. The Department of Agriculture has been breeding Anglo-Nubian goats for sale to farmers for upgrading the local goat as a better meat producing animal, and we support this activity.

5:121. More recently British Alpine goats have been introduced for milk production by the small farmer. This also deserves every encouragement since feeding will not be so difficult as with a cow. The management of the high producing milk goat is, however, an expert procedure and we suggest that the Department of Agriculture should supervise carefully the goat husbandry during the initial stages of issue to farmers. The contribution which a good milk goat can make to the prosperity of the small farmer can be considerable.

Sheep

5:122. The general climatic and other conditions prevailing on the island of Mauritius convinced us that it would be unwise to recommend any scheme involving government expenditure for the expansion of sheep breeding. This does not preclude interested private breeders expanding production of tropical-type sheep, although results elsewhere in the humid tropics have in general been disappointing. 7,050 sheep and lambs were imported in 1958 valued at Rs. 493,000 (£37,000).

Pigs

5:123. The pigs slaughtered in Mauritius during the period 1949 and 1955-1958 were as follows—

Table XLIII. Pigs Slaughtered Annually, 1949 and 1955-1958

Year					Rodrigues	Mauritius	Total
1949	..	..	..	..	..	1,543	3,837	5,380
1955	..	..	..	..	..	4,023	2,389	6,412
1956	..	..	..	..	..	3,005	3,436	6,441
1957	..	..	..	..	..	2,006	4,430	6,436
1958	..	..	..	..	..	1,683	3,608	5,291

These pigs were sold and consumed as pork and none was processed into bacon and ham. Forty-one metric tons of the latter valued at Rs. 277,000 were imported in 1958.

5:124. The estimated census figure of 7,000 presumably includes pigs of all age categories, and we were not supplied with the actual break-down. Taking an average slaughter figure for the past three years as a guide, there are probably 300 breeding sows and gilts which makes allowances for breeding stock replacements. We were informed that mature pigs in Mauritius sell at Rs. 1·50 per lb., live weight, and pork is retailed at Rs. 2·75. Pig keeping would, therefore, appear to be a profitable undertaking since an average sow is capable of producing and rearing 14 piglets per annum.

5:125. The recently erected Danish-type piggery at the Livestock Breeding Station, Curepipe, is a magnificent building which could not be copied by any commercial breeder on the island. Some excellent breeding stock has been imported from Australia and South Africa, and piglets of superb quality will soon be available. Interested breeders thus have an excellent opportunity of going ahead and expanding pig production on the island. Suitable pig rations are available from the Livestock Feed Factory and these could possibly be improved in both quality and cost. To encourage pig production further we recommend that consideration be given to the establishment of a small bacon factory. Present imports of bacon and ham represent a weekly throughput of 15 pigs a week. A small factory unit with an attached cold store can be profitably run on this alone producing bacon, ham, sausages, and other pig products, but it would be advisable to cater for three or even four times this throughput. The existence of such a factory established either by government in the first instance or by private enterprise would provide an assured market to breeders, who at the moment have no alternative except to sell to the butchers who, we have been informed, have from time to time formed a ring which keeps down the price offered to the producers.

Domestic Rabbits

5:126. In other island communities, and indeed in some larger countries, where fodder is a problem and meat is in short supply it has been demonstrated that the domestic rabbit can contribute greatly to such supplies. It is a type of production which can readily be carried out by poorer peasants without land and also in towns. We recommend that the Department of Agriculture should consider the importation of suitable rabbits for ultimate sale to the general public as breeding stock, advice being given on housing, management, and feeding. Apart from the contribution to meat supplies this activity will provide a source of income to people who are unable to manage other forms of livestock.

Poultry

5:127. The statistics of imported poultry given in Table XXXVIII show a rapid drop from 13,364 in 1956 to 9,800 in 1957, and only 1,100 in 1958. There is also a reduction, not quite so marked, in the imports of eggs. As far as we could ascertain local requirements are being met more and more by local production and principally by the small producer. We were informed by many, however, that they were now experiencing difficulty in disposing of poultry and eggs at an economic price.

5:128. With funds made available under the development plan for Mauritius a poultry breeding unit has been established at Reduit by

112

the Agricultural Department, and has recently opened. This in point of view of scale and magnificence is better than any we have seen in any overseas territory. The object of the unit is to supply high-class poultry to producers avoiding the necessity of importation with a possible disease risk involved. There is also a broiler production unit attached for demonstration purposes. The type of construction adopted generally could not be copied even by commercial breeders of wealth, but we understand simple prototype buildings are going to be erected in future. This unit should be capable of supplying the needs of all producers for some time to come.

5:129. In an island such as Mauritius, where land is scarce, production of poultry and eggs by modern intensive methods is a practical proposition. The feeding of poultry in this way is much more critical than is the case with any other form of livestock. It is essential that the feed should be completely balanced in all respects, and we recommend that particular attention be paid to this in the early experiments at the Reduit Poultry Unit so that suitable rations may be available at a reasonable price to producers who may wish to adopt intensive methods on a large scale. Experience elsewhere has shown that broiler poultry meat can compete successfully with other forms of meat and, indeed, influence the retail price of the latter. Eggs can also be produced by similar methods.

Sea Fishing

5:130. Nearly all the fresh fish eaten in the island is taken in the lagoons, or just outside the reefs, by in-shore fishermen using shallow-draft pirogues. In 1958 1,844 professional fishermen landed 1,986 tons. The average catch for the lagoons alone is more than 10 tons a square mile, but there is evidence that with more intense exploitation the total quantity would diminish. The Fisheries Division has to exercise strict control to prevent over-fishing. Surveys also indicate that the resources of the fishing banks near the coast, i.e. accessible to small craft, are probably limited. Nevertheless, fish is an article of diet eagerly sought by all communities, as recent imports show.—

Table XLIV. Imports of Fish, 1957 and 1958

Type of fish					1957	1958
Fresh and frozen	..	..	..	.. Metric tons	112	118
Salted ..	..	..	..	..	,,	1,166	667
Other, chiefly tinned		..	..	..	,,	720	995

If local supplies of good quality could be increased, they would find a ready sale. It therefore seems obvious that as home-grown food will always be limited by the land available, every possible effort ought to be made to exploit the resources of the sea.

5:131. This means that the remoter grounds must receive more attention. Mauritius is at the end of an arc of banks extending from the Seychelles Archipelago, and including in particular St. Brandon, the Nazareth bank, and the Saya de Malha. A two-year survey was made in 1948-49 by Wheeler and Ommaney, whose comprehensive report leaves no doubt that an abundance both of bottom-feeding and of pelagic fish is to be found in certain areas, and that, provided the many factors involved in fishing there are thoroughly appreciated, there is no reason why exploitation should not be successful. At least two commercial enterprises have confirmed these findings. For some years a Mauritius company has operated profitably a vessel of some 100 tons, which engages in fishing by hand-lines off St. Brandon and transporting guanao therefrom. A base has been established at St. Brandon where most of the catch is salted. The remainder is cleaned and packed in ice and finds an immediate sale when landed at Port Louis. On the average, 350 tons of salted and 120 tons of fresh fish are brought in every year (in addition to the imports given above).

5:132. Another venture was started in 1948 by local interests, helped by a substantial government loan. They bought and converted a naval corvette which proved to be quite unsuitable for the purpose. Although large catches were occasionally made, the fish could not be properly preserved before landing at Port Louis, and the company eventually went into liquidation. Most of the government loan is still outstanding.

5:133. This venture did at least confirm that fish could be caught in large quantities, and showed also that for successful commercial operation many factors have to be studied. Because of its failure, however, there has been reluctance to try again.

5:134. The bottom-feeding fish are best caught with hand-lines, since trawls suffer too much damage from coral obstructions. The pelagic fish (tunny, bonito, etc.) are plentiful enough to attract Japanese fishing fleets to Mauritian waters during the summer months. Mauritius itself has no sea-going craft suitable for this purpose. Suggestions have therefore been made from time to time for some kind of co-operation with the Japanese, and discussions are now at an early stage for the formation of a joint company with one of the leading fishing concerns in Tokyo. We believe this to be a practical and promising way of starting in earnest a deep-sea fishing industry based in the island. The Japanese have wide experience of all types of fishing in tropical waters, and such expert help is essential if another failure is to be avoided. We therefore recommend that this latest project be examined by United Kingdom fishery experts, and, if their report is favourable, that the government be prepared to give it financial backing. Even if this particular proposal is not acceptable for any reason, other ways and means of harvesting the known fishing banks should be vigorously sought. It is not too optimistic to think that, after satisfaction of local needs, a fish cannery producing for export might follow in due course.

5:135. An essential preliminary to plans of this sort is an extension of cold-storage capacity. The only plant now in existence is already too small for the many demands on it, and the owners have asked for government help to enlarge it. An independent and progressive group is also prepared to invest money for the purpose, and has made definite proposals. Quite apart from fish, Mauritius needs much more cold storage, not only for preserving imported foods (including such things as seed potatoes) but also for evening out gluts of local crops. We therefore recommend that the government should assist both ventures, either directly or through the Agricultural Bank, if private capital is not forthcoming.

THE ORGANISATION OF AGRICULTURE

The Department of Agriculture

5:136. As soon as a suitable opportunity offers we recommend that one post of Deputy should be dispensed with, and that below the Deputy level one or more posts of Assistant Director and one post of Chief Research Officer at the same appropriate salary level should be created. This would, we feel, create a clearer and more appropriate chain of command. On the research side we have already referred to the need for an officer to work on tea (paragraphs 5:39-40). We also feel that the filling of the proposed post of Chief Research Officer would result in a much better co-ordination of the work of the specialist officers not only with each other but also with the field officers and that it would result in a more definite direction being given to the work of specialist officers. In addition we cannot over-emphasise the importance we attach to the post of officer in charge of the extension services, which has shortly to be filled. It is our impression that the extension services have not yet found their feet and that contact with the farmer is very inadequate. We realise that steps are being taken to improve this including the construction of a series of extension centres but this most important branch of the Department's activities requires the organisation which only an experienced officer can give and it requires the drive of an enthusiast who is prepared to train the inexperienced and inadequately trained field staff.

5:137. In addition we think that the Department of Agriculture should divest itself of any activities that are or will be carried on by private individuals or autonomous bodies like the Tea Development Authority mentioned above (paragraph 5:43). In this connection, we are of the opinion that the Department should encourage private enterprise to undertake the extensive, and at present subsidised, service of satisfying Mauritius' seed requirements. This task might be undertaken either by independent but guided endeavour or by private individuals contracting with the government and its removal from the direct control of the Department would free the Department for more important work. We are strongly opposed to the Department's embarking on any commercial ventures (paragraph 5:140).

5:138. The College of Agriculture which has made such a notable contribution to Mauritian agriculture is, we feel, in danger of losing that reputation. A recently appointed committee has recommended that two streams, one for the sugar technologist and the other for the general agriculturalist should be instituted and we support this recommendation. The Department badly needs the trained practical agriculturalist and we doubt whether he is likely to be produced in present circumstances. The College should be directed by an experienced and practical agriculturalist. The extension officer must be able to turn his hand to all the jobs a farmer is called on to do and if he is to get the confidence of the farmer he must do these jobs well. He cannot learn to do this from textbooks and he must be taught by someone who knows.

Board of Agriculture, Fisheries, and Natural Resources

5:139. We make mention above of the function of the Chamber of Agriculture (paragraph 5:23). We gained the impression that the Chamber is so deeply and continuously involved with the interests of the sugar industry that it can have little time to devote to the needs of "other agriculture". Indeed, we doubt whether the membership of the Chamber is appropriate for this purpose. Under Ordinance No. 29 of 1957 there was established a Board of Agriculture, Fisheries, and Natural Resources, charged with the duties of advising the minister on all matters of general policy relating to agriculture, forestry, fisheries, and the utilisation and preservation of natural resources. In our view this Board has an extremely important and active part to play in the development and welfare of the agricultural industry. We understand that on the occasions that use has been made of the Board it has been largely in the form of a Committee of the Board set up on an *ad hoc* basis to deal with a specific question referred to it by the minister. In our view this is not how the Board should function. It should be the forum for discussion for all agricultural policy matters other than those directly and solely concerned with sugar. It should consider not only matters referred to it by the minister but should itself initiate discussion of all or any matters affecting the welfare of the industry and make its views known to the minister. Such a board can act as a tremendous stimulus and support to the minister and to the departments of government concerned. To fulfil these functions with energy and effect board members should be chosen from those who by experience and knowledge can make valuable contributions to discussions, who are public-minded and prepared to give their time and energy to this important work. We suggest that further consideration be given to the composition of the Board. In particular, we feel that the Director of Agriculture, who is already over-loaded with boards and committees, should be relieved of his responsibility as Chairman and that an unofficial chairman be appointed. We feel, too, that it is inappropriate that four members of Legislative Council should be members by virtue of that office and that sugar interests are over-represented on the Board. We recommend that the functions and composition of this potentially valuable board be reviewed.

Land Settlements and Allotments

5:140. Mauritius is not unique in having given way to clamour and rushed into the politically popular development of land settlements and allotments much too hurriedly. There was quite inadequate information on the system of agriculture to be followed by the settlers and none at all on the economics of the practices to be followed. Indeed, it seemed to us that even the suitability of the land for the purpose in view was regarded as a quite secondary consideration. The pious hopes that the land would be used for food crops and animal husbandry and that tenants would be required to pay economic rents very soon fell by the way. Rents have been reduced and one half to three-quarters of all arable land on settlements is now under sugar cane. We do not think that government-sponsored and subsidised schemes for the growing of sugar cane are in the best interests of Mauritius. Nor do we feel that because a man is landless he should have priority claims to become a tenant. The days when a man looked on it as a right that he should own some land have long gone by. Good land is at a premium in Mauritius and it will only produce its due quota if settlers of the right calibre are selected and if they are given the necessary informed guidance and help. There are many lessons to be learned from experience to date and to this end we strongly recommend that the whole position be reviewed, that the first task should be to consolidate and improve existing settlements, and that no new schemes be started until this has been done. New schemes should only be started when technical and economic doubts have been resolved. Except in so far as may be necessary to obtain information before the opening of settlements the Department of Agriculture should not be involved in schemes of direct food production. Commercial farming for profit by a government department is rarely, if ever, a lucrative occupation and in any case the time of the officers and the resources of the Department could be much better employed in other directions.

The Co-operative Movement

5:141. The Co-operative Movement has a long history in Mauritius, dating from 1913. It has some 30,000 members. Most of the primary societies, about 300 in number, are unlimited liability credit societies but there are nine other categories, of which the most important are retail stores and thrift and savings groups. There are four secondary societies, the Central Co-operative Bank, the Co-operative Wholesale Society, the Co-operative Agricultural Federation and the Co-operative Union. The movement finances the cultivation of sugar cane and tea (central bank funds), and tobacco and vegetables (from primary societies' own funds) up to about Rs. 5 million a year (£375,000) and distributes to members crop proceeds of about Rs. 15 million (£1,125,000) and consumer goods of about Rs. 6 million (£450,000). Other activities include thrift, housing, transport, and fishing societies.

5:142. It cannot be claimed that much of the pure spirit of co-operation exists but what can be claimed is that the movement provides the machinery for much-needed short-term credit and as such performs a most useful service to the community. We formed the opinion that small planters preferred that the financial transactions of the sale of cane should be through the society rather than direct with estates (this may, in part, be due to the disinclination of estates to provide cultivation loans) but that they preferred to retain their identity rather than market in bulk with their fellow members. Under existing legislation the membership of a credit society is limited to 75 and in these circumstances the meagre staff of the Registrar is largely employed in assisting with the book-keeping of societies. We recommend that in present-day circumstances, the permissible membership should be increased or some form of grouping arranged so that better accounting staff can be afforded by the societies.

5:143. The impression we gained was of a movement which runs reasonably smoothly along well-tried grooves but that the very limited staff of the Department of Co-operation was fully employed in maintaining this position and had no reserve strength to initiate improvements or expansion. If, as we suggest it should (paragraph

5:145), the Co-operative Movement is to play an important part in the development of organised marketing and possibly enter the field of medium-term credit, then some strengthening of the Department with well-trained staff will be necessary.

Marketing

5:144. In this chapter we have made frequent references to the need for organised marketing of primary products other than sugar. In some cases, e.g. tobacco, the existing marketing arrangements, subject to the qualifications we make (paragraph 5:45), appear satisfactory, in others like milk the establishment of satisfactory arrangements appears to be in hand (paragraph 5:59) and we would not suggest any interference where satisfactory arrangements already exist or are contemplated. We do recommend, however, that a central Agricultural Marketing Board should be set up to foster, through the provision of stable and secure market, the development of food crops, vegetables, oilseeds, the products of the livestock industry, and so on (see paragraphs 5:59-61).

5:145. The main purpose of the Board, as we see it, would be to offer guaranteed minimum prices for crops other than sugar. But it would be wise, initially at least, to restrict its activities to a limited number of non-perishable crops since such crops would raise fewer problems for it than would perishable crops. As far as perishable crops are concerned, we recommend organised supplies through co-operative societies to well-run municipal markets with as little interference as possible from the Board. To enable it to offer guaranteed minimum prices for the non-perishable crops with which it is dealing, the Board would have to receive a recurrent grant from the government to cover, up to a limited amount, the losses which it might make on such transactions. As long as the Board was acting in this way, as an agent for government subsidisation of the production of these crops, it should remain a government body independent of the co-operative movement, although even in these cases it should work as closely as possible with the co-operative movement. The Board should encourage the small producer to sell his produce to it through the co-operative societies and the co-operative societies should remain the main vehicle for bringing credit to the small producers.

5:146. In the case of imported products the success of a policy of guaranteed minimum prices may require some measure of protection either through the raising of an import duty or through the licensing of imports. Such import licensing may be needed to protect the producers of certain crops (e.g. potatoes and onions) against the risk of the untimely arrival of a shipload of imports. The imposition of an import duty or the licensing of imports must remain a function of the government but it would be an important function of the Board to advise the government on such controls over the import of agricultural products.

5:147. The Board or marketing organisation will have to be established by statute. It should have a controlling board which, because public funds are largely involved, must have appropriate government representation on it, and it should publish detailed accounts of all its transactions. The manager appointed to run it must be of the calibre necessary to ensure its success. The products to be dealt in by the board should be publicly announced as a schedule to the ordinance and we strongly advise that a limited and carefully selected list of products be agreed in the first instance. This list would be determined by the needs of the country for the product in question and the state of the existing marketing arrangements for it.

5:148. It will be charged with the duties of assisting and improving the marketing and processing of agricultural and fishery produce and, in particular, with assisting co-operative societies to dispose of their produce to the best advantage. It should be empowered in respect of certain produce to prescribe a maximum, minimum, or specific price to be paid to producers of such produce. It should have power to establish processing plants, depots and agencies and to enter into contracts for the purchase and sale of produce. It should have power to create a reserve fund but otherwise should be a non-profit-making organisation.

5:149. In price fixation we are in general in favour of the declaration of guaranteed minimum prices. Such prices must, however, be reasonably generous if they are to achieve their objective and they must be declared for a sufficiently long and appropriate period to make them effective. In addition they should be kept under constant review so that they will encourage production without sacrificing efficiency.

5:150. The Board will need some capital funds for working capital, for the provision of storage space, and for similar purposes. Such funds should be provided on commercial terms either by the banks on government guarantee or by the government itself. The Board will also have to receive a recurrent annual grant from the government for the purpose of offering guaranteed minimum prices. For the Board will clearly make a loss when the prices the consumer is prepared to pay fall below the guaranteed minima, although it may recoup part at least of this when these prices rise above the guaranteed minima. A strict limit should, however, be set to the size of this annual grant; and the Board should be required to revise the general level of its guaranteed prices in a downward direction if it were making a persistent annual loss in excess of this limit. We do not consider ourselves competent to say precisely what this limit should be; but we consider that the government should initiate the scheme by the appointment of a manager for the Board whose first task should be to draw up a scheme for the operation of the Board for approval by the government. This scheme should include a proposal for the amount of the annual grant to be paid by the government to the Board.

5:151. To help in the preparation of legislation for the organisation, we recommend that a study be made of existing legislation on the marketing of agricultural produce in other countries. Assistance in drawing up an ordinance suited to Mauritian needs may be obtained by reference to Ordinances No. 11 of 1948 and No. 26 of 1949 (British Honduras), Ordinance No. 7 of 1948 (Trinidad), Decrees No. 2 of 1934, No. 15 of 1937, No. 9 of 1939 and No. 25 of 1948 (Zanzibar), and Ordinance No. 39 of 1955 (Kenya), all of which deal with the establishment of marketing boards for agricultural produce.

CHAPTER 6

Industry

6: 1. Whilst we are confident that action on the lines set out in Chapter 5 will lead to an increase of employment in agriculture, we have already argued that any substantial increase in productive employment can be achieved only through the institution and expansion of manufactures (paragraph 2:51). In this chapter we survey the possibilities of such expansion, and it is clear from this survey that, given enterprise and initiative on the part of private businessmen in Mauritius and given a strengthening of the relevant parts of the administration, some measure of industrial expansion should be possible. It is equally clear, however, that there are many difficulties limiting the rate at which such expansion can take place and that Mauritius cannot hope by industrialisation to solve her population problem, unless the rate of growth of the population is itself greatly restrained.

6: 2. Before examining the particular industries, which we consider offer some hope of development in Mauritius, we would like first to outline some of the conditions which any industry, no matter where, needs for its inception and successful operation. There are six main factors to be considered:—

(1) raw materials,
(2) markets,
(3) capital,
(4) management,
(5) trained labour, and
(6) services, particularly electric power.

If industries are not to be wholly controlled by government, entrepreneurs are also vital—that is to say, men who can see the possibility of financial reward by starting new enterprises, are prepared to risk their own money in so doing, and are capable of assembling the necessary elements into a viable whole. There is no lack of such men in Mauritius. The record of the sugar industry in recent years shows what can be done, although it is to be regretted that so much energy and imagination has been devoted to one single end, to the neglect of other avenues of expansion. Mauritius does not lack ideas—in fact, we have found it difficult in the industrial sphere to suggest anything that has not already been thought of—and we believe strongly that given the right inducements, many of them can be brought to fruition. These inducements lie largely in the hands of the government to supply.

6: 3. In the above list, raw materials and markets have been placed first, because in Mauritius they are exceptionally important. The island has been well enough surveyed to make it certain that it contains no mineral resources worth exploiting. The industries can therefore only be based on materials either derived from its own animal and vegetable production, or else imported in a raw or semi-processed state. The very smallness of the country necessarily imposes limitations on the first, while its remoteness from sources must make imported raw materials, particularly those of high bulk and low prime cost, more expensive than in most other parts of the world. Further, the home market is still not large enough to support profitably and without tariff protection many of the commoner manufacturing industries.[1] The very substantial growth of the Mauritian population which will inevitably take place in the next decade or two (see paragraphs 2:2-4) will, however, enlarge the domestic market; and it is possible that for this reason some industries started now behind a tariff wall may find the protection less necessary or even unnecessary in the future. In saying this, we do not of course wish to imply that a large increase in the population is to be encouraged. On the contrary, as we have already argued, a large rate of increase in the population would make such demands on the limited resources of land and capital in Mauritius that the standard of living would inevitably fall; all that we are saying is that the larger domestic market would provide some small, but only very partial, offset to these undesirable effects of population growth.

6: 4. Another big difficulty is that risk capital is notoriously hard to come by in Mauritius. Again the exception is the sugar industry where some Rs. 330 million (£25 million) have been spent during the last ten years in modernising the mills and bringing marginal lands under cane cultivation. But in other directions, there has been little private investment. It is not that no funds are available, but rather that they are inadequate for any particular project, and more important, that the probable return is not attractive. The only credit institution available is the Agricultural Bank, whose limited resources have so far been devoted almost entirely to the sugar industry. Beyond this, it has been customary for entrepreneurs to have recourse direct to the government, in the hope of getting money

---

[1] Some idea of the size of the local market can be gathered from the scale of imports into Mauritius: See paragraphs 3:22 and 23, in particular Tables XX and XXI.

below commercial rates of interest. Few are successful, because official funds for this purpose are also scanty, and, moreover, the government has no machinery for properly investigating the applications. It is also noteworthy that there is very little overseas investment in Mauritius. We believe that outside the sugar industry only two foreign firms have erected factories, both for the manufacture of cigarettes. There is, in fact, a tendency for Mauritius to invest abroad rather than for foreigners to invest in Mauritius.

6:5. We have been struck too by the very general complaints that under existing legislation private investment in enterprises other than sugar is far from attractive. It is argued in some quarters that the main reasons for this are that at 40% company tax is too high, even after taking into account the 10% investment allowance, and that the tariff code is obsolete. We have heard of one case where a firm wishing to erect a block of flats in Mauritius has decided instead to build in Reunion, where the facilities offered by the French Government, particularly by way of tax relief, has made all the difference to the expected return on the investment.

6:6. We consider these matters in detail in Chapter 7, but we wish here to emphasise their supreme importance. It is axiomatic that risk capital will only go where the rewards are likely to be highest. Under-developed countries are realising the truth of this, and those that are slow or unwilling to take the necessary measures, are finding their industrial development lagging correspondingly behind their needs. In many ways, Mauritius is not under-developed. Some of its services are far advanced, but too many eggs are in one basket. The dominance of sugar has led to the neglect of the secondary industries, and this will continue unless the government takes much more positive action to guide private investors in other directions.

6:7. Management is a term not easy to define. Whether it is good or bad soon becomes obvious in the results of an undertaking. At least one essential ingredient is expertise in the kind of business managed. In Mauritius, the standard of technical management in the sugar industry is high beyond question, though as we have already said it is to be doubted whether its approach to the labour problem has been equally competent (see paragraph 4:17). In commerce too, as well as in some (but not all) departments of the public service, experience and skill are evidently not lacking, but in the field of industry generally, the position is not so satisfactory and, indeed, we cannot expect it to be otherwise, since outside the sugar industry, the island has no training grounds at any level of management. Those Mauritians who have gone overseas for higher education, mostly become doctors, lawyers, and the like. Few return as engineers or chemists, and those that do have a very limited scope for employment. Even the possession of a technical degree does not qualify its holder to become manager, say, of a soap or match factory; and he cannot obtain the necessary experience in the country of his birth. The point of these observations is that if a new industry is to have any chance of success, it must begin by employing experts from abroad who know their jobs. Neglect of this elementary principle has resulted in the past in more than one failure of a promising venture. The foreign managers can later be replaced by locally-trained men, always provided that there are enough people with a basic technical background and as we make clear in Chapter 8 radical changes are required in the educational system before this will be true of Mauritius.

6:8. As regards industrial services, transport and communications should present no particular problem. For many reasons, most new industries are likely to be concentrated in the vicinity of Port Louis. The planned development of the road net-work, together with the proposed improvements to the harbour, should serve all the foreseeable needs of industrial development. Water supplies in the Port Louis district are likely to be adequate for the kind of light industries that might be sited there; but heavy water-consumers, such as pulp and paper (which are not probable though not impossible) would have to go the the "wet" parts of the island. Electric power is of course essential for all forms of development, and we consider in a later section the programme of the Central Electricity Board.

6:9. Trained labour is the last of the desiderata listed above. We have already seen that the labour situation is complex and para-doxical, but that, as the working population rises and current attitudes to manual work change, there will be a growing number of people seeking employment—and if nothing is done, out of work. Although labour is plentiful and although wage-rates in Mauritius are low by western standards, it is still a high-cost country in comparison with others in the Far East, and if new industries are to succeed in the face of competition from this quarter, and without excessive tariff protection, their costs will have to be comparable.

6:10. While we can have no doubt about the future supply of unskilled labour, we are less certain about its quality. It is noticeable that workers are not themselves over-anxious to increase their earnings when paid on piece rates, or to perform satisfactorily if paid by time only. This is more noticeable in agriculture than in industry, though it is true in both. On the other hand, the average working-class Mauritian is not unskilful with his hands and is quite easily taught the simpler techniques needed to look after ordinary machinery. What strikes us forcibly is the lack of good foremen (as in so many under-developed countries) and of elementary technical education. The first results in poor supervision at the shop-floor and field levels; and the second means that new entrants into industry have no understanding of the processes they are called upon to operate. They may eventually become good workmen, but the odds are against them. Here again we come up against the need for educational reform.

6:11. Comparison is inevitable between Mauritius and other islands with a teeming population and few natural resources. Hong Kong and Puerto Rico spring at once to mind. Both have built up a prosperous export trade although they have to import nearly all their raw materials. But Mauritius does not have all the advantages possessed by these two islands. Hong Kong is peopled by one of the most industrious of all races. Risk capital has been plentiful and wages have remained very low. The island is the commercial gateway to the Chinese mainland, and being a free port, is able to obtain cheap raw materials and at the same time to enjoy free entry into the United Kingdom market for its manufactured goods. Puerto Rico, through its own efforts, has managed to persuade many American companies to set up subsidiaries whose products have free entry to the vast market of the United States mainland. Costs of production are less than in U.S.A., because of low wage-rates, and the help given by the government by way of tax reliefs, cheap factory sites and buildings, free services etc., enables the return on capital to be higher than from a similar investment on the mainland. Both these countries have a larger domestic market than Mauritius, and both have a homogeneous population with a greater sense of national unity.

6:12. Mauritius, it is true, *does* have free entry into the United Kingdom market as well as preferential treatment in some other Commonwealth markets, and *will* have a super-abundance of labour. But it is far from the main trade-routes and from other industrial communities—a handicap imposed by geography from which there is no escape. Yet freedom of entry for raw materials, government help for new industries, a greater spirit of enterprise and co-operation among all classes, and stable labour costs are all matters within its power to attain. Some only need legislation, others the intelligent co-operation of the people of all religions and political creeds. With them, Mauritius would have some chance of developing export industries based on the assembly or finishing of semi-fabricated components, and whilst never likely to become a second Hong Kong or Puerto Rico, it could at least emulate them in a small way.

6:13. A view of the general pattern can best be got by examining the figures of employment and registered establishments produced annually by the Central Statistical Office. Table XLV shows the number of skilled and unskilled workers employed in 24 principal industries including the public services in 1951 and 1958. It is by no means comprehensive, since it does not contain a number of occupations included in the 1952 census and listed in the Luce Report. According to the latter, the number employed in industry at the time

Table XLV. Employment of Skilled and Unskilled Workers in Industries, 1951 and 1959

Industries	1951			1958		
	Skilled workers	Un-skilled workers	Total	Skilled workers	Un-skilled workers	Total
Aloe fibre industry* ..	27	741	768	63	1,684	1,747
Aerated water works ..	10	45	55	82	124	206
Bakeries	350	83	433	320	227	547
Building trade	595	312	917	1,399	814	2,213
Bus coach building ..	55	28	83	92	61	153
Cigarette manufacture ..	27	193	220	46	166	212
Distilling industry.. ..	81	133	214	24	131	155
Docks	192	834	1,026	150	960	1,110
Electrical companies ..	112	218	330	479	275	754
Footwear manufacture ..	180	149	329	238	189	427
Jewellers' trade	172	78	250	370	78	448
Lime industry	182	358	540	187	369	556
Match industry	46	143	189	—	20	20
Oil industry	56	—	56	8	55	63
Printing establishments ..	291	107	398	251	88	339
Public services:						
Government	2,517	7,258	9,775	2,799	7,604	10,403
Municipal†	102	906	1,008	199	1,098	1,297
Salt manufacture	10	140	150	9	88	97
Saw mills	44	89	133	60	155	215
Stevedoring	6	817	823	826	—	826
Tanning industry	8	33	41	31	20	51
Tea industry	38	933	971	65	1,838	1,903
Wine manufacture ..	75	308	383	102	302	404
Tobacco plantations ..	53	1,750	1,803	127	1,952	2,079
Workshops:						
Engineering and motor	873	213	1,086	864	668	1,532
Total	6,102	15,869	21,971	8,791	18,966	27,757
Sugar	8,416	48,452	56,868	4,239	51,207	55,446
	14,518	64,321	78,389	13,030	70,173	83,203

* Inclusive of the sack factory.
† Exclusive of the sack factory.

of the review (March 1958) was in the region of 25,919 (Table 6) to 30,643 (Table 7) whereas, according to the year-book of statistics for 1958, the numbers in the 18 secondary industries listed, were only 10,139. The reason for the difference probably lies in the fact that the annual statistics are incomplete, while the Luce Report includes many industrial activities that are services rather than manufacturing.

Table XLVI. Employment in Secondary Industries and Public Services, 1959

Secondary industries	I.S.I.C. group	No. of establishments licensed	No. of workers
Aerated water works	214	11	222
Aloe fibre industry	231	20	1,232
Aloe fibre sack factory	233	1	340
Bakeries	206	82	575
Bricks, cement blocks, and tiles ..	331	43	N.A.
Building trade	400	22	2,955
Bus coach building	383,384	9	151
Cigarette manufacture	220	2	293
Cycle repairing	385	N.A.	N.A.
Distilling industry	211	3	147
Docks	720	2	1,131
Electrical companies	511	24	709
Footwear manufacture	241,300	34	427
Furniture and cabinet making ..	260	495	N.A.
Ice factories	209	7	30
Jewellers' trade	394	138	409
Lime industry	339	24	556
Match industry	319	1	20
Oil industry	312	1	44
Perfume providing plants	319	5	19
Printing establishments	280	54	300
Public services:			
Central government	810	N.A.	10,663
Local government	810	N.A.	1,152
Salt manufacture	191	7	142
Saw mills	251	83	302
Shoe repairs	242	222	N.A.
Soap manufacture	319	2	38
Stevedoring	716	4	1,013
Sugar mechanical pool	012	1	153
Tailors' workshops	243	912	N.A.
Tanning industry	291	9	41
Tea industry	011,209	284	2,003
Tinsmiths' trade	350	53	N.A.
Tobacco industry	011,220	479	2,214
Vinegar factories	209	2	4
Watch repairers' workshops	393	36	N.A.
Wine manufacture	212	12	352
Workshops:			
Engineering	381,382	126	1,538
Motor	383,384		
Totals		3,209	10,999

FIGURE I
Employment in Industry, 1951—1958

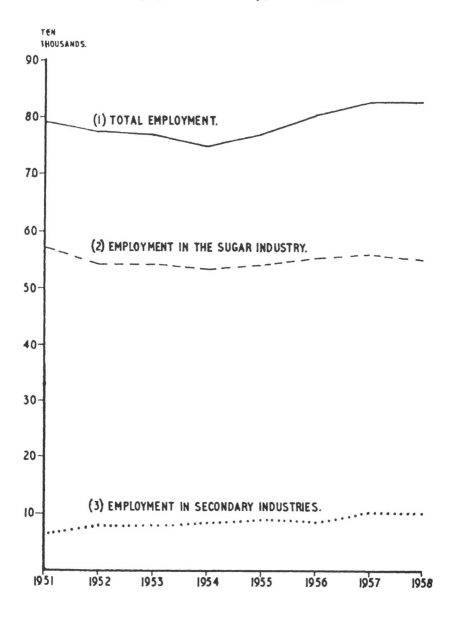

6:14. Table XLVI was specially prepared for us by the Department of Labour. It gives figures for 1959 correlated with registered establishments in accordance with the International Standard Industrial Classification (I.S.I.C.). This table contains 12 occupations not included in the annual returns, but in seven of them the employment is not known. We believe, however, that the annual returns (Table XLV) do give a reasonable indication of the trend in industrial employment, and they are therefore shown graphically in Figure I. In this are plotted—
   (i) total employment in all industries listed;
   (ii) total employment in the sugar industry; and
   (iii) total employment in secondary industries, by excluding sugar, docks, stevedores, public services, tea and tobacco plantation from the totals of (i).

6:15. We draw attention to the following points which appear from Table XLVI and Figure I.

(a) Employment in the sugar industry has remained remarkably static, although sugar production rose from 484,086 metric tons in 1951 to 525,842 metric tons in 1958.

(b) Between 1951 and 1958 total employment ((i) on Figure 1) rose by 4,364. This rise of 4,364 was made up of a fall of 1,422 in employment in the sugar industry ((ii) on Figure 1), a rise of 3,574 in employment in the secondary industries ((iii) on Figure 1), and a fall of 2,213 in employment in the remaining industries (i.e. in the industries other than sugar and the secondary industries). But within the secondary industries, employment in the building trades rose by 1,306, in the aloe fibre industry (including the sack factory) by 1,407, and in electrical and mechanical workshops (i.e. services) by 1,246—that is to say by a total of 3,959. Employment in the remaining secondary industries, i.e. in the manufacturing industries, therefore showed a slight drop.

(c) In the secondary industries appearing in (iii) of Figure I the average annual increase was about 450. Even with the inclusion of other secondary industries not appearing in (iii) of Figure I (i.e. of the industries appearing in Table XLVI but not in Table XLV), it is probable that the annual increase in all secondary industries has not much exceeded 500 during the last decade and that this has been concentrated at a very few points. Yet the annual increase in the economically active population has been some 3,000 between 1953 and 1958.

(d) These figures do not of course give a complete picture of economic activity in Mauritius, since they do not include commerce, retail trade, fishing, many forms of service, etc. The Luce Report gives the "economically active" section of the population

130

as numbering 205,281 in 1958. We can clearly deduce that manufacture makes very little contribution to the economy as a whole, and that it has made practically no progress during the last few years. This conclusion is borne out by the figures of national income discussed in Chapter 3. As we have shown there, there has been a downward trend in the proportion of manufacturing other than sugar in the gross national product (paragraph 3:11).

INDUSTRIES OF IMPORTANCE AND INTEREST

6:16. Having sketched the general background in terms of the conditions of development and the structure of industry in Mauritius we now turn to the prospects of developing or beginning those industries which, given some government encouragement, we believe might prosper. We make no mention of fibre and sack manufacture which is intimately connected with the growing of aloe and has been considered in detail in Chapter 5 (paragraphs 5:62-70).

SUGAR

(i) *General*

6:17. As we have already said (paragraphs 2:39 and 5:25) we have nothing but admiration for the efficiency of production and marketing. The mill owners are fully alive to the necessity of keeping Mauritian sugar competitive in the world markets, and have modernised accordingly.

6:18. Much money is still being spent on modernisation, so that the average overall recovery of the factories, now 87·6% ranks third among all the sugar-producing countries of the world. Vigorous research is carried out by the Sugar Industry Research Institute, not only on the development of new cane varieties and other field work, but also on improvements of factory operations and the utilisation of by-products. The industry is in close touch with the various international organisations and takes full advantage of knowledge derived therefrom.

6:19. However, in its efforts to keep down costs, the industry creates a dilemma for Mauritius. Any action it takes has repercussions on other dependent industries that are important employers of labour. We have in mind particularly the proposal to go over completely from sack to bulk handling. Another example is the importation and maintenance of sugar machinery.

(ii) *Transportation*

6:20. At present, all the sugar is bagged at the mills, taken by rail to storage sheds at the docks, and thence by lighters to ships moored in the harbour, when the bags are emptied into the holds. With all bulk handling it would leave the mills in covered lorries, be conveyed by road to silos at the quay-side, and loaded from there straight into the ships alongside. This scheme has been under study for years. Very heavy capital expenditure would be needed for extension of the deep-water quay, erection of silos, and provision of the special transport. The results would be a considerable reduction in the labour now employed by the dock and stevedore companies (now numbering 1,936) and probably the collapse of the government sack factory and, with it, of the aloe-fibre industry (see paragraphs 5:62 ff).

6:21. In these circumstances we think that the case for making a change must be proved overwhelmingly, and see nothing in the present situation to suggest that it can. Despite its rather primitive facilities, Port Louis compares very favourably with other ports in speed and cost of cargo handling and in 1958 the total tonnage moved was 995,000 of which more than half were sugar exports. Bulk installations would in some degree speed the handling of sugar, but the cost of dealing with all other cargo—in effect imports—would rise because most of the overheads will still have to be carried.

(iii) *By-products*

6:22. The by-products from sugar production, chiefly molasses and bagasse, might be important raw materials for secondary industries. This problem is constantly under study, not only in Mauritius but in all other sugar-producing countries.

6:23. One ton of molasses results from the production of about five tons of raw sugar. Average annual production in the last five years has been about 115,000 tons. 52% of this has been exported, 7%-8% used in three local distilleries for the production of industrial alcohol and of "colonial spirit" (the so-called local rum), and the remainder returned to the cane fields as fertiliser. Overseas, the molasses is used chiefly for making alcohol and for incorporation into animal food-stuffs. The market until recently has been good, with prices ranging up to Rs. 82 per ton f.o.b. in 1958. Recently, prices have fallen severely to below Rs. 40—the value at which it is held preferable to return all the molasses to the fields.

6:24. During and after the last war, a good deal of industrial alcohol was produced. Exports in 1951 were nearly 45 million litres, but thereafter the market deteriorated rapidly, for a variety of reasons, and exports are now negligible. The present production for internal use is around 1,600,000 litres. More than half of this is in the form of local rum, a relatively pure spirit, devoid of flavour and aroma, and quite unsuitable for export in competition, say, with West Indian rum. It is used locally for sale as such or for compounding into various other liquors, sold at 40% strength. Production of the rum from pot-stills is forbidden by law in order to stop illicit distillation. We believe, however, that lawless persons can easily reproduce the colonial spirit if they wish, and that the chief effect of the ordinance has been to kill a possible export. The overseas market may be difficult to enter, but at least there is no point in deliberately ignoring it. We recommend therefore that the law be amended.

6:25. A suggestion has recently been put forward for reviving alcohol production and exports by the erection of a large modern distillery, with a possible capacity of ten million litres yearly. Preliminary calculations show that with an investment of ten million rupees, and with world alcohol price at its 1960 level of some 52 cents a litre the undertaking should be profitable. The distillery would consume more than 30,000 tons a year of molasses, and the residues from the stills ("slops") which contain all the original manurial value would still be available for the cane-fields. Clearly the success of this scheme depends on arranging contracts with one or more overseas consumers. but if this can be done, we recommend strong official support.

6:26. It is most unlikely that Mauritius itself could support a chemical industry based on alcohol. Plants of this kind need cheap and abundant supplies of water and electric power, highly trained staff and labour and a complex chain of ancillary, particularly engineering industries ready to support them. But there are less ambitious possibilities such as the production of yeast for human and animal consumption, and of wax similar to Carnauba from the scum or filter-cakes. A promising enquiry, though now in abeyance, came recently from a British firm interested in producing calcium lactate from cane-juice. The Sugar Research Institute is alive to these problems, and with sucro-chemistry now making rapid strides, new uses for sugar and its derivatives may well eventuate.

6:27. In all sugar territories, bagasse (the fibrous material remaining after crushing the cane) is the primary fuel for generating the power needed by the mills. With an average crop in Mauritius, the production is of the order of 1,110,00 tons, with a calorific value of 3,000-3,500 B.T.U. While in former days the whole of it was needed as fuel, modernisation of the factories is beginning to yield a growing surplus available for other purposes. This might at present amount to 100,000 tons a year, though obviously it is dependent on the crop.

So far, the mills are not prepared to guarantee more than 28,000 tons.

6:28. Paper and various kinds of board have been successfully made from bagasse elsewhere. Experts from the U.S.A., the United Kingdom, and South Africa have studied the possibilities in Mauritius. We have not had access to their reports, but understand the conclusions are not favourable, probably because:—

   (i) the local demand is too small to justify the fairly heavy investment;

  (ii) bagasse needs expensive treatment with imported chemicals;

 (iii) the quality of the paper is not high, and it cannot be used for every purpose, including newsprint;

 (iv) it could not compete overseas with wood-pulp;

  (v) a steady supply of bagasse cannot yet be guaranteed;

 (vi) the large quantities of water needed for this industry will not be easily available.

6:29. We can best illustrate (i), by reference to the figures for the imports of paper, paper-board, and manufactures.—

Table XLVII. Imports of Paper, Paper-board, and Manufactures, 1957-1958

	1957		1958	
	Tons	Rupees	Tons	Rupees
Newsprint	294·8	303,042	334·6	301,445
Other papers, and paper-board	530·1	1,290,725	672·5	1,408,043
Articles made of paper ..	476·6	1,285,129	544·0	1,569,203
	1,301·5	2,878,896	1,551·1	3,278,691

We would not expect a paper factory to be economical with an output of less than 10,000 tons a year, unless it were heavily protected.

6:30. Consideration has been given to using bagasse for generating electricity in a central station, to be part of the Central Electricity Board's system. But the high cost of baling and transport, together with doubts about the reliability of supply, makes this an unlikely solution. On the other hand, several mills have now been connected to the C.E.B.'s distribution network, into which they feed surplus power during the crop season. At this time, shortage of water is apt to reduce the hydro-electric supply, so the load on the diesel generators rises. Power from the sugar mills provides a valuable relief; in 1959 four factories furnished 8·7 million kWh., an amount expected to rise in due course to over 25 million kWh. Despite some disagreement about its value, the consensus of opinion from which we are not in a position to differ, is that this will be the best method of utilising the whole surplus of bagasse.

6:31. Machinery imported for the sugar industry, as well as for some other specified purposes, comes in free under the preferential tariff, and pays only 5% under the general tariff. The value of such exemptions in 1958 was Rs. 20,210,917 (£1,515,820) of which the greater part must have been for the sugar estates. There are, however, at least three engineering workshops, reasonably well-equipped for handling heavy work and capable of building and repairing much of the sugar mill equipment. Since they have to pay duty on imported materials for fabrication, as well as on their own machine-tools, they feel they are losing business they could well undertake. They cannot find enough repetition work to justify re-organising the shops and mass-producing some of the smaller articles now imported. Consequently, the shops are not fully loaded and tend to work from hand to mouth with resultant high costs.

6:32. On the other hand, several of the large sugar mills have extremely good modern workshops which handle most if not all of their repair work and represent considerable capital expenditure. This situation has arisen because of the alleged inability of the independent firms to execute work as speedily and as satisfactorily as the exigencies of modern milling demand. With their present equipment, this is probably true and it is to be feared that their past failure to modernise, whether due to lack of capital, or inertia, or both, has now made it difficult for them to take effective action. Nevertheless, if these firms are to survive at all, they must be determined to bring themselves up-to-date, and they should receive government help in three ways they have recently sought, viz:

(*a*) by the abolition of the tariff on the importation of machine-tools, workshop, and foundry equipment;

(*b*) by helping them to obtain import licenses payable for exports of machinery to Reunion and Madagascar; and

(*c*) by ensuring that government departments should only import metal goods, machinery, and equipment which cannot be produced locally at equivalent cost and quality.

6:33. The railway workshops are also laid out for heavy maintenance work, but much of the equipment is old, even ancient, and will not be of much use when and if the railways close down. Indeed, unless this occurs fairly soon, some new machines will have to be bought. The P.W.D. shops are fairly well equipped for lighter work. Some other establishments, particularly those owned by the principal importers of specialised machines, including road transport have up-to-date facilities for maintaining them (e.g. tyre-retreading). These often have staff trained overseas in their special lines. In addition, there are many small garages and repair shops of varying degrees of efficiency, and Table XLVI lists no less than 53 tinsmiths' establishments, nearly all of which are in the one-man class, fabricating and repairing miscellaneous metal articles. As we have mentioned (paragraph 6:31), in general they have to operate under the handicap that all their materials and components are imported, and bear the same duty as, or even higher than, the finished articles.

6:34. As we have already said, there is no quantity production of metal goods for consumer use. Engineers who have studied the possibilities, report that the local market is too small as yet for most lines, though there may be a few exceptions such as nails, household utensils etc. Such manufactures would almost certainly need tariff protection at the start. For instance, the East African subsidiary of a well-known company is interested in starting the fabrication of aluminium goods in Mauritius, beginning with kitchenware, and in conjunction with a local firm. But they first need the assurance of greater help than the tariff code now provides, and we recommend that this should be given them.

6:35. Of other interest is the recent successful establishment of a small plant for making oxygen and acetylene, two of the most important industrial gases used by the engineering industry.[1]

TANNERIES AND FOOTWEAR

6:36. According to Table XLVI, there are nine licensed tanning establishments, employing in all only 41 workers. It is therefore a "back-yard" industry, with two tanneries responsible for most of the output. One of these is installing new equipment, but otherwise conditions and methods are antiquated. The hides come entirely from locally slaughtered animals, chiefly cattle and goats, and the quality of the leather is very variable (see paragraph 5:115).

6:37. Tables XLV and XLVI show 411 workers as employed in making and repairing footwear in 222 establishments. This industry too is in the hands chiefly of small craftsmen, though there are one or two workshops employing up to 20 persons, according to the volume of orders. One firm makes rubber shoes under a tariff protection of 70 cents a pair, and with a daily output of about 600 pairs, employs about 70, mainly women.

6:38. Leather to the value of Rs. 124,613 (£9,346) was imported in 1958, and leather footwear, chiefly from Hong Kong and India, to the value of Rs. 820,658 (£61,550). Imports of rubber footwear of all kinds were worth nearly Rs. 2,600,000 (£192,500) for 423,000

[1] It is noteworthy that although the facilities are quite good for the mechanical and general maintenance of all classes of property, neglect is only too obvious.

pairs. Clearly there is room for a large expansion of the local industry.

6:39. The shoemakers can and do produce good work, using imported materials for the best. In some lines they can compete with imports. But standards are going down in their losing efforts to compete with the mass-produced shoes from the Far East. The best makers fear that if this continues the craft will die out and vocational training being non-existent in Mauritius, except in the prison, there is no means of teaching this or any other trade.

6:40. An association of tanners and shoemakers is now in process of formation. Its first objects will be to improve the quality of local leather and to introduce trade marks for the better articles. It deserves whatever official support is required. The promoters contemplate that later it may be possible to centralise these two industries by building a modern tannery and shoe factory. Both schemes are laudable and should be encouraged, possibly by modifying the present duties and certainly by rationalising them. As an example of the anomalies of the tariff code, imported rubber soles pay a higher duty than the complete shoe.

SOAP, OIL, AND THE OIL ISLANDS

6:41. Only two soap producers are listed, employing 58 workers (1959). Both were closed down when visited. Equipment is primitive, output tiny, and quality very poor. Not surprisingly, imports have been rising.

Table XLVIII. Imports of Soap, 1957-1958

			1957		1958	
Type of soap			Tons	Value Rs.	Tons	Value Rs.
Household soap	..	..	2,904	3,035,000	3,275	3,330,000
Other	..	..	275	698,000	300	779,000
		Total	3,179	3,734,000	3,575	4,109,000

Local production in 1958 was only 154 tons, mostly from locally produced coconut oil. We think there may be room here for a small modern factory, but most of the raw materials would have to be imported. Consideration should be given to the protection that would be required.

6:42. Imports of edible oil in 1958 were 5,530 tons, principally cotton-seed and sun-flower seed. Coconut oil imports were 142

137

tons, but in addition 662 tons were produced from locally crushed copra. 118 tons were used for making soap.

6:43. The copra is brought in from the Chagos and Agalega Islands, which are worked by two private companies. Production in 1958 was 1,546 tons, of which 1,108 were crushed in Mauritius and the balance exported. The crushing plant, together with one of the soap plants, is owned by the same companies. It appears to be quite efficient and has a capacity of over 4,000 tons per year, a rate actually attained at times in the past. This is equivalent to some 2,500 tons of oil and 1,500 tons of oil-cake (poonac), used as an animal feeding stuff.

6:44. This plant is now closed, however, owing to shortage of copra, and seems likely to remain so. We have not visited the islands but on the information available to us it appears that the coconut plantations have deteriorated, and the two companies responsible for them have appealed to the government for help to save the industry, which otherwise will have to close down. We do not believe that the prospects are bright enough to warrant government aid and though we are loth to see one of Mauritius' few potential assets abandoned, we cannot support the application. Coconut oil is not essential to any future soap manufacture, and its consumption for household use depends on its price compared with other edible oils. If possible, the oil-extraction plant should be kept in good repair, either for crushing copra imported from the Seychelles or else for treating oil-bearing crops that might be produced in Mauritius itself.

MATCHES

6:45. The majority of the matches used in Mauritius are imported, despite a small preferential duty. In Mauritius itself there is only one small manufacturer employing about 20 persons and producing less than 10% of the total number of matches sold.

Table XLIX. Importation and Local Manufacture of Matches, 1957 and 1958

		Imports		Local manufacture	
Year		Gross boxes	Value in rupees including general and preferential duty averaging Rs. 3.48 per gross	Gross boxes	Value in rupees including excise
1957	..	103,743	371,548	7,786	27,600
1958	..	85,678	253,796	7,222	25,500

138

The capacity of the local company is said to be 1,000 gross per week but competition from imports has restricted output and the company is losing money. Established in 1939 it now has plans to modernise and extend its plant and to do this has asked the government for a loan.

6:46. A larger factory operated between 1929 and 1952 when it was shut down because of the rising cost of wages and resulting inability to compete with imports. The owners state that they would be prepared to restart provided they could get assurance of greater protection. They claim that with some additional machinery they could supply the whole market.

6:47. We are in no position to judge between merits of these two concerns, and cannot therefore pronounce definitely on the request of the first for a loan. We do however think that the colony ought to produce all the matches it needs and that the government ought to encourage any producers so far as it can. We recommend therefore that the government should forthwith abolish the excise duty on matches. This duty is only a relic from the distant past and there seems no particular reason why matches should be subject to it rather than other commodities. It is clearly a deterrent to larger production and the revenue it brings is not worth the collection

WOODWORKING

6:48. Furniture making, from both imported and local timber, is another of the widely diffused industries carried out by small craftsmen and others of varying competence. Table XLVI indicates that there are 495 such establishments with an unspecified number of employees. (A recent survey by the Conservator of Forests shows that there are 226 "better-class" establishments employing 785 people. Only three of these have more than 15 workmen.) As well, there are 83 sawmills, employing 302 workers. Most of the island's requirements of wood furniture appears to be locally made, since imports for 1957 and 1958 averaged only Rs. 450,000 in value. Shaped lumber for all purposes was worth Rs. 3.3 million for 15,500 cubic metres. Local production of round timber for 1958 is given as 15,430 cubic metres, which probably represents less than 7,500 cubic metres of shaped lumber.

6:49. Both the saw-milling and furniture industries are quite unorganised. As the Conservator of Forests pointed out to us, there is hardly one efficient or adequately powered saw-mill in the island, with the result that wastage is high and sizes are not standardised. Yet the island produces, in small quantities, a variety of pleasing hard-woods suitable for cabinet-making, as well as other woods which if properly seasoned and shaped, could be much more widely used for building purposes. The furniture makers work from hand to mouth; they have no capital for carrying stocks of timber in process of seasoning, nor for installing modern wood-working equipment. The standard of workmanship is not high on the whole, due in part to the complete absence of vocational training. The better craftsmen, who are mostly self-taught, are occupied too much with the simpler jobs of sawing and planing, instead of confining themselves to more skilled joinery work. All these factors have combined to restrict the progress of the wood-working industries, which we believe to be capable of considerable expansion.

6:50. One of the first and most important steps to be taken, of which we have already spoken (paragraph 5:74) is the erection of a modern saw-mill, alongside plants for the impregnation and/or seasoning, both by natural and artificial means, of local timber. This would tie in with the proposed programme of re-construction made necessary by the cyclone damage, for a new saw-mill and impregnation plant are essential preliminaries for the building of many thousands of timber houses. With a government factory supplying different kinds of well-seasoned and standardised timber at reasonable prices, the furniture makers, as well as the building trades, could be assured of the quality of the local materials and would be in a better position to expand and diversify their production. Some of the imports of steel furniture could be replaced, and outlets such as panelling, flooring, and other items for better-class buildings, might well be found.

6:51. But it will not be enough only to improve the materials. The carpenters and joiners will also have to raise their standards. This will involve not only a measure of capital re-equipment, but also a period of re-education that may be lengthy. New tools will need new techniques. The craftsmen of today are wedded to their traditional methods and designs, and newcomers to the trade can only copy the old ways and pick them up as best they can. It will hardly be practicable to equip each small workshop with modern machinery, if only because the premises are nearly always cramped, and the output would be too high for individual needs. Little loans to this end would certainly be wasted. We therefore recommend that failing the construction by private enterprise of a factory working from the start on commercial lines, the government should itself sponsor one to be run as far as possible as a co-operative effort by the members of the industry. It might well form part of the proposed industrial estate (paragraphs 2:60 and 6:102). Its objectives would be not only to make a profit, but also to provide a training ground both for established craftsmen and for apprentices, who would enter, we hope, with elementary knowledge already derived from vocational schools. The wood-working shop of the Prisons Department shows what can be done. It is spacious and well-equipped; the quality of instruction is good and the products excellent, despite the fact that the operatives are transient. If it were not for its unfortunate location, it might itself serve as the nucleus of a proper factory. But we believe that the knowledge and experience of what is required already exist in the island, and only await an energetic organiser with funds at his disposal.

BEVERAGES

6:52. Though complete figures are not available, the people of Mauritius are evidently drinking more and more, both alcoholic and non-alcoholic beverages. Two modern plants for making "cola" type drinks and "crushes" have appeared since the war, and both are obviously flourishing. Soda water and other minerals are made in a number of small establishments.

6:53. All locally produced spirits originate from "colonial spirit" (see paragraph 6:23). Sales from bond for this purpose in 1958 were 15,827,000 litres, at 50° Gay-Lussac, i.e. 50% of alcohol. After dilution to 40°, it is either consumed as such or compounded with flavouring matters into various kinds of liquor. Imports of other spirits approximate to one million rupees yearly.

6:54. No grapes are grown in the island, so that the true wines must be imported. Their value in 1958 was Rs. 953,000 (£66,500). But an interesting industry has developed for the manufacture of country wines—a cult that is growing rapidly in England. They are made by fermenting sugar solution and fruit juices with the correct yeast. After clarification and maturing, very tolerable imitations of various natural wines can be obtained. The largest producing firm, which probably has more than half of the market, is now making nearly three million litres yearly, and because of the rising demand, is now enlarging and improving the plant. Excise duty (at 30 cts. a litre) collected from the industry in 1958 was over Rs.1,200,000.

6:55. The same producer can make a sparkling wine from cane-juice closely resembling champagne, and believes there is a potential export market. He is also looking into the possibility of a brewery. Imports of all kinds of beer in 1958 exceeded two million litres, with a value of about Rs.1,900,000. Beer of the lager type is preferred. It can be made on quite a small scale, but it is usually found that provided the quality suits the local taste (which requires expertise at the start) a new brewery soon reaches its initial planned capacity and has to expand. We believe that this would happen in Mauritius, and recommend that every encouragement should be given to the idea.

6:56. This interesting suggestion originates from a local jeweller and watchmaker who was trained in Switzerland. Very large numbers of synthetic jewels are needed in industrialised countries for making bearings for watches and scientific instruments. The rough "ruby" can be bought easily, but the finished "jewels" require precision machinery and well trained and patient workers. They are produced chiefly in Europe, where the high cost of labour is a principal reason for their high price. Because both the raw material and the finished jewels have a very small volume, so that cost of transport is negligible, they are a perfect example of a labour-intensive industry needed in Mauritius. It is believed that local craftsmen could be quickly trained in the necessary techniques.

6:57. Two major problems would have to be solved before the industry could be started. First, the right kind of machines would have to be obtained from Switzerland, together with a first-class instructor. Second, prior arrangements would have to be made with potential buyers. Both would need a thorough and perhaps prolonged investigation in Europe. We believe that such a study would be well worth while. It could only be carried out by the proposer of the idea, and we recommend that if necessary, he be aided to do so.

6:58. From the same source comes another suggestion to produce and export heavy silver jewellery hand made to Indian designs. Some attractive specimens have been seen, though their appeal might depend upon fashion. Given good publicity, a profitable market might be established, and again we recommend that the idea should be investigated and encouraged.

TEXTILES AND CLOTHING

6:59. Mauritius has no spinning or weaving industries and therefore imports all its clothing either as fabrics or made-up goods. The quantity of both is considerable in relation to other imports, but still not large enough to justify local manufacture, with one or two possible exceptions. The values for 1957 and 1958 are given in Table L.

6:60. With so many races and consequently so many different tastes and needs the imports are of great diversity, particularly the fabrics, chiefly cotton, favoured by Indian women-folk. It is clear

Table L. Textile Imports, 1957 and 1958

Type of cloth	1957 Rs.	1958 Rs.
Fabrics, including wool yarns and cotton thread ..	24,126,189	19,030,272
Clothing of all kinds	4,467,183	5,194,645

from the above figures that most of the clothing is made up in the island, although there is no organised industry. The tailoring and dressmaking is done either at home or in a large number of little establishments, of which 912 were registered in 1959. It is somewhat strange that no spinning or weaving is carried out in the same small way. Elsewhere there are common cottage industries which are totally absent in Mauritius (see paragraphs 6:70-71).

6:61. The clothing trade conducted along its present lines affords employment to a good many people. Without very heavy protection, which might significantly increase the cost of living, it would not be possible at present to set up a viable mechanised industry that would compete with the cheap mass-produced goods from the Far East. Fabrics made from rayon or other artificial fibres may be an exception however as they already carry a high rate of duty. One prominent importer believes that with some tariff adjustment a small mill using imported yarn could be successful. Given this adjustment, the factory production of shirts and similar articles may also be possible before long.

BUILDING AND ALLIED TRADES

6:62. As Table XLV shows, building is one of the few industries that have expanded greatly during the last few years. Since 1951 the number of employees has risen from 910 to 2,955 in 1959, when there were 22 licensed establishments. The better of them maintain good standards, which unfortunately are not universal throughout the industry. Some of the faulty work to which our attention was drawn, evidently derives from poor supervision on the job—a general failing in Mauritius, due to lack of good foremen. But there is apparently need for a stricter application of recognised standards for materials and methods of construction. We recommend that the legislation on this matter should be tightened up.

6:63. Common bricks are not made in the island and most new buildings are constructed with concrete blocks, which are produced on a large scale by 43 licensed establishments, one or two of them being very well equipped. They crush and screen the local basaltic rock, obtaining road metal of all sizes and aggregate for concrete-mixing.

Table LI. Cement Imports, 1957 and 1958.

Year						Quantity, metric tons	Value, Rs.
1957 ..	..	..	..	..	..	42,987	6,307,414
1958 ..	..	..	..	..	..	51,455	6,740,772

6:64. All the cement is imported, mostly from England. These quantities are large enough to arouse the thought of local manufacture. Cost estimates have been submitted to the government by different makers of cement plants, and the problem was studied in detail by C. E. F. Williams in 1955. He found that the silica content of the local clays was too low, and proposed to correct this by the addition of bagasse ash. Laboratory trials showed that cement conforming to British standards could be produced in this way, and Williams concluded that a shaft-kiln plant with a capacity of 30,000 tons a year, ought to be profitable. We would doubt, however, whether a plant of this size and type would be an economic proposition. It is generally held that capacity should be not less than 100,000 tons a year, and that rotary kilns are much to be preferred. Neither should there be any shadow of doubt about the availability of the right raw materials. The cement market is highly competitive, and over-production has begun to appear. The capital needed would be very large and the labour employed relatively little. The saving of exchange on cement imports would to some extent be counterbalanced by the increased need for fuel and power. Therefore in our opinion the case is not strong for official encouragement of local manufacture.

6:65. There is more to be said in favour of importing clinker and grinding it into cement locally. This is a possibility which has already been studied and, although the conclusions were unfavourable, we recommend that the idea should be kept in mind by the Industrial Development Board which we propose should be established (see paragraphs 6:98-99).

6:66. We also recommend more vigorous investigation of the possibility of production of pozzolanic cements. These are inferior to Portland cements but can be used for many purposes in building; they have the advantage of requiring simpler plant and less fuel, and the raw materials are likely to present less difficulty in Mauritius. Some experiments have been made, but the problem needs to be tackled intensively by all concerned.

6:67. Except for refined table salt, the colony produces all its requirements by solar evaporation of sea-water from open pans. 3,900 tons were so obtained in 1958 with employment given as 97. The work is seasonal, however, and many more persons are engaged during the period of harvest. The pans are situated in the drier coastal zones and production could easily be increased if demand were to rise. But an export market is not likely to be found, since conditions are not so favourable as in regions such as Aden where the rainfall is negligible. Costs therefore tend to be higher, and it has been found necessary to protect the industry with a preferential tariff of Rs. 4 per 100 kgs.

6:68. In 1958 there were 25 licensed lime producers, employing 556 workers and producing 9,600 metric tons of various qualities. With one exception the kilns are of the old-fashioned stone-built batch type, situated on the coast and using sea-coral as raw material and wood for firing. The producers are small and independent, for the most part family concerns, and as is to be expected from their methods of working, the product is very variable. The best quality is used by the sugar industry for juice clarification, while the building trade absorbs the poorer grades, which yield inferior mortars and plasters. This partly accounts for some of the poor construction work.

6:69. A new shaft-kiln fired with anthracite is now in operation, and modern hydrating machinery is nearly completed. This plant uses an old coral deposit of excellent quality, and operating under controlled conditions can produce lime to uniform specifications. The company expects to meet all the requirements of the sugar industry and hopes later to develop a market for agricultural lime. Some soils in Mauritius are known to be lime-deficient and could be profitably improved if local supplies were available cheaply. But owing to limitation of capital the company cannot immediately undertake expansion for this purpose. We believe this to be another case where financial help from a credit institution would make a valuable contribution to industrial development.

6:70. In a country so much influenced as is Mauritius by its oriental background one would have expected that rural crafts such as weaving, pottery, basket-making, metal-working, etc. would be flourishing outside the towns, either as part-time occupations of the cottagers or as the full-time trade of village craftsmen. Yet at present there is an almost complete absence of cottage industries, which cannot be attributed solely to lack of indigenous materials. Pottery, for instance, is hardly made at all—we were only able to discover one potter working in a very primitive way—although it is most likely that suitable clay is to be found in the island (and that there is in addition a large market for simple household ware, all of which is now imported). In any case the existence of raw materials in Mauritius is not a *sine qua non* of the development of cottage industries: in Thailand, for instance, a thriving industry in silk fabrics has been built up on home looms using imported Japanese yarn, and it has now reached the stage of factory production. Some basket-ware can be seen in the towns of Mauritius, but the Prison Department has met with no success in its efforts to persuade ex-prisoners who have been trained in the art, to use it as a means of supplementing their incomes after release.

6:71. We do not believe that cottage industries as such can make a substantial contribution to the national income, but in an economy such as Mauritius they might be useful in eking out the earnings of an under-developed rural population. It may not be easy, however, to inculcate the necessary skills, or to maintain continued interest. Organised help would also be needed for getting raw materials and for marketing. We were not able to examine the problem in detail, but we think it important enough to justify expert advice, and we recommend that this should be sought from one of the United Nations agencies.

TOURISM

6:72. Stimulated perhaps by the success of some West Indian islands in building up a lucrative tourist industry, the desire to do the same in Mauritius is not hard to understand. Its natural attractions are undeniable; its physical amenities on the other hand leave much to be desired, and they would have to be vastly improved before the island could become a popular tourist centre. It is a matter of hot debate as to whether the potentialities justify the considerable expenditure on hotels, restaurants, and recreational facilities that would have to be provided, largely at government expense.

6:73. Visitors now have only one hotel to go to with any pretensions to comfort. It is situated at Curepipe in the centre of the island, and was originally started, with an old mansion as its nucleus, to provide transit accommodation for passengers and air-crews of the three international air-lines serving the colony. It therefore has structural defects not improved by the two recent cyclones. But making allowance for these, we were poorly impressed by the quality of the management. The cuisine in particular is lamentable, prices are very high, and many important details appear to receive no attention. This hotel is owned by a company in which the government holds a 20 % interest, and to which is being entrusted the building of two new hotels, with the aid of a government loan of Rs. 1,600,000 (£145,000). One is to be primarily for tourists at Grande Baie on the north coast, and the other for air-crews at Le Chaland on the south coast near the air-port.

6:74. We do not doubt the necessity for improving the present hotel accommodation, but we do question the new plans. The hotel at Grande Baie, with fifty double bedrooms, is being urged forward so as to be ready for the International Sugar Conference, scheduled to be held in Mauritius in mid-1962. Without it, the conference with over 200 participants, could hardly take place, and the sugar industry holds strongly that cancellation would mean a great loss of prestige. On the other hand, there is doubt about completing the construction in time, and even if it is finished the hotel could not accommodate the whole conference. To us it appears unwise to force an immediate decision solely for this purpose, particularly as the destruction caused by the cyclones would give Mauritius an excellent reason for deferring its claim to the conference.

6:75. After the conference the hotel would be open to tourists and other visitors. To make a profit at least 60 % of the rooms would have to be let throughout the year. It is difficult to see where the occupants are to come from. The clientele of the existing hotel is composed of business-men, officials, and air-crews, together with a few casual tourists stopping off en route between South Africa and Australia. The new hotel at La Chaland, the building of which is justified, would cater for the air-crews and occasionally for residents. Business-men and official visitors will probably prefer to stay at Curepipe, which is the residential centre of the island. The new hotel will have to depend almost entirely on new tourist business plus whatever is diverted from the other. Therefore neither is likely to operate at a profit.

6:76. While it is true to say that tourists will never come to Mauritius in any number if they cannot find a first-class hotel in agreeable surroundings, it is also true that such an amenity will not in itself attract many people to a place so far off the beaten track. We ourselves feel that the time is not yet ripe for the hotel at Grande Baie. It would be better first to build the hotel at La Chaland, so releasing space at the existing hotel now reserved for air-crews, and concentrate on improving the latter, together with various minor but important measures already recommended by the recently-formed Tourist Advisory Bureau.

The Provision of Industrial Services

6:77. (i) *Electricity.* The Central Electricity Board (C.E.B.) is now the sole producer and distributor of electricity in the island having been formed in 1953 to take over the assets of several existing undertakings. It is a statutory body deriving most of its capital from long-term government loans and the remainder from private institutional investors. The capital is heavily watered, because too high a price was paid (under Mauritian law) for the plant of the private companies. Hence, although the Board is able to make a reasonable trading profit, this converts to a nett loss after paying interest charges. Nevertheless, the objective, under ordinance, is to operate on a commercial basis.

6:78. The graphs in Figure II (page 149) show the growth of demand in relation to installed capacity. At the end of 1959 the capacity was:

       8,910 kW. from four hydro electric stations, and
       7,000 kW. from one diesel station (St. Louis)

Total 15,910

During 1960 the following capacity will be added:

       6,375 from three new hydro-electric stations, and
       5,000 from two new diesel generators

Total 11,375

The total at the end of 1960 will therefore be 27,285 kW. It is to be noted that the full hydro-capacity is not available during the dry season, when the load has to be taken up by the diesel installation, aided to an increasing extent by power supplied from sugar mills.

6:79. The new machines soon to be commissioned will just avert another crisis in supply similar to those occurring in 1959 and 1952, when power cuts and other forms of rationing were frequent. The C.E.B believes that the new capacity will only meet expected demands up to the end of 1962; as can be seen from the curves of the graphs in Figure II, they are rising very rapidly. They consider it urgent to begin without delay the construction of one or more new stations to be ready for operation by 1963. Even as it is, they are unwilling to accept new consumers and to undertake more development into unelectrified areas. They estimate essential expenditure

FIGURE II
Growth of Electricity in relation to Installed Capacity

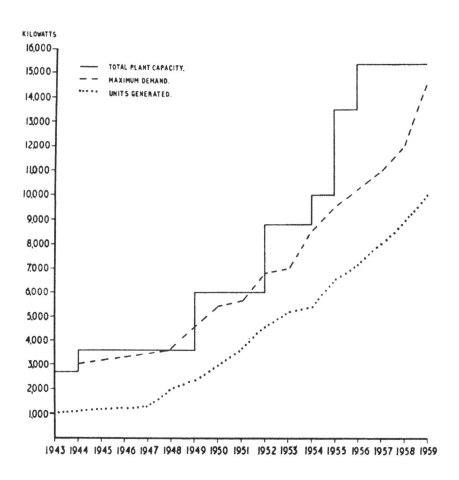

to meet commitments to exceed Rs. 33 million (£2·5 million) up to June 1962, with a further Rs. 2 million (£150,000), as desirable, to meet new demands. These figures include about Rs. 5 million (£375,000) for repair and replacement of plant damaged during the cyclones (see paragraph 7:46, Table LVIII).

6:80. We have noted that the loss between generation and consumption is exceptionally high—apparently 34%. The explanation given is that many parts of the transmission system are grossly overloaded, and that this being in part an inheritance from the previous owners, the Board has not yet had the time or the funds to put matters right. On the face of it, if the transmission loss were reduced to normal, the new capacity now coming into service should meet requirements for more than three years. It is not possible to estimate what these might be, more accurately than by extrapolating the maximum demand curves.

6:81. The Board has the expert advice of prominent consulting engineers, and we have no reason to suppose that the necessary expenditure will be appreciably less than that given above. It is understoon that the government hopes to allocate Rs. 23 million (£1·7 million) to this end, leaving about Rs. 10 million (£0·75 million) possibly to be financed by contractor credits. One disadvantage of the present programme is that, owing to shortage of funds and other reasons, the Board has had to abandon a new hydro-electric scheme, Riviere de Creoles, which is at an advanced stage of planning. Instead, the new plant for 1963 will have to be either steam or diesel-driven generators at Fort George, near Port Louis. This will mean an increase in the imports of fuel, an unfortunate necessity when the hydro resources of the island are not yet fully tapped.

6:82. We are of the opinion that the time has come for the government of Mauritius to seek outside aid not only for the development of electricity supplies but for other purposes as well. The C.E.B. has suffered from a chronic shortage of money ever since its formation, despite the fact that it has had its full share of government funds. Even to meet its minimum future requirements the strain on the hard-pressed budget will be severe. With some capital re-organisation the C.E.B. could become a viable commercial entity, and as such, might be able to enlist financial help from say, the Colonial Development Corporation (C.D.C.) or the International Bank. We understand that the Government of Mauritius has already approached the International Bank. We support this action but we do not think that this should stand in the way of an immediate approach to the C.D.C. or private organisations to participate in the financing of this and other projects.

6:83. The general manager of the C.E.B. has propounded an

ingenious scheme for obtaining electrical energy from the sea. In brief, the proposal is to convert a selected part of the coral reef into a sea-wall of special design; waves breaking over it would be allowed to fill up the lagoons behind, to a height sufficient to run very low-head turbines. Consulting engineers consider the proposal to be feasible, but likely to prove too costly. One obvious disadvantage is that, because of periods of relative calm, the power obtained would be seasonal, so that full stand-by plant of orthodox type would still be needed. Nevertheless the idea is interesting enough to warrant certain experimental work now being financed by the government. If the results are encouraging, the next stage would have to be a pilot plant on a sufficient scale to solve the many problems of design and construction. The expenditure on this would be quite beyond the resources of the government, but if it were successful the knowledge obtained might be of great value outside Mauritius. The pilot plant would appear to come within the scope of the United Nations Special Fund, to which it should be referred if the results of the experiments now in progress are promising.

6:84. (ii) *Transport and communications*. For a small island, both the rail and road networks are surprisingly extensive. The roads are often narrow and winding, but for the most part are well-surfaced and maintained. As elsewhere, they are having to carry a fast-growing volume of traffic; thus, the number of registered vehicles rose from 9,209 in 1954 to 13,172 in 1959. Congestion is sometimes evident in Port Louis and through the densely-populated districts up to Curepipe, but is only mild in comparison with the towns of Europe and America.

6:85. It has been decided gradually to close down the railways which have been running at a loss for some years. Passenger services have already been discontinued, and the burden on the roads has consequently increased. New roads are being built and others improved, and all goods traffic, of which sugar constitutes the major part, will eventually be transferred from one system to the other. Many more heavy lorries will then be operating, especially during the crop-season. It is intended apparently that most of the movement will take place at night, but on the whole traffic must converge on Port Louis and very careful organisation will be necessary. The change-over obviously cannot be completed without heavy capital expenditure both on roads and vehicles.

6:86. When the railway passenger services were stopped, the responsibility for passenger transport was handed over to private bus-owners. They now allege that they have not had enough official help towards acquiring and maintaining the many extra vehicles needed for efficient service. They also complain of unfair competition from taxis, despite legislation to control this. Certainly, the number of licensed taxis does appear to be greatly in excess of ordinary requirements.

6:87. We are inclined to doubt whether the change-over from rail to road transport is really an economic proposition, but were informed that the governing factors were the value of the property occupied by the railways which could be released for other purposes and the heavy cost of future replacements of railway equipment. An economic commission was set up in 1958 to enquire into the efficiency of public transport, but it has not yet published a report. The problems are too complex for us to form a considered opinion, but we do believe that with a good deal of public money at stake, they are important enough to warrant the appointment of an expert transport controller with wide experience—an office that was capably filled up to 1955 but has now been allowed to lapse.

6:88. (iii) *Water*. The new industries that may come to Mauritius are not likely to be abnormal consumers of water; though the possibility of paper and similar manufactures cannot be entirely discounted. As we have already pointed out (paragraph 5:1) the rainfall on the central plateau is high enough to supply other parts of the island with much more water than they now receive. There should be no great difficulty in integrating the needs of industry with those of agriculture and domestic consumers. In so far as hydro-electric generation is concerned and subject to the requirements of agriculture, we would emphasise the great importance of utilising to the maximum the water resources of the colony, since every unit produced in this way means a saving in imported fuel. We therefore repeat here our recommendation (paragraph 5:11) that a Water Resources Authority be established without delay, in order to obtain the greatest beneficial use from a natural source of wealth that is far from completely tapped.

GOVERNMENT AND PRODUCTIVE INDUSTRY

6:89. The public utilities for which the government is responsible, e.g. electricity, railways, harbours, telephones, water-supply, etc., comprise in themselves a considerable volume of industrial activity. In the purely manufacturing field, i.e. the production of goods for sale, it controls only the sack factory, a tea factory managed by outside agents, the tobacco warehouse, and a few products such as animal food-stuffs and timber, of the Department of Agriculture. Mention should also be made of the Prisons Department, which has among other training facilities, the finest wood-working shop in the island, and produces a quantity of good quality furniture, boots and shoes, clothing, metal ware, baskets, concrete blocks, and other articles for the use of government departments. We were much impressed by its activities.

6:90. Otherwise, the government has assisted a number of private industries, not always successfully, by loans at low rates of interest, and has an approximate 20% holding in the equity of the hotel company. A list of loans is given in Table LII below.

Table LII. Government Loans to Industrial and Commercial Enterprises

	Amount, Rs.	Rate of Interest, %
1. Mauritius Cold Storage	484,000	3
2. Indian Ocean Trading Co. Ltd.	634,000	3½
3. Albert Oil Factory	85,000	4
4. Evershine Wax Polish Factory	60,000	4
5. Rodrigues Salt Produce	15,000	4½
6. Les Gas Industrial Co. Ltd.	125,000	4½
7. Ommilit Hardboard Factory	225,000	4
8. Loans to fishermen	64,000	6
9. Aloe Fibre Industry	493,000	5½
10. Colonial Steamship Co. Ltd.	3,500,000	3½
11. Mauritius Hotels Ltd.	290,000	5½
12. Tobacco Board	600,000	4
13. Bois Cheri Tea Estate	750,000	5
14. La Flora Tea Estate	958,000	4½
15. Agricultural Bank	10,500,000	3½–4½
16. Central Electricity Board	30,000,000	5
17. Government Sack Factory	5,350,000	—

N.B.: Enterprises 2, 3, and 7 were complete failures, and have been wound up.
    11—loan converted into shares.
    17—loan is interest free, repayable after 30 years.

Other than the Treasury and the Agricultural Bank there is no institution to which entrepreneurs can normally go for middle or long-term credits.

6:91. The Ministry of Industry, Commerce, and Communications which was formed in 1959, is generally responsible for the government's industrial and commercial interests, as well as for a number of miscellaneous departments such as civil aviation, meteorology, tourism, etc., that do not conveniently fall under other ministries. It has not yet had time to organise itself for the proper execution of its somewhat nebulous duties. It has only a small staff, none of them with practical experience of industry, and it is now the channel through which must go all private applications seeking government help for new or expanding industrial ventures. This is

153

perfectly proper procedure. Previously, applications were submitted in a variety of quarters, and though they eventually reached the Financial Secretary, there was evidently no machinery for properly examining and dealing with them. It still does not exist, but at least a start has been made. We have in consequence found difficulty in tracing the history of projects put forward for official assistance.

6:92. No industrial survey has ever been carried out. The Department of Labour has a good deal of information derived from its powers under the factory acts, and some can be got from study of the trading licences issued by the Police Department. Data on the major, particularly agricultural, industries are relatively complete, but not so on those, such as furniture-making, tailoring, etc., where production takes place in a large number of small establishments. Thus Table XLVI contains several industries where the employment is not known. Some, such as pottery and basket-making, are not mentioned at all in published statistics. Figures on value of output, total wages paid, power consumed, etc., would have been valuable. We do not think that our conclusions on the progress of industrial development are vitiated by the lack of such information, but it should be made available in the future. The Ministry of Industry (or the Industrial Development Board to which we refer later, paragraphs 6:98-99) should be responsible for compiling and keeping up-to-date the necessary records.

6:93. We take it as accepted that the government does not wish to extend its direct participation in industry if only because it will have little money to spare from the tasks that are its proper responsibility. Indeed, the allocation under the original five-year plan was less than 3% of the total of Rs. 210 million (£15·75 million), and of this tourism was to take half. But if industrial development, without which economic development in general cannot advance, is to be left to private enterprise, vigorous action must be taken to encourage the entrepreneurs. Clearly, the island has a very great need for capital. Equally clearly, the attempts so far made to attract it, whether from institutional or private sources, have met with little success. We have already said that the programme of the C.E.B. might well be financed from outside the colony. Other projects such as deep-water fishing, building societies, harbour development, hotels, etc., are all within the scope and experience of the Colonial Development Corporation. Several United Nations agencies and private foundations assist in the promotion of agriculture, social services, and other forms of development in backward countries. If the government could be relieved of the financial burden of only a few items in the five-year plan, it would be better able to tackle its other problems. For instance, it could (and should) strengthen the borrowing powers of the Agricultural Bank, which received nothing at all under the five-year plan (see paragraph 7:88 ff). We are well aware that the Government of Mauritius has had the problem of attracting outside capital much in mind. But the negotiations involved in raising funds from overseas, whatever their source, are prolonged and exacting. They can only be undertaken by one or two individuals who are already deeply occupied with the normal financial administration of the island. The establishment of an Industrial Development Board and the reorganisation of the Agricultural Bank, and other measures which we propose elsewhere (in Chapter 9), should do much to lessen the burden of routine, and so enable even more attention to the vital problem of attracting capital.

6:94. With regard to private capital, we have remarked that there is money in the island awaiting profitable investment; and we have evidence to believe that financial houses and private firms from overseas, particularly East and South Africa, would be interested in Mauritius provided they could look forward to a good return—if not immediately, at least within a reasonable period. What particularly is wanted by both local and overseas investors is:

(*a*) generous relief from import duties both on equipment and raw materials;

(*b*) protection against imports, at any rate in the early stages; and

(*c*) an income-tax holiday for at least five years after starting.

6:95. On the first point, the government does have powers and claims they are freely used, to grant concessions. Undoubtedly, the sugar, tea, and a few other industries have benefited therefrom. But each new application has to be studied by a number of different departments, whose attitude is often too conservative. A decision may take a long time to reach, and in the interval, applicants are liable to lose interest. No doubt they are sometimes themselves to blame, through not properly presenting their case, but the point is that there is no recognised procedure to enable these matters to be dealt with expeditiously and sympathetically.

6:96. Both (*a*) and (*b*) raise the question of the Customs Tariff Code which we believe to be in urgent need of drastic overhaul. We have met several instances of local manufacture being discouraged by the fact that duty on raw or semi-finished materials is higher than on the finished articles made from them, and we have cited a number of cases in which assistance is needed either in the form of lower import duties or greater protection.

6:97. On the question of tax holidays, the Income Tax Department maintains that the 10% investment allowance now granted for industrial (but *not* commercial) investments, ought to be quite adequate, and is preferable to a tax holiday on grounds of greater ease of administration. But the fact remains that in the eyes of people with risk capital to invest, this allowance is *not* enough even when added to the initial allowance granted for industrial, but not commercial, buildings and plant. The proof is that the rate of industrial development has been far slower than it might have been. The businessmen are still holding back, and will continue to do so until the conditions for investment are made more attractive.

6:98. We discuss the changes required in detail in the following chapter, but one fact stands out as central, that as we have already observed (paragraph 6:91), the Ministry of Industry is not properly equipped to deal with the multifarious problems which face it and which will become more numerous and perhaps more difficult as industrialisation proceeds. We recommend, therefore, that as the lynch-pin of all industrial development, the government should set up an Industrial Development Board, which should be a statutory body as far removed as possible from political influence. Its head must be a man with the widest possible experience of industry in other parts of the world (and will, therefore, be neither cheap nor easy to find). The staff need not be large, but it must be both experienced and enthusiastic.

6:99. The duties of this Board should include the following:

(1) to compile and keep up-to-date the industrial records now lacking;

(2) to advise the government on legislation and other action needed to foster industrial expansion and grant concessions;

(3) to advise and help all applicants for special concessions and/or loans in this field;

(4) to investigate new possibilities, and when they show promise, to interest local and foreign capital in their development;

(5) to take part in the administration of the wholly-owned government industries, other than those purely agricultural;

(6) to set up and administer a government-owned industrial trading estate, for which there is need in the vicinity of Port Louis;

(7) to advise the Agricultural Bank (or such other industrial credit institution as may later be formed) on the credit-worthiness of applicants for loans; and

(8) to keep watch on expenditure after loans have been granted.

6:100. This list of duties is not necessarily comprehensive, but it deliberately excludes the power actually to make loans. We recommend that this should be vested in a separate financial authority, responsible for advancing money in accordance with the recommendations of the Board. We suggest below (paragraphs 7:88-89) that the government should increase the borrowing powers of the Agricultural Bank so that the Agricultural Bank may develop its dual role of industrial as well as agricultural development bank.

6:101. If it is to be effective, the Board will need to work closely with the Agricultural Bank and with those government departments most directly concerned with economic policy. We therefore recommend that a Government Advisory Committee should be established, consisting of representatives of the Board, the Agriculture Bank, the Ministry of Finance, the Ministry of Commerce and Industry, the Customs and Excise Department, and the Inland Revenue Department. The principal function of this Committee should be to consider all applications by industrialists for concessions (e.g. tariff concessions, tax holidays, etc.) and to make recommendations to the relevant ministers as to whether such concessions should be given.

6:102. The industrial trading estate referred to above (paragraphs 2:60 and 6:51) should prove an effective means of helping small industries. Even in highly industrialised countries, both national and local authorities try to attract new industries in this way. The trading estate can take many forms, but the essence of it is that the government sets aside an area of land in a suitable locality where communications are good, and prepares it for development by levelling, if necessary, and laying on water, power, roads, and drains. It may go further and erect standardised factory buildings, with or without central administration offices, and sell or rent them to small manufacturers at prices dependent on the services wanted. In some cases, a larger manufacturer might only wish to lease a site and erect his own factory, or the government might do this for him and even accept payment in shares in the equity. We believe that in Mauritius there would be a real demand for small, ready-to-occupy, workshops, not only from new industries, but also from established businesses that would like to move out from the congested environment of Port Louis. Proposals for two such industrial estates were actually made in 1952, in Thornton White's report on a Master Plan for Port Louis, but nothing has been done. We recommend that urgent action should be taken in concert with the Industrial Board when established.

6:103. In addition we recommend that discussions with the Colonial Development Corporation should be initiated officially and without delay. If the C.D.C. were to take an active interest in Mauritius, it might do so through the medium of an Industrial Development Corporation, similar to those it has sponsored elsewhere. Conceivably, such a corporation might become responsible for a large part of the programme of industrialisation, in which case it might take over many of the functions of the Industrial Development Board enumerated above. We cannot at this stage suggest the exact form which such participation might take. It clearly depends on the outcome of negotiations between the C.D.C., the Government of Mauritius, and private interests, but we do recommend that official discussions to this end should take place at once. At the same time we urge that negotiations with C.D.C. should not be allowed to hinder or delay in any way the immediate action required for the establishment of the local Board and Bank.

6:104. In conclusion we wish to draw attention to one other matter on which we have heard many criticisms of government policy. It is alleged that government departments do not make as much use as they should of supplies and services available in the colony. Importers complain that tenders are often not put out to public enquiry, or that departments ask them for information about goods which are then ordered through the Crown Agents. The island is well served by its merchant houses, which between them hold an immense number of overseas agencies. They contend that for most commodities they can quote prices at least equal to the Crown Agents, and point out that they themselves bear the losses arising from damage and deficiencies. They further maintain that for bulk shipments such as rice and flour, they can often arrange cheaper freight rates, and have suggested that this trade could be handed back to private enterprise to the advantage of all concerned. The engineering firms previously mentioned feel that they are not given enough opportunity to quote for metal goods, and others, including the printing trade and the Booksellers Association, share this belief. Professional men too, such as architects, say that the government does not make full use of the services they have to offer.

6:105. On the other hand, government officials maintain that there is little justification for these allegations. They have given us several examples where prices quoted by local suppliers have been considerably higher than those quoted by the Crown Agents. Nevertheless, this is clearly causing concern in business quarters, and we recommend that the government should review its policy of local purchases. In particular, there should be a far wider use of the system of open tenders. Supplies should be purchased locally even if there is a slight margin in favour of purchase through the Crown Agents, since this margin may represent a higher addition to local incomes. But it is important for government to retain its use of the Crown Agents as a check against over-charging by local suppliers.

6:106. In many of the foregoing paragraphs, we have laid emphasis on the necessity for positive action by the government to encourage entrepreneurs. But in the ultimate analysis, industrial development in a free economy must depend on the personal efforts of individuals. Therefore the businessmen of Mauritius must themselves be realistic. They cannot expect large loans at less than commercial rates, unlimited protection, or carte blanche to charge government departments uneconomic prices for goods and services. Inertia is just as much the enemy of progress whether it is present in private or official circles. What must be created is an atmosphere of confidence, in which a man with the ability and determination to exploit a good idea wherever it comes from, can expect the whole-hearted co-operation of the government in all reasonable ways.

CHAPTER 7

Finance

INTRODUCTORY

7:1. In preceding chapters we have considered the factors which have been holding back economic growth in Mauritius, and have made a number of recommendations designed to overcome them. Many of our proposals, however, involve the need for finance of one kind or another; moreover, the structure of Mauritius' public and private financial systems has an important effect on the growth of the economy. A faulty tax system may discourage enterprise; the credit system may not be designed to promote the kind of investment which is required. Moreover, government's own capital expenditure has a key position in promoting economic development.

7:2. In this chapter, therefore, we consider the structure of public and private finance. In the public sector, we examine the tax system, and make recommendations designed both to lessen the inherent bias which exists in favour of investing in sugar and to encourage other forms of investment. Next we consider the trends of government's recurrent expenditure, and relate this to the growth of recurrent revenue. We then examine current plans for capital expenditure in the public sector, and consider ways in which a suitable programme could be financed. Lastly, we consider the suitability of the system of private finance for the encouragement of productive investment, and suggest ways in which the gap in the financial structure might be filled.

PUBLIC FINANCE

The Principal Sources of Government Revenue

7:3. The principal sources of government revenue are taxes on incomes of individuals and companies, import duties, excise duties, and a variety of licence and other fees. The following table shows the principal sources of government's estimated *tax* revenue in 1959-60 (that is, government recurrent revenues excluding receipts from public utilities, public services, rent, and interest).

Nearly a third of tax revenue is derived from import duties and nearly a quarter from the tax on companies. Income tax on individuals accounts for nearly a sixth of revenue, and excise duties

160

Table LIII. Estimated Tax Receipts, 1959/1960

Tax					Rs. million	%
Income tax:						
Companies	..	..	..	..	28·5	24·0
Individuals	..	..	..	..	19·5	16·4
Import duties	..	..	..	..	38·5	32·5
Excise duties ..	..	..	..	..	17·5	14·8
Other taxes ..	..	..	..	..	14·6	12·3
		Total tax receipts			118·6 (£8·9 million)	100·0

for a little less. The balance is made up by trading licences, motor vehicle licences, registration fees, a tax on lotteries, sweepstakes, and bets, contributions for widows' and orphans' pensions, and a number of minor taxes and licences.

Company Tax

7:4. Companies are taxed on their undistributed profits at a rate of 40%. Dividends are taxed in the hands of shareholders at the rates of personal income tax applicable to the individual holder. There are several allowances which companies may set against their chargeable income, these being mainly based on past or present practice in the United Kingdom. The most important of these are initial and annual allowances, investment allowances, and agricultural allowances.

7:5. There are initial allowances of 10% on the value of expenditure on industrial buildings (including hotels) and 20% on the value of machinery and plant, with subsequent annual allowances based on the written down value of the assets. There is a similar system of agricultural allowances, whereby a quarter of capital expenditure on agricultural land and buildings or other agricultural works may be set off against income in the year in which it is incurred, the remainder being written off at a rate of 5% per annum over the succeeding fifteen years.

7:6. In addition to these capital allowances, which involve a postponement of taxation from the company's point of view, or an interest-free loan from the government's point of view, there is also an investment allowance, under which one tenth of capital expenditure on industrial building and plant may be set against chargeable income in the year in which it is incurred. This differs from an initial allowance in that the capital value of the asset is not written down by this amount. Thus it is a complete remission of tax to this extent, and not merely a postponement of tax. The investment allowance since April 1960 has not been given on the purchase of vehicles.

7:7. We have received several complaints to the effect that the rate of company tax is too high and we believe that these are justified. We would not suggest that the level of company tax is the sole, or even the principal, factor which has discouraged the growth of industry in Mauritius, since, as we have already shown in Chapter 6, the difficulties facing industrial development are legion, but we do believe that a level of company tax of 40% must be a powerfully discouraging influence on enterprise and that it is far too high a rate for Mauritius. It is true that about three quarters of this tax is borne by the sugar industry, which can easily afford it, but this is no justification for 40% level of tax on all companies. It is significant that, out of 264 companies assessed to company tax in 1958-9, 96 had taxable incomes of less than Rs. 5,000, and a further 58 companies had taxable incomes of less than Rs. 25,000. The typical Mauritian company is small, and a 40% company tax bears hardly on it.

7:8. Clearly the government is not in a position to forego more than a part of a tax which is easily assessed and raised, but we think that a reduction of 10% from 40% to 30%, would be reasonable, involving as it would (on the basis of the 1958-59 assessments) a loss of revenue of about Rs. $9\frac{1}{2}$ million. This is probably a slightly conservative estimate of the loss since, by widening the gap between the marginal rates of tax on the highest level of personal incomes (currently at 70%) and the rate of company tax, the reduction would encourage a certain amount of tax evasion by smaller companies, which might tend to retain a higher proportion of their profits in the business than was warranted by the needs of the concern. Under Section 55 of the Income Tax Ordinance, as amended in 1958, the Income Tax Commissioner has power to assess the shareholders in companies controlled by not more than five persons as though any undistributed profits which could, without detriment to the business, be distributed, had been distributed, but it is possible that action under this section would not be completely effective. We therefore estimate that the total loss of revenue from this concession would be Rs. 10 million (£750,000).

7:9. However, if the rate of company tax is reduced, we recommend that it should be accompanied by a reconsideration of the company-tax allowances, in particular the investment allowance. The concessions granted under this allowance increase according to the amount of capital invested and thus place a premium on capital-intensive methods of operation—that is, methods which employ a great deal of capital to a little labour, rather than those which employ a great deal of labour to a little capital. Since we have already argued that one of the major problems facing Mauritius is to increase the level of employment in the most economical possible way in terms of the use of land and capital, such concessions appear to us to give the wrong kind of encouragement to investment. We do not propose the abolition of the initial allowance—indeed, in view of the shortage of long-term credit in Mauritius a system of government investment-free loans of this kind has something to recommend it. We are, however, opposed to direct government subsidies on capital investment which are proportionate to the value of such investment, particularly since we understand that the principal beneficiary of the investment allowance has been the sugar industry. It is doubtful whether the allowance has had any substantial effect on the industry's scale of investment, and this concession has in effect been unnecessary. We therefore recommend that the investment allowance be withdrawn, which would, on present rates of company tax, provide a saving of Rs. 2 million per annum to government (£150,000).

7:10. We have also considered the possibility of granting complete relief from company tax for an initial period for selected new industries. Tax holidays of this kind, for varying periods, have been adopted by many territories, especially in the West Indies. There is little definite evidence of their effectiveness in stimulating investment. Jamaica and Puerto Rico, which granted them, have also experienced a rapid rate of industrial development, but many other Caribbean territories which have also granted them, have had little or no advantage from them and we doubt whether tax holidays, as such, have more than a marginal influence on the rate of investment. They are, however, of some psychological value as demonstrating that the government is in earnest in its desire for a growth of industrial investment, and in so far as they create confidence in government's intentions, they are of value. They suffer from the disadvantage, from the point of view of the firm, that little or no profit may be expected in the first year or two of operation, and the concession is accordingly of little value for that period. We therefore recommend that any tax holiday granted should be of a form which should grant freedom from company tax for any five of the first eight years of a company's operation. The question whether a tax holiday should be given in any particular instance should be referred to the Government Advisory Committee (paragraphs 6:98, 99 and 101).

Personal Income Tax

7:11. The rates of personal income tax vary from 10% for the first Rs. 5,000 of chargeable income (£375), up to 70% on all chargeable income in excess of Rs. 100,000 (£7,500). The principal allowances are as follows:—

(i) personal allowance .. .. .. Rs. 2,500 (£187·5);
(ii) wife .. .. Rs. 2,000 (£150);
(iii) children's allowances
     for the first child .. .. Rs. 800 (£60),
     for the second child .. .. Rs. 700 (£52·5),
     for the third child .. .. Rs. 600 (£45), and
     for each succeeding child .. Rs. 500 (£37·5);
(iv) earned income relief
     on the first Rs. 10,000 (£750) .. 25%, and
     on the next Rs. 15,000 (£1,125) 20%;
(v) allowance for children educated
    outside the colony (in addition to
    above allowances) .. .. Rs. 1,000 (£75)
                            (per child);
(vi) overseas leave allowance; and
(vii) allowance on life insurance premiums and premiums paid to
     secure annuities on retirement.

7:12. We do not consider that there is any substance in the charge that these rates of tax are too high. On the lower and medium incomes at least, the rates are substantially lower than in the United Kingdom, and when eligibility for allowances is taken into consideration, there can be no doubt that many people who are well able to pay income tax do not do so. It has, for example, been pointed out to us that only about a half of the individuals owning and running cars pay income tax. We were greatly impressed by the efficiency of the Income Tax Department, and we doubt whether there is a great deal of outright tax evasion. It is, however, probable that the workings of the income-tax allowances provide considerable scope for more or less legitimate tax avoidance, and that has led us to particular consideration of the children's allowances and the leave-passage allowances. We should also mention the allowances given for the education of children over-seas. We support the view of the Titmuss Report that these allow-ances should be withdrawn and suggest that the savings which accrue should go towards financing an increased number of overseas scholarships (see paragraph 8:46).

7:13. The Titmuss Report recommends that children's allowances should be withdrawn, on the grounds that, first, they give a positive incentive for large families, and that, second, a system of family allowances, which they propose, is incompatible with a system of income-tax allowances for children. The second of these arguments does not appear to us to carry much weight. Several countries, in-cluding the United Kingdom, both grant family allowances and give tax allowances for children. On the other hand, we see great force in the first, that the present system of allowances in Mauritius provides a considerable incentive for the production of large families. The Government of Mauritius has announced its intention of encouraging and assisting the "three-child family" and it would appear to us to be in line with this policy to restrict the number of children for whom allowance was made to three. This would not provide an incentive for having large families, but would at the same time give some relief for the moderately sized family. No detailed estimates are available as to the additional revenue which might be obtained from this change but we are informed that an additional Rs. 500,000-Rs. 1,000,000 (£37,500-£75,000) might be raised.

7:14. The allowances for overseas leave are provided for in Section 35B of the Income Tax Ordinance, as amended in 1958. Deductions are made from chargeable income for the cost of passages for leave outside Mauritius for a man, his wife, and children, on condition that the total cost shall not exceed three return fares by air in tourist class to the United Kingdom, and that it shall not be allowed more than once in five years. We understand that this concession was given in order that the private income-tax payer should enjoy similar privileges to civil servants in respect of overseas leave. We recommend above (paragraph 2:83) that the overseas leave privilege for local civil servants be greatly curtailed, and we also recommend that this concession under the income-tax ordinance be withdrawn. We estimate the additional revenue to be gained by so doing at Rs. 400,000 (£30,000), plus an additional Rs. 600,000 (£45,000) if leave passages provided by employers are also charged as income. In so far as such passages are, in effect, part of the remuneration for employment, it would seem to us to be logical that tax should be charged on it.

Import Duties

7:15. The Mauritian tariff is primarily revenue raising. There are certain duties which are intended to be protective, including those on rubber footwear and tobacco, but so far tariff protection has been little used, although the high level of certain revenue duties could in certain circumstances provide a measure of protection for local industry. Certain articles of mass consumption, such as rice and other cereals, and salted and dried fish, carry very low rates of duty, in order to reduce the cost of living to the poor, and for reasons which we have elaborated elsewhere (paragraphs 2:70-72) we support this policy, although it does not appear to us that it has been consistently carried out. For instance, the non-preferential rate of 75% on rayon piece-goods and made-up garments does not appear to us to be in line with this policy, although it might provide protection if a rayon weaving industry were to be established in Mauritius. In general, apart from the fairly high duties on certain luxury items, such as motor spirit and liquor, which are regarded as major sources of government revenue, it is difficult to find either system or consistency in the tariff schedule, which appears to us to be a combination of *ad hoc* expedients and historical relics.

7:16. Moreover, as we have already observed (paragraph 6:96) there are several instances where the customs tariff has a definitely disincentive effect on local enterprise. For example, the rates on some raw materials or semi-manufactures are higher than the rates on the finished goods which are made from them, with the result that there are specific duties of varying amounts on different iron and steel semi-manufactures, whilst machinery and plant for the sugar industry enters duty free. Local firms which manufacture machinery for the sugar industry are thus at a direct disadvantage in relation to imports. Again, a number of potential raw materials for industry carry rates of $12\frac{1}{2}\%$ or more, rayon yarn for instance carrying a preferential duty of 25% and a general duty of 75%. We do not suggest that raw materials or potential raw materials should always be imported free of duty since this would involve a very considerable loss of revenue, and might encourage the growth of industry which added little to employment or the national product—for example, the finishing of products imported in nearly finished condition. Some such industries can be of value, but it is also possible that the cost to government of free entry of raw materials or semi-finished products for industries of this kind could far outweigh the benefit of the industry to the economy as a whole. We do believe, however, that duties on raw materials and semi-finished products should in general be lower than those on articles of final consumption into which these raw materials and semi-finished products enter. There are difficulties of definition in applying this rule—what is a raw material for one purpose may be an article of final consumption for another—but we recommend that every attempt should be made to apply this principle as far as is practicable in individual circumstances.

7:17. To some extent it can already be applied under the present customs tariff. Under Section 4 of the Customs Tariff Ordinance of 1954, the Governor in Council may, on the report of the Comptroller of Customs remit or refund the whole or any portion of a duty in the case of any goods imported under special circumstances "or imported for an object or an enterprise beneficial to the colony". In addition there are a number of exemptions from import duty in the first schedule of the Ordinance, such as chemicals, which may be imported free of duty, if they are to be employed on specified industries, including the sugar industry. It seems to us, however, that these procedures are not entirely satisfactory. Although, under Section 4 procedure, the Governor in Council acts on the report of the Comptroller, no rules are laid down for the Comptroller's guidance in the matter, nor is he required to obtain advice or assistance from any outside body or person, which in our opinion places too heavy a responsibility on the Comptroller. Amendments to the first schedule of the Ordinance may be made by resolution of the Legislative Council, but again there is no requirement that the advice of any particular persons be obtained before a resolution is laid before the Legislative Council. We consider that, when any special concessions are given to particular concerns, as under Section 4, or for particular industries, as in amendments to the list of exemptions to the schedule, there should be a statutory requirement that the advice of the Government Advisory Committee should be obtained (see paragraph 6:101).

7:18. The present import duties on machinery show a curious dichotomy. On the one hand a fairly wide range of machinery, including machine tools, metal-working machinery, pumps, wood-working machinery, paper-mill and pulp-mill machinery, and textile machinery, carries a general rate of 37% and a preferential rate of 15%. On the other hand, under Serial No. E.3 of the schedule, machinery, plant, and apparatus imported for a wide variety of industries, such as sugar, aloe fibre, tanning, tobacco, hardboard, edible oils, and aerated waters, may be admitted at a general rate of 5% and duty free under the preferential tariff. We see no justification for this division between machinery which effectively enters free of duty and that which carries duties of 15% and upwards. We have not seen any arguments which would tend to the view that machinery imported under Serial No. E.3 was of any greater value to the economy than machinery imported outside this schedule, and we propose that the distinction be abandoned. The duties on all machinery should be at a fairly low level, and Serial E.3 should be omitted from the list of exemptions. It should be open to government to remit duties on machinery altogether for any particular firm if, in the opinion of the Government Advisory Committee, this is desirable.

7:19. As we have already argued (paragraphs 2:70-72 and 6:94-96), we consider that there is a case in Mauritian conditions for some measure of protection for new, and even for some established, industries. We recommend that, where a protective tariff is imposed, this should be done for a period of five years in the first instance, and renewable if a case can be made out at the end of the period for a further five years. This protection, as with remissions of duty, should be considered by the Government Advisory Committee, which should make recommendations to the minister concerned. We understand that at present, since the Customs Tariff Advisory Board is virtually a dead letter, it is granted almost solely on the advice of the Comptroller of Customs.

7:20. In deciding whether an industry should be given protection, there are a number of relevant questions which should always be considered. The case for protection should be considered favourably in so far as:—

(i) there is no prospect of making a profit, at least in the initial stages, without some measure of protection;

(ii) there is a good prospect of obtaining on reasonable terms the necessary raw materials;

(iii) there is a good prospect of developing a market, at home or overseas, on a scale sufficient to make production reasonably efficient;

(iv) there is a good prospect that, in time, as the necessary new skills and techniques are acquired by experience, the industry's costs will become competitive with overseas producers;

(v) the industry is one that is likely to employ an appreciable amount of labour of the kind available in Mauritius, without making great demands on the use of land or of capital;

(vi) the establishment of the industry will attract capital and/or enterprise from overseas, or local capital and/or enterprise that would otherwise go overseas;

(vii) the establishment of the industry is likely to give experience to managers, engineers, foremen, and other workers in techniques and skills which will be useful in other lines of industrial development in Mauritius; and

(viii) the protection is not likely seriously to affect the cost of living.

7:21. So far as the general revision of the customs tariff is concerned, which we understand is at present being prepared, we suggest that the following considerations should be borne in mind:—

(a) The schedule should as far as possible follow the principles already suggested above (7:15-19); in particular that raw materials and semi-manufactures should in general be taxed at a lower level than finished goods and that machinery should be admitted at a low rate of duty.

(b) The schedule should be as simple as possible. At present there is a great variety of charges and a most confusing mixture of *ad valorem* and specific rates.

(c) Finally the revision must involve some modification of preferences. Any increase in preferences is ruled out under the G.A.T.T., so that modifications tend to be in a downward direction. Preferences given by Mauritius to other Commonwealth countries, on the one hand, and, on the other hand, the preferences given by other Commonwealth countries to Mauritian sugar (including the Negotiated Price paid by the United Kingdom for such sugar) make up together a joint commercial system of mutual benefit. It is important, therefore, that any unavoidable reductions which Mauritius may have to make in the tariff preferences which she offers should not be made without considering their effect on this system.

Other Taxes

7:22. The proposals which we have made so far would mean a net loss of more than Rs. 6 million in revenue (£450,000). On the other hand, there is, as we shall see, need for government to provide funds for a large measure of investment in industry and agriculture, and, whatever savings might be possible on government recurrent expenditure and however much it may be possible to raise from abroad, there will undoubtedly remain a need to maintain, and if possible increase, the level of revenue from taxation. We have therefore considered what alternative form of taxation might compensate for the loss of revenue, and came to the conclusion that for taxation as well as for economic reasons the export duty on sugar, which varies between 10 cents and 30 cents per metric ton, should be replaced by a 5% *ad valorem* duty on the production of sugar.

7:23. There are several arguments supporting such a change. In the first place, there is at present an almost irresistible upward trend in the output of sugar and, as we have already argued, some brake must be placed on it if over-production is to be avoided (paragraphs 2:35 ff). In the second place, it is one of the principal features of the present system for selling sugar that because of the system of averaging out the returns on sugar among the different producers it is more profitable for the individual producer to expand his production than it is for the industry as a whole, and it is clear that part of the profitability of investing in expanding the sugar acreage depends on this fortuitous arrangement. To some extent (though by no means completely) a 5% duty on the production of sugar will bring the marginal return for the individual producer per ton of sugar nearer the marginal return for Mauritius as a whole, and in effect will do something to correct the distortion of the pattern of investment in Mauritius arising from these arrangements. Finally, there is some evidence that it is particularly difficult to assess small planters fairly for income tax, and, in so far as this is so, the imposition of a duty on sugar will fall on those who are able to pay income tax but do not do so. In all, then, we consider that a 5% duty on sugar production would be both economically sound and socially just. We estimate that the gross yield from such a tax would be Rs. 15 million, but that there would be a reduction in income tax receipts amounting to some Rs. 3 million as a result, and that the net yield would therefore be about Rs. 12 million (£900,000).

Summary of Taxation Proposals

7:24. The total effect of our tax proposals on revenue can be summarised as follows:—

	Rs. million
Lowering of company tax to 30% ..	− 10
Abolition of investment allowance ..	+ 2
Restriction of child allowance to first three	+ 0·5- + 1
Abolition of overseas leave allowance plus charging as income leave passages ..	+ 1·0
5% tax on sugar production	+ 12
Total between	+ 5 and + 6
(between	+ £375,000 and + £450,000).

Government Expenditure

7:25. There has been a steady rise in the recurrent expenditure of government during the past few years. In 1952-53, current expenditure (excluding public debt charges, loans and advances, and transfers to special funds) totalled Rs. 77·36 million: by 1958-59 this had risen to Rs. 117·4 million—an increase of 52%. The following table shows the major headings accounting for this increase:

Table LIV. Major Increases in Government Expenditure, 1952-1959

Head	Expenditure in Rs. million		
	1952–53	1955–56	1958–59
Central administration	1·19	0·853	5·34
Police	5·17	5·67	7·35
Public works and surveys establishment ..	2·53	1·78	4·61
Education	12·1	13·2	18·6
Health	8·41	11·0	14·9
Public assistance	3·10	8·41	15·8
Agriculture	2·04	2·47	4·02

These seven heads account for 90% of the increase in recurrent expenditure over the period. Over 60% of the increase was under the three heads of education, health, and public assistance.

7:26. By far the greater part of this increase has taken place since

1956-57. Expenditure in 1958-59 was 40% higher than it had been two years earlier. This was partly the result of arrears of pay under salary revisions, but a large part of the rise reflects genuine increases in the cost of services. A rise in recurrent expenditure of this order in such a short period is disquieting. If this trend were to continue, it would both involve a degree of taxation which would impose a heavy burden on the country and would render it impossible for government to make any savings from its recurrent budget for financing capital expenditure. Elsewhere in this report we have indicated various activities which government should undertake to support and in order to encourage economic growth, but unless some check is placed on the expansion of the recurrent budget, it will be in no position to do so. It is possible that some part of the necessary finance can be found from external sources, but it is unreasonable to expect the United Kingdom Government or international agencies to meet a financial gap which arises largely because of the unwillingness of the Government of Mauritius to face the problem of rising current costs.

7:27. To some extent these increases are the inevitable result of the growing need for services arising from an expanding population. For example, the number of children between five and fourteen years of age rose from 114,464 in 1952 to 153,294 in 1957. The number is expected to increase to 194,500 in 1962 and, if fertility remains constant (that is, if there is no fall in the birth-rate) to 223,000 in 1967. Thus the population of this age group will have doubled in fifteen years. In the face of such an increase it is inevitable that the cost of education should rise steeply. If the cost per child remains constant, as compared with 1957, the recurrent education bill will rise from Rs. 18·6 million (£1·395 million) in 1958-59 to over Rs. 21 million (£1·525 million) in 1962 and over Rs. 24 million (£1·8 million) in 1967. The cost per child will increase however if there are further salary revisions, some improvement in the standard of the schools, and an increase in the proportion of children over twelve years of age receiving education in government or aided schools. We discuss the education system as such in Chapter 8, and at this stage we are concerned only to suggest the strains which will inevitably fall on the recurrent budget as a result of the growth in the number of children of school age—a burden which will become ever heavier if the birth-rate does not fall considerably in the near future.

7:28. But in addition to the inevitable increases in expenditure to meet the growth in population, we believe that there is a large unnecessary element in government's recurrent expenditure. Most departments are heavily overstaffed in relation to the size of the country, the work that has to be done, or the ability of Mauritius to afford their services, some being worse offenders than others. This overstaffing occurs at all levels, and although some departments like the Statistics Department and Tea Division of the Department of Agriculture are certainly understaffed at the top levels they are exceptions. Our attention has been drawn to departments with as large a staff as can be found for the whole of the Federation of Nigeria, with a population fifty times as great as that of Mauritius. We make certain suggestions which we believe will increase the efficiency of the public services in Chapter 9. Here we are concerned only with the financial implications of the present size and structure of the public service. Personal emoluments and pensions for government employees amount to about a half of government's recurrent expenditure, and although this includes the cost of teachers in government schools, nurses in hospitals, and other people who would not normally be classified as civil servants, the size and structure of the civil service is a very important element in the government's recurrent budget.

7:29. One important element in the rise in recurrent budget is the steady increase in the cost of public assistance. This problem is examined in detail by the Titmuss Report and we are in general agreement with the analysis of the problem presented in it. The Titmuss Report proposes the introduction of a number of social security measures, the most important of which is a system of family allowances, which should have the effect, *inter alia*, of containing this increase in expenditure on public assistance. We are not competent to judge how far these measures would have this effect. We must, however, emphasise that the proposals will involve a substantial and immediate net addition to the recurrent budget. We estimate that the total cost of the measures proposed in the Titmuss Report would be of the order of Rs. 12 million per annum (£900,000) of which some Rs. 4 million per annum (£300,000) should be saved on the cost of public assistance, leaving a net additional cost of Rs. 8 million per annum (£600,000) or nearly 7 % of actual expenditure in 1958-59. We do not wish to comment on the merits of these proposals, but it is very necessary that the Government of Mauritius, when examining them, should place them in the context of the total demand on their resources and of the recurrent budget in particular. Although we are not competent to judge the merits of the proposals in any detail, we consider that, if the additional Rs. 8 million per annum placed on the recurrent budget is the necessary price of an effective programme of family limitation, the price would be well worth-while.

7:30. There is one further important element in the rise in government recurrent expenditure. We believe that there is a tendency for government in Mauritius to undertake a number of functions which in most countries would normally fall to the private sector. This is partly a reflection of the paternalist tradition inherited by the present Government of Mauritius, but it is also a reflection of that compartmentalism of Mauritian life, which makes it very difficult for citizens of different racial groups to combine together voluntarily for a common purpose. We encountered several examples of this attitude. For example, we heard complaints from the Chambers of Commerce—the Mauritius Chamber of Commerce, the Mauritius Chamber of Merchants, and the Chinese Chamber of Commerce—which represent different racial groups, that it was difficult to obtain commercial intelligence in Mauritius, with the suggestion that government should do something to meet this need. This gap could easily be filled if the three chambers of commerce combined together to produce a periodical with commercial intelligence, but because of their inability to combine, nothing is done unless government does it. We cannot measure the importance of this attitude in financial terms, but we consider that any examination of the government machine which is undertaken for the purpose of increasing its efficiency should also consider how essential are some of the functions carried out by government. We have already mentioned one or two particular activities which we think should be handed over to the private sector (see, for instance, paragraphs 5:73 and 137).

7:31. To these we should like to add one more, namely, government finance of the rice trade. Because of the fall in the world price of rice the government is not at present making a loss on the trade but this has not always been so. In 1958-59 the government lost Rs. 3·36 million (which was only slightly offset by a profit of Rs. 0·5 million on its trade in flour). However, even this net loss of Rs. 2·86 million does not represent the total cost to government. Granary, stacking, and delivery costs total about Rs. 450,000 per annum, and since government provides its own finance for the trade, something between Rs. 15 million and Rs. 20 million of its funds are generally immobilised. The question of the government's continuation in the rice trade is thus of some financial importance. We have already pointed out that, at the current (1960) world price of rice, the government trade in rice involves no subsidy to the consumer (paragraph 2:27); but two questions remain, first whether the trade should be returned to private hands and second whether, if the government decides to retain the trade in its own hands, the necessary finance could be raised in other ways.

7:32. The principal reasons for the retention of the trade in public hands are to maintain stocks adequate to Mauritian isolation and to keep down the price of rice to the consumer, both by subsidising it and by controlling the price at wholesale and retail levels. The latter is perhaps the more important and for reasons we explain elsewhere, we are in general sympathy with it. Private traders with whom we have discussed this have claimed that there would be no increase in prices if the trade were returned to them. They argue that the government is inexperienced in trading matters, and has not always bought its rice on the most favourable terms possible. Moreover, they claim that private traders could obtain shipping space cheaper because they would be negotiating for shipping both for imports and exports. They deny that there would be excessive price margins in rice imported by the trade. Members of the Ministry of Finance with whom we have discussed the problem argue that the quality of rice would fall and its price would rise if it were returned to private trade.

7:33. It is difficult for us to judge between these views. There are, however, other considerations. First, if the government decides to go ahead with its scheme for family allowances, the case for subsidising essential foodstuffs becomes weaker. The proposals of the Titmuss Report, in so far as they relate to non-contributory social security schemes, amount in effect to a redistribution of Rs. 8 million from the general body of taxpayers to those in particular need—that is, to families with three or more children. A rice subsidy also involves a redistribution of income from taxpayers to rice consumers. It could be claimed that the two are alternative means of meeting similar needs and it is open to question whether the tax structure should be called on to effect both these forms of redistribution. Secondly, the Report on the Purchasing Power of the Rupee does not provide much evidence to suggest that margins in the private wholesale and retail trades are excessive. There are certain exceptions—especially where sole agencies have been granted by the supplying firms abroad or where competition is restricted for other reasons. It does not appear to us probable that competition among importers would be greatly restricted if the rice trade were returned to private hands, and we have no reason to suppose that price margins would be excessive.

7:34. On the other hand, as we have emphasised elsewhere, we consider that it is of the greatest importance that wage costs be kept stable. In so far as stability in the cost of living contributes to this end, we believe that government should do all it can to keep down the prices of essential articles of consumption. It is possible that the freeing of the rice trade would not, in the immediate future, cause an increase in the price of rice. If, however, world prices rise again, and a measure of subsidisation is again required to keep the internal price of rice steady, it may be very difficult to implement such a policy if government is no longer in the trade. Government, then, should not lightly throw away this important potential means of stabilising the cost of living.

7:35. On balance, then, we are inclined to support the retention of the trade in rice (although not necessarily that in flour) in government hands. We believe, however, that there is no case for their financing these imports from their own resources. We have discussed the problem with the three commercial banks, and we understand that there would be no difficulty in obtaining bank advances on reasonable terms to finance the trade. We recommend that, whether the rice trade is returned to private hands or not, government should cease to finance the trade from its own funds, but should employ a system of fluctuating overdrafts from the commercial banks.

7:36. We do not wish to make further detailed recommendations on the elimination of unnecessary government functions, but we suggest that, as part of a general survey of the efficiency of government there should also be a close examination of the importance of the work being carried on by departments. In the last resort decisions on what government should or should not do must be made on grounds of public policy, but there is a tendency for departments to carry out many minor functions without any general decision by government to do so. It is therefore necessary that the examination of the working of government should cover both functions and methods; any reasonable measure of economy in public expenditure requires a constant review of both.

The Current Surplus

7:37. So far we have considered the tax structure, suggesting amendments which will produce a modest increase in revenue, and the trends in expenditure, noting the tendency for the costs of the social services and administration to increase. We now consider the relation between current revenue and expenditure and the surplus on current account.

7:38. The following table shows the trend of recurrent revenue and expenditure in recent years. The expenditure figures have been adjusted to exclude payments into special funds or transfers to the capital budget (where relevant). Public utilities are treated on a gross basis; that is, their gross receipts are included in revenue, and their gross expenditure is included on the expenditure side. Public debt charges are excluded from the expenditure side, since a good deal of these consists of payments into special funds.

7:39. As can be seen, until 1957-58 the Government of Mauritius had a very substantial effective surplus on current account. But in 1958-59 there was a substantial reduction in the surplus and in 1959-60—mainly because of the cyclones—the surplus

175

Table LV. Current Revenue and Expenditure, 1952-1959

Rs. million

Year					Revenue	Expenditure	Surplus
1952–53 ..	..	..	..	..	93·7	84·9	8·8
1953–54 ..	..	..	..	..	101·4	88·7	12·7
1954–55 ..	..	..	..	..	109·2	84·5	24·7
1955–56 ..	..	..	..	..	115·0	85·5	29·5
1956–57 ..	..	..	..	..	119·1	89·7	29·4
1957–58 ..	..	..	..	..	131·5	107·7	23·8
1958–59 ..	..	..	..	..	133·2	123·4	9·8

is expected to be negligible. Government must normally maintain a surplus on current account, to help finance capital development, to service the public debt, and to build reserves against disasters. This last function is of special importance in Mauritius; it would be the height of imprudence to assume that external financial assistance will always be forthcoming to meet the cost of cyclones. The building up of reserves against cyclones must be counted as a normal cost of government. It is difficult to be precise, but we consider that government should normally aim at a surplus of some Rs. 20 million per annum on current account to meet these requirements. Of this sum, some Rs. 12 million per annum—or about 10% of current revenue—might reasonably be devoted to capital expenditure, and the remainder for debt servicing and the building up of reserves.

7:40. As Table LV shows, the surplus on recurrent account was substantially in excess of this figure until 1957-58. This situation was reflected in a sizeable accumulation of sterling assets by government during this period. Indeed, policy during this period might be criticised on the grounds that it was excessively cautious, and the export of capital on government account was unnecessarily high. Whether this was so or not, the changes during the past two years are a matter of serious concern. The problem we have to examine is how far this fall in the current surplus is the result of temporary factors, and how far it represents a long-term trend.

7:41. The immediate cause of the change lies in the failure of revenue to rise at a period when expenditure was increasing very rapidly. We have seen earlier that the principal reasons for the rise in expenditure have been salary awards to civil servants and the steady increase in expenditure on the social services—especially education, health, and public assistance. We have also seen that expenditure on the social services will almost certainly continue to increase. Between 1956-57 and 1958-59, expenditure rose by 37·6%, or over 17% per annum. The rate at which expenditure rises in future will depend on a number of factors, including the rise in population and the demand for social and other government services, policy decisions concerning the functions of government, and the efficiency and economy with which these functions are carried out. An annual increase of 17% could not possibly be tolerated for more than a short period, and it is reasonable to assume that this rate of increase will be somewhat reduced. The rate of increase which might be judged bearable must depend on our forecasts of the future of government revenue. During the period 1952-53 to 1958-59, current revenue increased at a rate of a little more than 6% per annum. During the same period, the gross national product rose by less than 4% per annum. Thus government revenues were accounting for an increasing share of the national income. Future revenues will depend on the growth of taxable capacity and changes in rates of tax. Tax increases announced in April 1960 are estimated to raise a further Rs. 12 million per annum, and our tax proposals are estimated at a further Rs. 5-6 million. Thus, if our proposals are accepted and there is no increase in the national income, there will be an increase of Rs. 17-18 million in revenue—or about 13% of revenue in 1958-59, less than one year's rate of increase in expenditure between 1957 and 1959. Indeed, far more important than the increase in tax rates is the increase in taxable capacity—that is, in the national income, and it is on the growth of the national income that government will depend for meeting the growth in public expenditure.

7:42. We have already given our reasons for supposing that increases in the national income will be more difficult to achieve in future than in the past. We believe that Mauritius will do well to increase her national income by 5% per annum (if prices remain constant). In other words, unless tax rates are raised still further, that is, if the ratio of government revenue to national income remains constant, we cannot expect government revenue to increase by more than 5% per annum in the next few years. If, then, the tax increases proposed in the April 1960 budget and in our report are sufficient to provide the necessary surplus on current account on present levels of recurrent expenditure, they will do no more than allow for a 5% per annum increase in recurrent expenditure in future. *It should therefore be the aim of government to restrict rises in recurrent expenditure to 5% per annum.* As we have suggested, this may be no easy task, but some limitation is essential if sufficient resources are to be made available for necessary investment and for maintaining reserves. This 5% increase should not be interpreted in a mechanical way; that is, we are not proposing that increases on each heading in the budget should be limited to 5%. On the contrary; we consider that expenditure under a number of headings should be increased by far more than 5%, while that under other headings should be reduced or even abolished. Our proposal is that *total* recurrent expenditure should rise by no more than 5% per annum, and this total must accommodate any necessary larger increases than this under individual headings.

The Capital Budget

7:43. The original Capital Expenditure Programme of the Government of Mauritius for the period 1957-62 totalled some Rs. 210 million; this total was revised to Rs. 223 million in 1959. Of the original total, some 12% was capital expenditure connected with administration, 30% was on the social services, and 22% was on communications. The plan envisaged phasing of expenditure as in the following table.—

Table LVI. Capital Expenditure Programme, 1957-1962

Year				Rs. million
1957–58 ..	..	..	..	36·5
1958–59 ..	..	..	..	53·3
1959–60 ..	..	..	..	47·8
1960–61 ..	..	..	..	41·0
1961–62 ..	..	..	..	31·6

7:44. In the event, expenditure in the first two years of the plan was well below the estimates, being Rs. 25·6 million in 1957-58 and Rs. 28·6 million in 1958-59. The reasons for the shortfalls may be summarised as follows:—

(*a*) the plan over-estimated the ability of departments to prepare projects and get them to the operational stage;

(*b*) delays in arrival of essential equipment from overseas; and

(*c*) delays in acquisition of sites for public works.

Table LVII shows progress on the major items in the plan.

7:45. Progress is estimated to have been more rapid in 1959-60: expenditure under the programme is believed to have been over Rs. 40 million. Schemes were being brought to the spending stage; contracts had been let; sites had been acquired; equipment had arrived from overseas. The whole future of the development programme was, however, put in doubt by the two cyclones of 1960. The principal effects of these from the development point of view were, first, that the financial resources of government would be subject to heavy calls to repair the damage, and, in particular, to carry out a programme of cyclone-proof housing; second, that the ability of government to plan and carry out development work would be

178

Table LVII. Capital Expenditure Programme: Major Items

Items	Rs. million		
	Total Estimate	Actual Expenditure	
	1957–62	1957–58	1958–59
Agriculture	22	2·8	4·5
Water supplies and irrigation ..	14	2·0	4·0
Secondary industries	5	—	0·02
Electricity	30	6·7	6·0
Roads	23	2·3	3·1
Harbours and quays	11	0·45	0·2
Telecommunications	9	0·7	0·5
Education	24	3·6	3·5
Medical	13	2·2	0·9
Housing	10	0·6	1·1
Sewerage	19	0·3	0·4
Local authorities (except housing) ..	9	1·15	1·15
Police	6	0·7	0·5
Others	15	2·1	2·7
Total	210	25·6	28·6

stretched to the uttermost; and third, that government would suffer a loss of revenue as a result of the cyclones, and would thus be less able to appropriate funds from the recurrent to the capital budget.

7:46. After discussions with members of the mission and the Ministry of Finance, the Government of Mauritius decided to prepare a new Capital Expenditure Programme to cover the period 1960-65. This programme would, on the expenditure side, include uncompleted projects from the 1957-62 programme, and some new projects, as well as necessary reconstruction following the cyclones. On the revenue side, an estimate would be made of available reserves, revenue surpluses, local loans and funds which might be made available from overseas. Table LVIII summarises the proposed expenditure suggested in this rough outline.

7:47. The table is not intended as a detailed programme for the period: some of the projects are at little more than the most preliminary stage. Moreover, there is some doubt as to whether all of these items could be completed in the five-year period; as we have seen, the Government of Mauritius has so far spent no more than Rs. 40 million in a year on development and it may be doubted whether this could be increased to an average of Rs. 70 million a year over the period. In particular, we understand that the Housing Adviser to the Secretary of State for the Colonies doubts whether the whole of the re-housing programme can be completed in five years.

Table LVIII. Skeleton Reconstruction and Development Programme,
1960-1965

Rs. million

	Development			Total
	Carry-over of old schemes	New provision	Recon-struction	
Administration	6·6	4·4	7·2*	18·2
Economic Services:				
Agriculture	10·5	—	—†	10·5
Forests	0·6	0·05	—	0·65
Fisheries	0·6	—	—‡	0·6
Secondary industries	3·45	0·25	—	3·7
Miscellaneous economic ..	—	—	0·9	0·9
Total economic services ..	15·2	0·3	0·9	16·4
Infrastructure:				
Roads	17·0	15·6	—	32·6
Harbour	9·9	0·1	—	10·0
Telecommunications	6·0	2·0	—	8·0
Civil aviation	1·5	5·0	—	6·5
Electricity	11·0	30·0	4·7	45·7
Water supplies and irrigation ..	7·0	15·0	—	22·0
Sewerage	20·0	—	—	20·0
Miscellaneous infrastructure ..	2·8	2·2	—	5·0
Total infrastructure	75·2	69·9	4·7	149·8
Social Services:				
Education	13·5	2·0	3·0	18·5
Health	7·5	1·0	—	8·5
Housing	—	—	125·0§	125·0
Miscellaneous social services ..	0·6	0·1	—	0·7
Total social services	21·6	3·1	128·0	152·7
Other Expenditure:				
Loans and subventions‖ ..	5·5	3·0	—	8·5
Local government	5·0	2·0	0·9	7·9
Miscellaneous	0·5	—	—	0·5
Total other expenditure	11·0	5·0	0·9	16·9
Grand total	129·6	82·7	141·7	354·0

* Including some repairs to schools, telephones, and other public services.
† Some expenditure included under "miscellaneous economic".
‡ Some development expenditure should now be re-classified as reconstruction, but we have ignored this change.
§ Includes a substantial development element.
‖ Mainly to the Mauritius Agricultural Bank.

7:48. The capital programme in the next five years is dominated by the demand for re-housing after the cyclones. The Rs. 125 million allocated in the table may indeed be an under-estimate; we are informed that the demand for loans for middle-class housing (for which this total includes Rs. 15 million) may be far higher, and that it may be as much as Rs. 30 million. During the current five-year period, however, this may, as we have suggested, be set off by under-spending on the other part of the re-housing programme. If we take the figures as they have been given to us, housing accounts for over 35% of proposed expenditure. As we have suggested earlier (see paragraphs 2:1-4), the rapid increase in population may be expected to cause a substantial increase in the demand for housing in the normal course of events, but if there had been no cyclone a programme on this scale would scarcely have been envisaged. Secondly, expenditure on direct economic services accounts for less than 5% of total expenditure, including nearly 3% on agriculture, and just over 1% on secondary industries. Apart from housing, the other major items of expenditure are infrastructure services (mainly electricity, roads, water supplies, and sewerage), which account for 42% of total expenditure.

7:49. As we show elsewhere the Government of Mauritius will have severe financial pressure on capital account over the next quinquennium, both as a result of the cyclones and because of the trends of recurrent expenditure. Moreover, the pressure on the government's ability to formulate and carry out development works will be equally great, even if, as we understand, a separate organisation is established to carry out the housing programme. For these reasons we consider that every attempt should be made to postpone any item of expenditure which can be postponed without great loss. Any development programme will include some items which are essential, others which are merely desirable, and yet others which are unnecessary luxuries. It is essential in present Mauritian circumstances that the programme be analysed in terms of relative urgency, and that items of low priority be abandoned for the time being. On the other hand, we consider that there are certain classes of expenditure for which insufficient provision is made in the programme. We would suggest that those projects be given first priority which either will assist directly in the expansion of productive employment in the island or will provide urgently needed social services (especially housing and higher and technical education). We believe that it will be necessary for the Government of Mauritius to adopt an austere attitude to many projects in the present plan if sufficient emphasis is to be placed on those of greatest importance.

7:50. We have not examined in detail all the projects in the programme, but we have considered the major items with these considerations in mind.

(a) As we show elsewhere, a far greater participation of public funds in the private section of the economy will be necessary over the next few years. This must come primarily through increasing the resources of the Agricultural Bank. We understand that some Rs. 8 million is allowed in the present outline for this purpose; we should expect the demand for government finance for the next quinquennium to be between Rs. 30 million and Rs. 50 million. To some extent, this does not represent a net addition to the total funds required. Certain projects, including the improvement of agricultural marketing and loans for middle-class housing and to secondary industries, are already included in the programme, and the fact that they are to be channelled through the banks will not make any difference except in the allocation of funds as between different items. But we consider that the provision for these items is seriously inadequate. In particular, we consider that Rs. 3·7 million is far less than will be required over the quinquennium for the promotion of manufacturing industries, if an active and efficient Industrial Development Board is set up (paragraphs 6:98-9). Moreover, some amount should be included to finance the setting up of an industrial estate (see paragraphs 2:60, 6:51 and 102). Again, we have not made any estimate of the capital cost of establishing agricultural marketing organisations (paragraph 5:144), but we would expect the allocation of Rs.0·4 million in the present plan to be seriously inadequate. Thus, although an increase in funds available to the Agricultural Bank will be partly balanced by savings elsewhere, there should be a substantial net addition—depending in part on the funds which can be raised elsewhere for this purpose.

(b) The proposed expenditure on infrastructure services is very substantial. We do not wish to comment on the estimates for electricity development, since we have seen no detailed break-down of the additional Rs. 30 millions allocated under the new plan. We understand however that the International Bank is being approached for finance for this project, and we assume that no action will be taken on it until the Bank's views are known. The other substantial item under this heading is expenditure on roads. Some capital expenditure on roads is inescapable. The demand arises principally from the proposed closing of the railway. The main item in the original programme is a new trunk road from Port Louis to Forest Side, at a cost of Rs. 10 million. Contracts for this have already been awarded and work will commence shortly. The new project is for a road from Trianon to Cluny at a cost of Rs. 15·6 million. It is argued by supporters of this project that the roads are already inadequate and that the closing down of the railway will make them even more so, especially during the sugar crop season when all the sugar will have to be shifted by lorry from the factories to Port Louis. On the other hand, Mauritius has a fairly well developed road system. Moreover, if it were possible to move the sugar by night, the present roads should be adequate for the time being. We understand that one of the difficulties is that the workers at the docks are unwilling to work at night, but it would seem to us to be worth investigating whether some means, such as special bonuses, would encourage them to do so. We would suggest that this project be postponed, at least until the present financial and other pressures are relieved. We understand that, of the other major infrastructure schemes, contracts have already been let for the sewerage and harbour projects, and that the need for work at the airport is most urgent. The large additional expenditure under water supplies is for the Midlands Reservoir to which we would give our strongest support.

(c) Although there is a substantial allocation for education, we do not believe that it can be substantially reduced. In the following chapter we stress the inadequacy of the schools, and although this is as much a question of educational policy as of school buildings, the general increase in the number of children makes some capital expenditure essential. If, however, our proposal for postponing the school entry age till six (paragraph 8:33) is adopted there should be some relaxation of the pressure on accommodation. We strongly support the proposed expenditure on a technical institute.

7:51. No attempt has been made to phase expenditure under the programme. As we have seen, the proposed phasing under the original 1957-62 programme was highly optimistic. We appreciate the difficulties of phasing expenditure over a period of five years ahead; there may be a change in relative priorities or costs; experience may show certain types of project to be more or less useful. For this reason, although a five-year capital expenditure programme is of value, it should not be treated as a fixed scheme of things. Several countries have found the "rolling" five-year plan to be a useful device. Under this, a list of projects is drawn up for the next five years, with some general indications of costs. Detailed estimates are, however, prepared only for the first two years of the programme, with perhaps rather less detailed estimates for the third year. At the end of the first year, the whole plan is shifted on a year, and detailed estimates again prepared for the first years of the plan. By this means, the country always has a plan in general outline for five years ahead, and a more detailed plan for the next year or two, and there is no hiatus between the end of one plan and the beginning of another. The Capital Expenditure Programme for 1957-62 did propose that a review of the whole programme be carried out each year; our proposal is that this review should involve the preparation of a new programme. We do not consider that this would place an undue burden on the bodies concerned with planning, since substantial revisions already take place at frequent intervals.

Revenue for the Capital Development Programme

7:52. The sources of revenue for the capital programme are revenue surpluses from the annual budget (that is, government's current savings), loans raised by government on the local market, the sterling balances of government and other public bodies, and other external sources of finance such as donations from the United Kingdom Government and external loans. In considering the resources available for capital expenditure we have ignored the various technical devices used by the Government of Mauritius in mobilising its resources. For example, in so far as the Tap Loan and the Consolidated Sinking Fund are methods by which sterling assets are withdrawn and used for local purposes, we have preferred to look at the actual resources used rather than the devices by which they are used. We consider these seriatim.

Budget Contributions

7:53. The Ministry of Finance estimates that some Rs. 7½ million per annum can be saved from the recurrent budget. As we have explained earlier, it should be the aim of the government to achieve a surplus[1] on its recurrent budget of some Rs. 20 million a year, to meet debt charges, necessary additions to reserves and contributions to the capital budget. We do not consider that it will be easy to do more than this, at least in the next two or three years. Of this, debt charges (interest and sinking fund) are estimated at Rs. 8·7 million in 1960-61, including Rs. 5·4 million in interest and Rs. 2·8 million in sinking fund payments, with some additional management charges and capital repayment. Although we cannot make any accurate estimate of the contributions which can be made for the recurrent budget over the next five years, we believe it would be unsafe to rely on a larger contribution than that estimated by the Ministry of Finance, at present levels of taxation. We have, however, suggested above (paragraph 7:24) that additional tax revenue of Rs. 5-6 million per annum would be raised. If these recom-

---

[1] We have defined the surplus on recurrent account as including debt charges, because in practice debt charges in the budget include both interest and provision for repayment of loans.

mendations are accepted, this should provide an additional Rs. 25 million over the quinquennium, thus making possible a budgetary contribution of about Rs. 60 million towards the plan.

Reserves

7:54. The sterling assets held by the Government of Mauritius on its own behalf and on behalf of other public bodies in May 1960 (excluding Cyclone and Drought Insurance Funds and the Currency Fund) amounted to over Rs. 110 million. Some part of these funds is committed for various purposes (such as the reserves of the Post Office Savings Bank) and genuinely disposable funds probably total no more than Rs. 70 million. We have considered with the Ministry of Finance the various funds available. As we have emphasised before the Government of Mauritius has to maintain a safe level of external reserves in view of the ever-present danger of cyclones. Bearing this in mind, we estimate the amount of sterling assets which could be employed in financing the development programme as at June 1960 as follows.—

Table LIX. Sterling Assets Available for the Financing of the Development Programme, June 1960

Assets	Rs. million
Capital Fund..	17·6
Note and Coin Security Fund	5·0
Other Funds	30·0
Total	52·6

7:55. The note and coin security fund already holds Rs. 10 million of local stock; this further investment would bring the proportion of local stock in its portfolio up to about a quarter of the currency in circulation at the period in the year with the smallest currency demand. It may be that this proportion could be increased with complete safety, but we understand that Mauritius may obtain internal self-government in the not too distant future, and the new Government of Mauritius may reasonably wish to retain a large external backing for its currency so as to maintain confidence. We would, therefore, not propose that the proportion of local backing should be increased more than is here allowed for at the present time.

7:56. In examining the other reserves under government control, we have borne in mind the ability of the Government of Mauritius to raise external capital. Mauritius, like all other colonial territories, has free access to the London loan market, and, as long as loans could be easily raised in London, the Government of Mauritius had no particular reason to dispose of sterling assets in order to finance development. Whether it was worthwhile to dispose of sterling assets or to raise loans depended on current and expected long-term rates of interest. For the past three or four years, however, it has been very difficult for colonial governments to raise loans on the London market. The demand for fixed-interest securities in general, and for colonial securities in particular, has been weak. If, then, the Government of Mauritius is to finance a large-scale development programme, it must rely on its own reserves. The estimate of Rs. 30 million in the foregoing table was arrived at after considering in turn each of the funds for which the government is responsible, and estimating how much of the funds could be invested locally with safety. We are satisfied that this figure is not unduly conservative, and the government could not with safety raise more from this source.

Internal Loans

7:57. We are concerned here only with those internal loans which represent a net addition to government resources; we are not concerned with loans which merely transfer liabilities from one government fund to another. The distinction is an important one. Of the local loans issued by government amounting to Rs. 52·7 million in June 1959, only Rs. 14½ million was held by the public, including Rs. 2·87 million held by insurance companies. The rest was held by various funds under government control. The genuine public demand for government stock is very small, and we are satisfied that it has already been fully exploited. The Ministry of Finance do not consider that more than Rs. 2½ million per annum can be raised from the public for government loans. We are not able to judge the validity of this estimate, but we have no evidence on which to dispute it. We draw attention elsewhere to the general shortage of long-term capital in Mauritius; this estimate seems *prima facie* a reasonable one. The total available from this source over the quinquennium, then, would be Rs. 12½ million.

External Finance

7:58. The only assured source of finance from abroad is aid which has been promised by the United Kingdom Government. This consists of Rs. 17·5 million of grant allocated under the Colonial Development and Welfare Acts (excluding C.D.W. funds offered as assistance after the cyclones) and Rs. 84·4 million of grant and loan for cyclone relief and reconstruction—a total of Rs. 102 million. Of

186

this total of Rs. 102 million, about Rs. 63·5 million is to be in the form of grants, and Rs. 38·4 million will be loans.

7:59. If these estimates are correct, funds in sight for the capital programme are as in the following table.—

Table LX. Sources of Funds for the Capital Development Programme

	Rs. million
Revenue surpluses	60·0
Reserves	52·6
Local loans	12·5
Assistance from the United Kingdom Government ..	102·0
Total	227·1

Thus, for a programme of some Rs. 354 millions, some Rs. 227 million is in sight, leaving an apparent gap of Rs. 127 million. We do not know how far this gap is likely to emerge in practice. First, we have proposed that the plan itself be revised so as to postpone the less urgent projects, and we cannot at this stage estimate how large the plan will be when thus revised. Secondly, there are other possible sources of finance. The most important of these are assistance under the Colonial Development and Welfare Acts, the Colonial Development Corporation, the International Bank, the International Development Association, contractor finance, and loans raised on the London market.

7:60. Assistance for colonial development is normally given by the United Kingdom government under the Colonial Development and Welfare Acts, the present Act running until March 1964. Assistance is given either by grant or by Exchequer Loans. The Government of Mauritius has already been assured some Rs. 24 million in grants and Rs. 23 million in loans under existing Acts. We do not know how far Mauritius can count on further assistance under the present Acts; this must be a matter for negotiation when the financial requirement is more clearly known. It is, however, important to note from Mauritius' point of view that, in the past, Colonial Development and Welfare Acts have normally been renewed a year before they were due to expire, and additional funds have been made available. There can be no assurance that this precedent will be followed in future, but if it is, further funds should be made available from this source in April 1963.

7:61. We understand that the Colonial Development Corporation has already been informally approached for assistance. We believe that, in addition to anything the Corporation may wish to undertake

187

in the field of private industry, special efforts should be made to interest the Corporation in the finance of middle-class housing and the proposed industrial estate. The International Bank is already being approached for aid for electricity development, although it should be emphasised that the Bank will meet only the import costs of any project, and will wish to lay down strict conditions on the financial operations of the Central Electricity Board as a condition for any loans it makes. The International Development Association (I.D.A.) has been established only recently, and it is too soon to tell the kind of project in which it might be interested. Its purpose is to provide finance for the kind of infrastructure project which, although economically beneficial in the long run, does not yield sufficient revenue in the short run to enable it to meet heavy interest and amortisation charges, and therefore requires loans on easier terms than those made available by the International Bank. It is possible that the Midlands Reservoir might be a suitable project to put to the I.D.A. for financial assistance. We understand that the Government of Mauritius is already exploring the possibility of contractor finance for some of its projects. It should, however, be realised that such finance tends to be expensive, either because interest rates are high or because the cost of the project itself may be slightly inflated. We do not know what are the possibilities that Mauritius might raise a loan on the London market in the next quinquennium, but we see no reason to rule out the possibility of her doing so. The credit of the Government of Mauritius is good, and, if its reputation remains sound, there should be some possibility of a market loan.

7:62. In all, then, although there appears to be a sizeable gap in capital finance over the next quinquennium, we do not consider that it is unbridgeable, although some part of the bridging may be the result either of a reduction in the size of the programme or its extension over a longer period of time. We should, however, emphasise that a good deal of the finance will have to be found by loans, and care will have to be taken to avoid an excessive increase in public debt charges unmatched by additional revenues. The public debt at the end of June 1959 totalled Rs. 126·4 million; of this total Rs. 73·65 million was London loan, and Rs. 52·7 million was local loan of which, as we have pointed out, Rs. 14½ million was held by the public and Rs. 38 million was held by public funds. In other words, the debt owed by government to outside bodies was some Rs. 88 million—or about eight months revenue. This is a very modest amount of debt, and we consider that it could be considerably increased with safety. We do not suggest that there is any "correct" level of public debt which a government should aim at, but the Government of Mauritius can well afford to raise further loans for worth-while projects. But, as we have already emphasised, there has been during the past few years a very strong tendency for recurrent expenditure to increase, and any addition to loan charges must be carefully controlled unless it is matched by additional revenue, either arising directly from the project or resulting from the increase in national income and taxable capacity resulting from the expenditure.

Private Finance

7:63. We have considered the organisation of public finance in relation to the need to promote a high level of investment in activities other than the sugar industry. We now examine the system of private finance from the same point of view. The principal suppliers of finance for the private sector of the economy are the commercial banks, the Mauritius Agricultural Bank, the co-operative movement, a large number of small lenders (including money-lenders, shop-keepers, and wholesalers who give credit), and members of the general public who invest in issues of shares. Of these we have not looked into the suppliers of credit for consumption—money-lenders, shop-keepers, and so on—since these did not appear relevant to our enquiry.[1] We have attempted to establish whether there is a gap in the financial structure, as a result of which worthwhile investment is being prevented or restricted. As a result of our investigations, we are convinced that there is such a gap, and we have therefore considered the most suitable method by which it might be bridged.

The Commercial Banks

7:64. There are three commercial banks operating in Mauritius; two of these are branches of banks with headquarters elsewhere, while the third is an old-established local bank which has close affiliations with one of the major United Kingdom banks. The principal functions of the banks are to provide finance for the sugar crop and to finance the import trade. The importance of the sugar crop in the work of the banks can be seen from Figure III below, which shows the seasonal variations in bank deposits, advances and cash held during the past four years.

7:65. As Figure III shows, deposits are normally at their minimum in July, before the beginning of the sugar harvest. Then they rise steeply to reach a peak about the beginning of the year, and then fall again until the beginning of the next sugar crop. Not only are the seasonal fluctuations in deposits determined by the sugar crop, but the level of the peaks and troughs in deposits in particular years

---

[1] For a description of the system of consumers' credit see Dr. Burton Benedict's "Cash and Credit in Mauritius", *South African Journal of Economics*, volume 26, number 3, September 1958, pp. 213–221.

FIGURE III

Commercial Banks : Deposits, Advances and Overseas Balances,
1956—1959

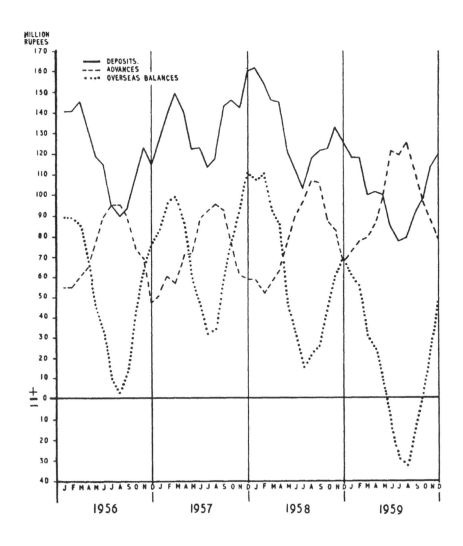

appears to reflect the level of incomes from sugar in the previous year. Thus the high level of both peak and trough in the second half of 1957 followed on the record output of sugar in 1956, combined with the temporary freeing of the world sugar market in 1957. The decline in both peaks and troughs since then reflects the smaller sugar crops of 1957 and 1958.

7:66. Similarly advances reach a peak at the beginning of the sugar crop and fall to a minimum at about the end of the year. Whereas there has been some downward movement in the level of deposits since 1956, the level of advances has been rising. It is, however, not possible to say whether this is related to the fall in sugar output or is part of a long-term trend. The overseas balances of the banks show similar seasonal variations, reaching their minimum at the beginning of the crop and their maximum around the end of the year. These balances have fallen since 1957, and for about four months in 1959 the balances were negative—that is, the banks had borrowed abroad.

7:67. It is reasonable to assume that the difference between the maximum and the minimum in the level of advances during a year is roughly equivalent to the amount of funds engaged in financing the sugar crop. Between 1956 and 1959, this difference averaged Rs. 45 million—some 37% of the average level of deposits. This, however, is by no means all of the amount of bank funds engaged in financing the sugar industry. Loans have also been made for capital expenditure by the industry. These are usually in the form of overdrafts for fairly short periods, but we have been informed of loans which have been made to the industry for periods up to ten years. These, however, are exceptional.

7:68. The other principal seasonal element in the banks' finances is provided by the tea industry. Since the main part of the tea crop is plucked in the first quarter of the year, demands for crop finance by the tea industry do not normally conflict with the seasonal demands of the sugar industry. As Figure III shows, the impact of the tea industry on the pattern of deposits and advances is very small in relation to that of the sugar industry.

7:69. Apart from the sugar and tea industries, the greater part of the banks' advances are to trade and industry. A typical form of advance is the three-month renewable loan. Thus the banks provide the working capital for the import trade as well as for a number of small manufacturing industries. They do not normally provide long-term capital, although they have informed us that they would lend long-term against adequate security such as mortgages. The banks will not normally subscribe the initial capital required for starting an industrial enterprise. This partly reflects their general policy; being modelled on, and in some part attached to, the English banking system, they see their role as that of providing working capital rather than fixed capital. There is also the difficulty of security. The banks claim that adequate security for long-term loans is difficult to obtain. We are informed that, under Mauritian law, it is not possible to obtain a lien on the assets of a company; mortgages may be obtained only on immovable property—that is, on buildings and land. There is no evidence that the banks are restrained from granting long-term credit either by a lack of funds or by a desire to maintain a particular degree of liquidity.

7:70. The commercial banks are, however, indirectly providers of long-term capital. The Mauritius Commercial Bank has established a Finance Corporation with a capital of Rs. 5 million, Rs. 3 million of which is subscribed by themselves and Rs. 2 million by the British Bank with which they have affiliations. The Mauritius manager of Barclay's (D.C. & O.) is also the local agent for Barclay's Overseas Development Corporation. These two bodies make loans for longer periods than the commercial banks; a period of five years was stated to be fairly typical. We understand that loans have been made for constructional ventures, housing, and service and other industry.

7:71. The commercial banks, both directly and through these special finance or development corporations, are the most important source of credit in Mauritius. In spite of the limitations which they apply in their making of loans, we have the impression that they do in practice provide a fair amount of medium-term credit. Advances are frequently renewed for quite considerable periods. Moreover, the demand for security is not always rigidly adhered to. In a small community like Mauritius, where a good banker may be expected to be able to make a fair estimate of the credit-worthiness of his clients, the most important type of security may well be the banker's knowledge of the trading community. We have been informed of cases where the demand for security has been waived, or where the security has consisted in the personal guarantee of some other customer of the bank. But, in spite of these relaxations, we consider (and the commercial banks would agree) that there is a large demand for medium- and long-term capital which is not met by the banks. Either the potential borrower has insufficient security or the banks are unwilling to commit funds for more than a limited period ahead. There is in practice considerable difference between a three-month renewable loan which is regularly renewed and a loan made for a longer period such as five years in the first instance. Loans of the first kind cannot normally be used for medium- or long-term investment, since there is no guarantee that the loan will be renewed at the end of any given period.

The Co-operative Movement

7:72. The principal source of credit to small planters is the Co-operative Movement. There were 144 unlimited liability Credit Societies in 1958, which operated on credit advanced by the Co-operative Central Bank whose funds are supplied by one of the Commercial banks. About 95 % of the societies' advances are for crop finance—almost entirely for cane cultivation. Small amounts are also advanced for capital development, but the societies do not regard this as one of their principal functions. Although we consider that the societies perform a valuable function, and that their work could usefully be extended—especially in financing a wider range of crops—we do not believe that they can fill the gap in long-term finance to any substantial extent.

The Local Share Market

7:73. Thus there is a gap in the machinery for the supply of medium- and long-term capital. This gap is partly filled in two principal ways; first, by the issue of shares, and second, through the Agricultural Bank. The issue of shares in Mauritius is an exceptional process. There is a local share market—the Bourse—but transactions on it are few and there is not a ready market in locally issued shares. But this narrowness of the local market may not be the only reason why share issues are rare. As we have emphasised earlier, one of the features of Mauritius which most strikes an outsider is the compartmentalism of its economic and social life. Association between the various racial groups is at a minimum. The idea of an issue to the general public of shares in a concern may in such a situation meet with resistances of two kinds. The proprietors of the concern may be unwilling to face the danger that control might eventually fall into the hands of members of a different racial group; the subscribing public may be unwilling to finance a concern belonging to a different racial group from their own. We met industrialists who were in need of capital for development, but who were unwilling to convert their concerns into public companies and appeal to the public for capital in case this led to control being gained by some other racial group.

7:74. The principal exception to this confirms our general view. Early in 1960 the most important sugar company in Mauritius raised Rs. 7 million through a public issue of non-voting shares. The published offer of shares included neither a prospectus nor a balance sheet of the company.[1] And yet the offer raised more than twice as

[1] We have not examined the question of the desirability of amending a system of company law which permits share issues to be made in such conditions, but if public share issues become more common, it may be necessary to consider legislation to protect the investing public.

193

much as was asked for. There appear to be several reasons for the success of the issue. First, the company itself is known to be very efficient and progressive; in other words, the balance sheet and prospectus which would be needed in a larger community were here replaced by public knowledge of the company and of those in control of it. Secondly, this company is the only one in which members of different racial groups are associated, and its appeal was thus country-wide rather than to members of one community. We have been informed by several people that it would be impossible for any other company to issue shares in Mauritius on anything like the same scale. We consider, however, that, even after allowances are made for the special personal circumstances in the recent issue, it would be possible for other companies to go to the market if they were willing to abandon their racial exclusiveness and adopt a Mauritian, rather than a communal attitude. In saying this, we are not criticising the attitude of any particular community; our evidence suggests that these attitudes are shared by all the communities in Mauritius.

7:75. Although, however, we consider that a lessening of racial exclusiveness in Mauritius would do much to foster a capital market, no amount of exhortation will change attitudes which are deeply embedded in the social structure of the island. Although we believe that these attitudes will change under the impact of economic advance, we are forced to take them into account in considering the problem of the provision of capital for development in the private sector. In other words, we have assumed that the mutual exclusiveness of the different communities in Mauritius will not be substantially lessened in the next few years, and that the capital market will continue to be restricted in its scope and effectiveness by these attitudes. But although we are forced to accept the situation, we must point to the disadvantages arising from it. Apart from the burden it throws on government to meet the capital gap, it is also an important factor in keeping the structure of the Mauritian economy unchanged —and in particular, in perpetuating the dominance of the sugar industry. As we have shown elsewhere, the greater part of investment in the sugar industry has been made by the ploughing back of profits, and, in default of a wide capital market, it has been inevitable that this should be so. Thus the lack of a Mauritian, as opposed to a Franco-Mauritian, or Indo-Mauritian, or Sino-Mauritian, capital market, means that the industries which are most likely to expand are those which have resources of their own for investment. Therefore successful industries can grow still further, but new industries are seriously handicapped.

The Agricultural Bank

7:76. In face of the inadequacy of the local capital market, government has been compelled to meet the need to some extent. It has done so through the Agricultural Bank. The Bank, which was established before the war, at present operates under the Agricultural Bank Ordinance of 1950, as subsequently amended. The principal part of the Bank's funds are provided by government, mainly in the form of debentures. The Bank also accepts fixed deposits and savings deposits, and is empowered to obtain overdrafts from the local banks and to borrow money on long-term loans. The upper limit for debentures which the Agricultural Bank might issue was fixed at Rs. 17 million in 1954. The following table shows the capital funds of the Bank at the end of 1958.—

Table LXI. Agricultural Bank: Capital Funds

	Rs. million
Government loans	9·6
Government bills	1·0
Debentures	17·0
Subscription debentures	0·3
Fixed deposits	2·1
Savings deposits	2·0
Long term loans	3·0
Short term bills	2·5
Total	37·5

The bank also had reserves, sinking funds and appropriations totalling Rs. 4·2 million.

7:77. The purposes for which the Bank may lend money are stated in Section 62 of the 1950 Ordinance, as subsequently amended. They are as follows:—

(*a*) The purchase of agricultural land, its development and improvement and the incurring of capital expenditure necessary for the preparation of its product for the market.

(*b*) The purchase, construction, or repair of any building, factory, mill, machinery or equipment used or to be used in connection with any agricultural undertaking.

(*c*) The manufacture or preparation of any agricultural or industrial product or commodity for sale in the market.

(*d*) The purchase of any building or the land appurtenant thereto or of any land suitable for building purposes.

(*e*) The erection of a building on any land.

(*f*) The repair or improvement, or both the repair and improvement, of any building . . .

(*g*) The purchase . . . of shares or interests in any company or partnership carrying on any business which is mainly connected with agriculture, industry or housing . . . provided that the purchaser has or obtains as a result of such a purchase a controlling interest in the company or partnership whose shares are purchased.

(*h*) Any purpose incidental . . . to any of the above purposes, including the payment of any premium in respect of the policy of an assurance contracted under a scheme approved by the Bank for the purpose of furnishing to the Bank additional security for the repayment of a loan . . .

7:78. Although the Bank was originally established for the purpose of financing agriculture, its activities in providing housing finance have become of major importance in recent years. Loans to industry however, have been comparatively small. Applications received and loans made since 1951 are shown in the following table.—

Table LXII. Agricultural Bank Loans, 1951-1958

Rs. million

Year	Agriculture		Housing		Industry		Total	
	Applications received	Loans paid	Applications received	Loans paid	Applications received	Loans paid	Applications received	Loans paid
1951	6·74	2·74	11·45	1·53	0·31	0·2	18·51	4·47
1952	2·58	4·54	5·66	2·19	0·24	0·06	8·48	6·79
1953	0·07	4·42	0·71	1·91	—	0·02	0·79	6·35
1954	5·80	1·43	5·48	1·66	0·82	—	12·10	3·09
1955	8·24	1·27	4·12	1·54	0·22	—	12·58	2·82
1956	2·77	1·33	3·81	1·39	0·23	—	6·82	2·72
1957	2·36	1·29	3·42	1·20	—	0·3	5·78	2·79
1958	4·37	1·98	1·62	1·29	0·63	0·34	6·61	3·61
Total	32·95	19·0	36·27	12·71	2·44	0·92	71·66	32·63

7:79. Several points should be noted in this table. First the level of applications has varied sharply from year to year. These variations normally result not from changes in the demand for loans, but from changes in the ability of the Bank to make loans. In May 1952 for example the Bank was so heavily committed for loans that it was decided not to accept further applications other than for small loans —a situation which remained unchanged till November 1953. When applications were resumed, they were limited to Rs. 4,990 for the purchase of buildings, Rs. 20,000 for the construction of new residential buildings, or Rs. 1,000 per arpent for the purchase of development of agricultural land. In 1958 a shortage of funds compelled the Bank to reduce its maximum for housing loans from Rs. 20,000 to Rs. 15,000. We understand that the Bank at present does not have any remaining capital funds available for lending, apart from some Rs. 2½ million per annum from the repayment of past loans.

7:80. Second, although the level of applications has been reduced as a result of the knowledge that the Bank was not able to make loans other than on a limited scale, less than half of all applications over this period were met. Although the applications received necessarily include some which could not be justified, there seems to be no doubt that if the Bank had more funds, it would make more loans. At the end of 1958, about Rs. 7½ million of applications were carried forward—three times the annual amount of loan capital at present available.

7:81. Third, although agricultural loans predominate in the business of the Bank, housing loans are also substantial and in some years have been larger in total than agricultural loans. Loans to industry have, by comparison been very small, amounting in all to less than 3 % of all loans issued over this period.

7:82. We understand that a large part of the agricultural loans have gone to the sugar industry, for such purposes as the purchase price of land and the capital expenditure required to put it under cane. Rates of interest charged have been between 5 % and 6 % for large estates and 5½ % and 6½ % for small estates. The development of the tea industry has also been largely financed by the Bank, which also provided loans for the construction of tea factories. The housing loans have been predominantly for middle-class borrowers. Industrial loans have been mainly on a small scale, and have been limited by the need for adequate security. Loans have been made to a variety of industries including wire, matches, dry cleaning, and salt.

7:83. We have seen the report on the Agricultural Bank by Mr. W. J. Jackson of the Bank of England, and are in general agreement with his criticisms of the Bank's operations—in particular with his emphasis on the need to make proper allowance for the repayment of capital. We consider, however, that the policies of the Bank have been open to wide objections, from the point of view of the Mauritian economy as a whole. As we have already stressed, there is a shortage of long-term capital in Mauritius, and we consider that the Agricultural Bank has an important part to play in meeting this need. As we have seen, the demand for loans has been almost continuously greater than the ability of the Bank to meet it. We have

197

seen no evidence that the Bank has ever worked out any system of priorities in allocating its scarce funds, or has adopted any other rational means of applying its resources to the best effect. As far as we can judge, applications for loans have been considered on purely commercial principles—that is, on whether it seemed probable that the interest charges could be met and capital could be repaid. Although we consider that this is a necessary criterion in the granting of loans, we do not believe that it is a sufficient one for an organisation working primarily with public funds in the circumstances of Mauritius. In saying this we do not wish to attach any blame to those who have been charged with the management of the Bank. The Bank is a body corporate whose functions are prescribed by various ordinances, and nowhere in these ordinances is there any guidance on the problem of allocating scarce funds to the best advantage from the point of view of the Mauritian economy as a whole. It is for government, not the Bank, to consider the wider implications of the Bank's activities and to lay down any necessary principles.

7:84. The most obvious feature of the Bank's activities is the predominance of the sugar industry among its borrowers. Of some Rs. 26 million in agricultural loan balances outstanding in 1958, about Rs. 25 million was owed by the sugar industry. In other words, the principal function of the Agricultural Bank has been to provide government capital for the sugar industry. Even if housing and industrial loans are taken into account, the sugar industry accounted for over two thirds of outstanding loan balances—and probably of loans made. We believe that this is a mistaken use for public funds, for two reasons. First, the sugar industry can raise capital in other ways. The main attraction of Agricultural Bank loans is that they are cheaper than funds from other sources, but we see no reason why the sugar industry should be given loans at favourable rates of interest. The industry is a highly profitable one, and could, if it so desired, raise capital through public share issues or other means. It can offer the kind of security which could secure loans from many other sources. We consider that government funds should be used only where a real need can be established—that is, where capital cannot be raised in other ways. Secondly, as we have emphasised elsewhere, it is of the greatest importance for Mauritius to correct the current bias in the direction of investing in sugar. Several of our other recommendations, especially in the tax field, are designed to correct this bias, and it seems wrong that public funds should be employed in such a way as to intensify it.

7:85. We would not propose that the Agricultural Bank should be compelled to abandon altogether its policy of making loans to the sugar industry. It is of great importance that sugar should be grown efficiently, and we have shown that there is a wide spread between the most efficient and the least efficient members of the industry. But we recommend that the Agricultural Bank Ordinance be amended to make it clear that the Bank should act only as a lender of last resort—that is, where it is impossible for the borrower to obtain capital elsewhere on reasonable terms—the word "reasonable" being interpreted in such a way as to include public share issues, bank loans or overseas sources of capital. The Bank should be required to interpret this requirement as strictly as possible. We also believe that there is no justification for lending money to the sugar industry at favourable rates of interest; rates of interest should be slightly higher than rates for equivalent loans from other sources, so that all industry, and in particular the sugar industry, is encouraged to make full use of other finance before coming to the Agricultural Bank.

7:86. Just as we consider that the Agricultural Bank should lend less to the sugar industry, so we believe that it should lend more to promote other agricultural development. For example, the capital which will be required by the proposed agricultural marketing organisation (see paragraphs 5:144/145) could be provided through the Agricultural Bank. Similarly the Bank could help in other agricultural finance such as in the marketing of milk or the provision of proper cattle sheds. Loans of this kind are more difficult to make and administer than are loans to the sugar industry, but they would be of far more relevance to the island's needs.

7:87. We consider that the work which the Bank is doing in the field of housing is of great importance. The need for finance of this kind is especially urgent in view of the 1960 cyclones—we understand that over Rs. 30 million will probably be required in loans from the Bank to finance repairs and reconstructions of middle-class housing. We understand that a separate organisation is being established to provide mass housing and this will not come within the scope of the Agricultural Bank. We support the policy of the Bank in enforcing the condition that all houses financed from these loans should be built under the supervision of the Bank and should be fully covered by cyclone and other insurance.

7:88. Given the establishment of the Industrial Development Board which we propose above (paragraphs 6:98/99), there should be an increased demand for loans for worth-while industrial projects. As we stated there, we do not consider that the Industrial Development Board should act as a bank, since Mauritius is too small and the supply of qualified people too limited to make it worth-while to have two development banks. We would suggest that industrial loans continue to be made through the Agricultural Bank, but that the

Bank should rely on the advice of the Industrial Development Board on the making of individual loans and on the terms on which such loans should be made. We recommend that, when an application is received by the Bank for an industrial loan, it should be referred to the Industrial Development Board for advice. Similarly, if the Board wishes to promote an industrial project, it should approach the Bank for finance. In these circumstances the Bank should be willing to view the project sympathetically and to make any necessary loan, on condition that the scheme meets the technical requirements of the Bank. Where a scheme has the backing of the Industrial Development Board, the Bank should also be prepared to waive its requirements on security for the loan; we assume that the Board would not give its support unless the project had good chances for success and the Board was prepared to provide continuing advice and assistance to the enterprise. In these circumstances, the need for a formal security such as a mortgage should become less important.

7:89. Although we suggest that the Bank should reduce the amount of its loans to the sugar industry, the additional demands for capital in other agriculture, housing and industry should far outweigh any savings which the Bank made on sugar. We believe that the Bank will require a considerable addition to its capital resources —the greater part of which will necessarily have to be provided by government. We recommend that government should immediately increase the borrowing powers of the Bank by Rs. 50 million, and should be prepared to meet the greater part of this sum itself. Attempts should also be made to attract outside capital. It may, for example, be possible to associate the Colonial Development Corporation with the housing side of the Bank's activities. If this were done, it would probably be necessary to reorganise the Bank's financial structure; the C.D.C. would certainly not invest in the Agricultural Bank with its present financial structure. But it might be possible to establish a separate housing corporation, half of whose capital was provided by the Agricultural Bank and the other half by some organisation, such as the C.D.C. This could be under the same day-to-day management as the Agricultural Bank, although the other suppliers of capital would doubtless desire some say in its running. Similarly, it may be possible to attract outside capital into industrial finance, although this may most suitably be done for individual projects. The Industrial Development Board should attempt wherever possible to obtain Mauritian or other capital for any project where finance is being supplied by the Agricultural Bank.

7:90. Suggestions have been made for changing the name of the Mauritius Agricultural Bank, so as to bring it more into line with its actual functions. We have, however, been told that Mauritius is a conservative place, and that people would lose confidence in the Bank if it changed its name. Consideration might, however, be given to changing the name sufficiently to indicate its wider functions, but not so much as to suggest a complete break with the past. Some such name as The Mauritius Agricultural and Development Bank might be suitable. Eventually, we would consider that it might be simply called "The Mauritius Development Bank", but some years may elapse before Mauritius is ready to accept this change.

7:91. We consider that the Agricultural Bank has a central role to play in the economic development of the island. To do this, it requires progressive management, further finance, a new lending policy on the lines we have suggested, and close co-operation with the Industrial Development Board. Without these, the capital gap will remain unfilled, and Mauritius will be unable to face the challenge of finding productive employment for its growing population.

CHAPTER 8

Education

8:1. We have so far discussed the problems of the Mauritius economy in almost solely economic terms, and we have recommended a number of measures both direct and indirect, designed to overcome them. In so doing, however, we have frequently touched upon a failing in the social services of Mauritius, which we regard as one of the gravest disabilities from which the country is suffering—namely the almost total lack of facilities for technical education, and indeed the bias of the educational system in the opposite direction. In our view this is central to the Mauritian problem and we are convinced that if the schools are to help the process of material development— as they should—rather than to hinder it—as in so many cases they do at present—the government will have to take firm and often unpopular decisions in this vital sphere. We therefore discuss the issue at some length. We begin with a sketch of the present system or lack of system, and all that that implies, and then go on to consider in detail the situation and requirements in the spheres of primary and secondary education, teacher training, and technical instruction.

8:2. The primary school system at present consists of 189 schools, 113 of them "government" schools, and the remaining 76 "aided" schools, owned and administered by four educational "Authorities". These "Authorities" are central boards of management, responsible for the administration of the schools belonging to their respective denominations or lay groups, Roman Catholics, Church of England, Hindu, and Muslim. There are in addition no less than 370 unaided schools, private fee-charging schools attended by nearly 19,000 pupils who are either unable or unwilling to find places in the government or aided schools, where education is free. The total enrolment in the government schools is 60,500 and in the aided schools 47,000, the ratio of boys to girls among the whole 107,000 being six to five. The minimum age for admission is five, and the normal leaving age is 12 plus. The course is one of six "standards", promotion being automatic at the end of each year of school life. The last year's work may be and often is repeated by pupils who fail at their first attempt to obtain the primary school leaving certificate which is awarded on the results of an examination normally taken

202

at 11 plus and serves as a qualifying test for admission to the Junior Scholarship examination, on the results of which are awarded a limited number of scholarships to the government or aided secondary schools.

8:3. Secondary education is almost entirely academic in character and is provided for 4,000 pupils in three government and eight aided schools, and for 14,700 pupils in 58 private schools. All pupils pay fees, except those who hold the Junior Scholarships mentioned above, who receive not only free tuition and books but a small allowance in cash as well. A small beginning has been made with a less academic type of post-primary schooling in the small "Central" schools, one for boys with 84 pupils and one for girls with 29 pupils. Education in these schools is free, but little enthusiasm is felt for them by parents or pupils.

8:4. The glittering prizes on which the ambition of most secondary school pupils is fixed are the English Scholarships, six in number, four for boys and two for girls, which are competed for in a special examination by students who have already passed the Higher School Certificate examination. They are extremely valuable and provide more than adequately for the needs of the holders during their studies at any British university. The students' choice of course is quite unfettered, and the great majority, we were told, enrol as students of medicine or of law. So great is the competition for these scholarships that countless children are intensively "crammed" from quite an early age, their parents paying heavily for private coaching which they believe is essential to reinforce normal school teaching.

8:5. Higher education is not available in Mauritius except at the College of Agriculture, but the strength of the island's academic tradition is shown by the relatively large number of Mauritian students who enter universities and colleges in the United Kingdom.

8:6. There has hitherto been very little in the way of practical training at any level. Handicraft centres have been established to serve the needs of 94 primary schools; in them elementary woodwork and metalwork are taught to boys in the top classes. Apprenticeship training has been available for a small number of boys in the railway workshops as mechanical engineers and in the Central Electricity Board's workshops as electrical engineers, but of technical education as such there was none until the Technical Institute was opened in January, 1959 in very inadequate and temporary premises. The total full-time enrolment in the Institute is at present 50, and this small figure is unlikely to increase until the government presses on vigorously with the plan to provide satisfactory premises, staff, and equipment.

8:7. The total recurrent expenditure of the Education Department was estimated at Rs. 20,795,000 (£1,559,600) for the financial year 1959-60. This figure, which is considerably higher than the corresponding figure for any other department of the government and represents about 15% of all government expenditure, is an increase of more than 50% on the figure for 1955-56 and shows clearly the financial effect of recent policy decisions.

8:8. The situation today presents a number of striking contrasts. In an island which has been subject to European influences for well over 250 years, and which also shares by inheritance the great cultures of the Indian sub-continent, there is on the one hand a desire for education which is obsessional in its strength, and on the other startling ignorance of modern ideas about education and of its true purpose. A country whose only resources are its land and its people devotes most of its educational effort to persuading children, by implication if not explicitly, that of all forms of human activity the least meritorious and the least dignified is manual work, and that of manual work the lowest form is cultivation of the land. As we have seen, this attitude to some extent stems from the conditions under which manual workers are employed (paragraphs 4:9 and 4:10 ff). Further it is by no means confined to Mauritius, and may be expected to exist in greater or less degree in any country where field work was once performed by slaves or by the indentured labourers who replaced the slaves. However, there must be few countries in the entire world where the prospect of creating large numbers of new "white-collar and clean-hands" jobs is more remote than it is in Mauritius, and the traditional attitude to labour is therefore more dangerous and more of a handicap to all attempts to develop or diversify employment than it is elsewhere.

8:9. To overcome some of the deep-rooted prejudices which now exist and to replace obsolete and anti-social attitudes by more enlightened ideas is a task which will tax to the uttermost the resources of all concerned with education, professional and layman, administrator and politician alike, Of all branches of governmental activity, perhaps education is the one in which there is most need for a lively and enlightened public relations service. By this we mean something more than the occasional article in the press and talk over the wireless which often pass for educational publicity; we mean an unremitting all-out effort to gain the understanding and support of every teacher and every parent in Mauritius for a sound and realistic educational policy, in the framing of which no vested interests, no radial or sectional affiliation, must be allowed to obscure the country's real needs. Other countries, with much less acute problems to solve than Mauritius, have succeeded in getting education withdrawn from the arena of political conflict and in winning national rather than party support for a policy in which all believe and which is kept constantly in the mind of the entire population. Unless Mauritius can successfully emulate them, her hopes of evolving a decently planned educational system from the jungle of cut-throat academic competition which passes for education today are slender indeed.

8:10. There are various legitimate and well-tried tricks of the propagandist's trade which can be used to good effect in securing widespread understanding and support for a wise national educational policy, once the policy has been agreed upon. "Education Weeks", "Open Days", conferences at village, district, and national level are all useful instruments in the kind of educational campaign which we believe should be waged in Mauritius. But in present conditions there is a considerable risk that such a campaign might easily degenerate into a series of "stunts", spectacular, but useless because the essential agreement and unity of purpose which should give them meaning are lacking. The wounds inflicted upon education in Mauritius by recent quarrels and disagreements in the service are very grave, but they are no graver than is the less obvious but more lasting damage caused by the prejudices and animosities arising from the racial and political loyalties which mock the idea of community and nationhood in Mauritius. We should be less than honest if we did not record our deep disquiet at the extent to which we have ourselves seen professional judgement warped and sound administration undermined by unworthy devotion to the interests, real or supposed, of this or that group.

8:11. We therefore regard it as important to build up in all possible ways a sense of unity among the different elements in the education service and to reduce to the minimum the separatist influences which at present exist. One such is the artificial distinction now drawn in the primary school system between those teachers who are employed in "government" schools and those employed in "Authority" schools. Though we appreciate the advantages which seem to follow for the members of what are in effect two "company unions", we are strongly of the opinion that the real disadvantage for Mauritius as a whole is much greater. What the island needs is a single professional association with a strong professional conscience and sense of purpose, rather than two bodies each inevitably as much occupied with bargaining for its own members' rights as with the broader issues which should be the concern of both. We have no hesitation in saying that there should be a single primary school teaching service, with common conditions, salaries, pensions, etc. In such a service, all the teachers would be employed by the government, some to teach in government schools, others "seconded" or lent to the Authorities to teach in their schools, and all would enjoy equal chances of promotion.

8:12. It has been suggested that the Education Authorities may view this proposal as a first step towards enabling the government to destroy the influence of the churches in education, but we find it difficult to believe that any responsible group could so grossly misinterpret the intention either of the mission in recommending or of the government in accepting, if they do accept, the proposed change. Admittedly there will at first be considerable calls on the tact and good sense of the government, the Authorities, and the teachers themselves, but we are confident that given the will to co-operate the new system could work without friction and to the great benefit of education as a whole.

8:13. In the following sections, it will be found that we have little that is new to say about the various stages of education in Mauritius. For that we offer no apology. Mauritius has for many years not lacked advice, but only the will to accept it and act on it.

PRIMARY EDUCATION

The Pressure on Places

8:14. At present following a rapid increase in the last four years there are something like 80% of the children of primary school age enrolled in the primary schools of the island. The table below shows just how rapid the rise has been.

Table LXIII. Increase in Number of Primary School Pupils,
1955 to 1959

	1955–56	1956–57	1957–58	1958–59	1959–60	Percentage increase 1955–59
In all schools ..	85,446	89,434	102,291	115,629	126,173	48
In government and aided schools ..	73,510	74,288	89,845	100,551	107,487	46
In private schools ..	11,936	15,146	12,446	15,078	18,686	60
Cost to government in rupees	9,435,285	9,939,345	10,833,595	14,009,265	15,139,630	57

As is said in paragraph 104 of "The Plan for Mauritius", this is "a record which by any standard in the world is a good one". In paragraph 105, the plan goes on to say: "On the principle that a literate and intelligent population is the best guarantee of future economic wisdom, the basic aim of the educational programme is to ensure primary education for every child". In enunciating this basic aim, the assumption is made that primary education will produce a literate and intelligent population. There is no reason to doubt the intelligence of the future citizens of Mauritius, but there is unfortunately very good reason for doubting whether the present primary school system will produce literacy. In fact it is not too much to say that the system at present operating is more likely to produce illiteracy.

8:15. The general picture of education today affords a good illustration of the ill consequences which can so easily follow undue or too early preoccupation with primary schooling for all as opposed to a more evenly balanced programme of educational development at all levels. When Mauritius decided a few years ago to concentrate a very high proportion of all the resources which could be made available for education on the expansion of the primary school system, she was in fact deciding, because her resources were never adequate to meet every need, that she would have quantity even if she could not have quality. The decision not to refuse admission to a primary school to any youngster applying for it sounds praiseworthy indeed, and nobody could possibly quarrel with the motives for making the decision. Unfortunately, however, the number of children in Mauritius, always large enough in all conscience, has in recent years been increasing at such a rapid rate that the country never really had a chance to provide the buildings, equipment, and in particular the teachers necessary if universal primary schooling was to be worth-while.

8:16. In the opening section of the Education Department's Annual Report for the year 1958, the following sentences occur: "A record total of 24,558 children entered the government and aided primary schools in January, 1958. The immediate price paid for this implementation of the new policy that no child seeking admission should be refused entry was that 360 (in 1959, 394) classes went on 'double shift'. This means that the children in those classes have had half a day's schooling, and that 190 teachers have had to work with one batch of children in the mornings and another batch in the afternoons. A further 247 (in 1959, 254) classes were on single shift. *The problems created by these massive annual intakes can be solved if enough new schools can be built, enough new teachers trained in time, and if the country can afford the capital and recurrent cost. Three big 'ifs!'* " (The italics are ours, as are the figures in the brackets.)

8:17. It needs no great wisdom in 1960 to see that the "ifs" were indeed great, too great in fact for Mauritius to meet them. In the matter of accommodation, the vigour and enterprise put into the building of additional schools and classrooms have been remarkable and it represents no small achievement that early this year the government should feel able to say that they are within measurable distance of being able to insist upon compulsory primary schooling for all children. Yet even before two disastrous cyclones, congestion was still acute and it was estimated that a further 268 classrooms were still needed to deal with children already in attendance.

8:18. In order to get enough teachers to keep the size of classes within anything like reasonable limits (and Mauritius had to accept 50 as a "reasonable" size of a class), it was necessary to reduce the training-college course from two years to one, to give full responsibility for a class to many a young man and woman who really were only half trained, and to push many others through "short courses" which could only aim at standards far below those which had previously been regarded as acceptable.

8:19. When one bears in mind that the estimated number of children of primary school age (five plus to 12 plus) was 134,000 in 1958, is now 146,000, and will be 172,000 in 1965, the magnitude of the commitment which Mauritius accepted, too readily it now seems, is clearly seen. As the problems with which a young Mauritian teacher has to cope are in many respects more difficult than those which face his colleagues in many more advanced countries, it is small wonder that during the past few years many of the new entrants to the profession have been quite unable to do justice to their own good intentions and to the hopes of their pupils.

8:20. It is true that the severest pressure on the schools came in 1958 and that the resulting overall drop in quality of primary schooling has already been checked. It may even be claimed by the super-optimist that Mauritius can and should afford the new buildings and the additional salaries and that the quality of teacher training can be expected to recover as quickly as it fell. This is a view which we can merely recognise without being able to share it.

THE LANGUAGE PROBLEM

8:21. We are, however, much more worried by one other factor which makes the teacher's task in a Mauritian primary school extremely difficult and is in great measure responsible for much of the undoubted inefficiency in the primary school system, and which is much more intractable than pressure of numbers, congestion and so on, since it springs from the complicated social and racial pattern of Mauritian life. We do not believe that we exaggerate when we say that the greatest handicap to successful education in Mauritius is that imposed by the multiplicity of languages in use.

8:22. Everybody or practically everybody in the island can speak (though many would think it undignified to do so) Creole, a French-based "patois" which can do no more than serve as a rough-and-ready means of oral communication. Mauritius is a British colony—it has therefore long been agreed that English is and must remain the official language and as such should be learnt by all children. Mauritius has had a background of French culture—it is therefore claimed that the French language should continue to be taught to all Mauritian children in order that they may not be cut off from their cultural heritage. Most children in Mauritius today are of Indian extraction—it therefore seems reasonable that they should be taught an oriental language, be it Hindi, Urdu or any other, because only by learning the language will they be able to retain the cultural background of their people. These arguments seem at first sight reasonable enough. When, however, they are applied to the primary schools of Mauritius and result in little children of seven and eight years of age attempting to learn three languages at the hands of teachers who are themselves masters of none of the three, the absurdity of the present system is clearly seen. Children leave the primary schools in large numbers without having acquired anything worth calling literacy in any one language, though they have spent an intolerable amount of time dabbling in all three.

8:23. This problem has been commented on often enough in the past, and all we can do at this stage is to repeat advice which may be unpalatable for various political or social reasons but will have to be accepted sooner or later by Mauritius, if she wishes to get anything like value for the large sum of money which she is at present spending to little or no purpose on her primary schools. The only workable solution to this language problem is to accept fully the implications of the decision (which nobody at this stage would wish to argue against) that English should be learnt by all children in the primary schools, because it is the official language of the country and because it is and must remain the medium of instruction in all post-primary establishments. Clearly in the first years of the primary school, the medium of instruction should be whatever is the appropriate vernacular, whether that be Creole with its close affinity to French or the hybridised forms of various oriental languages which are currently in use. As soon as possible, English should become the medium of instruction. This may be after three years or four years or in the case of some children even five years, but there is nothing whatsoever to be said in favour of the present arrangement whereby at one stage French replaces the vernacular as the medium of instruction, only to be replaced itself by English at a later stage.

8:24. If these two propositions are accepted, it would follow that the formal teaching of any language but English should disappear from the primary school. Those parents who were genuinely anxious for religious, cultural, or social reasons to have their children learn French or an oriental language should be responsible for making private arrangements for the instruction of their children out of school hours, though there would be considerable justification for the payment of a government subsidy to reputable establishments where such instruction was given.

8:25. When the question of language teaching in primary schools is discussed in Mauritius, strong feelings are inevitably aroused, since the points in question are generally viewed not as educational issues but as factors affecting either the status or the prospects of some group or other. The Indian elements in Mauritius are well aware that since French but not Hindi is examined, their children are handicapped at the stage of passing on from the primary to the secondary school, and the Franco-Mauritian population must be equally well aware that its children are specially favoured by present arrangements. It would, therefore, seem equitable as well as educationally desirable to omit French from the subjects offered in the Junior Scholarships Examinations. If that examination is restricted, as it should be, to English, arithmetic and geography or general knowledge, with or without a paper incorporating intelligence tests, all children would have a fair chance, and Mauritius being as examination-conscious as she is, the artificially-fostered demands for other languages than English would probably disappear overnight.

8:26. We have no wish to minimise the difficulty of the problem nor the consequential difficulties which may well follow acceptance of our recommendation. We realise in fact that opinion in Mauritius has for twenty years been well aware of the problem and has only been deterred from taking a difficult decision by dislike of the consequences. That dislike is quite naturally strongest among French-speaking Mauritians, who see in a threat to the French language a weakening not only of their own dominant position in Mauritius but of the whole influence of the French thought, ideas, and culture to which they are themselves so deeply attached. It must be remembered too that on purely educational grounds, there are very strong arguments in favour of giving to French the dominant position in the primary schools which we suggest should be given to English. "Creole" is so like the French language of which it is a debased form that mastery of the parent tongue comes fairly easily to the Creole-speaking child. The learning of French is therefore much easier than is the learning of English, and to that extent French would probably be a more suitable vehicle for instruction at any stage in Mauritian schools. French again is so much the normal language of Mauritians that many children who learn English in school may well hear and read little of it outside school, and will therefore be learning something which must remain to them artificial and largely incomprehensible.

8:27. If those who advance these arguments would follow them to their logical conclusion and argue that French should become the official language of Mauritius, and should be the only language formally taught in the primary schools and the medium of instruction in the secondary schools, we might be tempted to take the easy course and agree with them. In fact, however, the argument is not pressed, because nobody so far as we could discover wants French to replace English as the official language or as the vehicle of instruction in the secondary schools. Even if there are some logical souls whom we did not meet and who would face the social, economic, and political consequences of their devotion to the French language, there is no chance whatsoever of their ideas being accepted by the majority of the people of Mauritius, who are determined that English shall retain its official status and its dominance in the secondary schools.

8:28. We are, therefore, after very careful consideration of all the issues involved driven back to a restatement of the principles which should govern the decision which we believe must be taken.

(1) It is universally agreed that English must remain the official language of Mauritius and the medium of instruction in her secondary schools. *Therefore*

(2) English should be taught at the earliest possible stage in the primary schools and should become the medium of instruction when it has been adequately mastered. *Therefore*

(3) No other language should be formally taught in the primary schools or examined at the end of the primary course.

(4) French and oriental languages might be taught out of school to those pupils whose parents so desired and should in any event be taught as second languages in the secondary schools.

THE NEED FOR CENTRAL SCHOOLS

8:29. This change would do more than any other to improve the quality of primary education, but by itself it will not be enough to ensure that Mauritian children grow up with the kind of attitude and abilities which the country needs in its citizens. The intensive competition which is a feature of Mauritian education from a child's earliest years to the end of school life is itself a reflection of Mauritian life as a whole. There is nothing to be surprised at in the fervid desire of humble Mauritian parents to acquire for their children an education which will lead to some kind of a certificate and, if at all

211

possible, a job of some kind in the service of the Government of Mauritius, so long as the prevailing attitude to hard work and to manual dexterity remains. To change these attitudes will take a long time. Something can be done by modifications of the school curriculum, but the schools themselves cannot make the change complete. When Mauritius is prepared to agree that a young man who can mend a motor car is a more useful citizen than the man who can only sell one, and when the man who can drive a tractor is recognised as a more valuable member of the community than the man who can only drive a pen, school attitudes can be expected to change correspondingly. In the meantime something could be done by encouraging respect for manual skill, for proficient agriculture and for those forms of human activity which are at present despised. Some at least of the time made available by cutting out a lot of the language teaching should be devoted to handwork of various kinds, and among the more senior pupils to activity in the school garden where a garden exists.

8:30. Since, however, most children are going to end their formal education at the age of 12, it cannot be expected that many of them will develop any great personal skills in practical activities. It seems desirable therefore that the policy of establishing the type of secondary schools that Mauritius knows as Central Schools, where selected pupils from the primary schools could take courses biased in favour of woodwork, metalwork, and agriculture in the case of boys and of the domestic arts in the case of girls, should be revived.

8:31. In an island where agriculture is of paramount importance, it is clearly essential that an appreciation of the agriculturalist's contribution and of the importance of good cultivation should be fostered in the primary schools. It is, however, vain to expect the schools to be able to check a tendency which is by now world-wide, for the rural population to drift to the towns in search of the supposed extra comfort and additional amenities which the towns offer. The gradual spread to rural areas of the advantages at present enjoyed by town dwellers will do more than all the efforts of the schools could do. In this connection, however, the provision of good school facilities in areas at present ill-served could have very great effect, and we would strongly urge the establishment of Central Schools in areas where at present no facilities exist for any form of post-primary schooling, except those offered by private schools of doubtful quality.

8.32. The need for schools of this type was stressed as long ago as 1941 in the Report on Mauritian Education presented by the then Director of Education, Mr. W. E. F. Ward. Varying degrees of attention were paid to Mr. Ward's wise recommendations, and it is not too much to say that if they had all been accepted and acted upon, the present picture would be a much brighter one. In the case of Central Schools, the Education Department has been able to establish two, one for boys which has been in existence for some few years and is now attended by 84 pupils, and one for girls, which was established only last year and has an enrolment of 29. Unfortunately the building, equipment, and other provisions available for these two schools show what a low estimate is taken of their value by those responsible for educational policy. So strong is the obsession with purely academic schooling that it would be quite unrealistic to suggest that Central Schools should be treated as one of the main elements in the secondary system, but we believe that half a dozen Central Schools, suitable sited and adequately housed, equipped, and staffed, could help considerably in introducing new ideas and in providing potential students for any institution of technical education which may be created. Admission to these Central Schools should in our opinion be free, though pupils should be selected on the basis of an entrance examination.

THE AGE OF ENTRY

8:33. In its Sessional Paper No. 3 of 1960 the government expressed the hope that compulsory primary schooling could soon be insisted upon. We recommend that this aim, laudable though it is in many respects, should not be pressed. In our view the urgent need now is not for any further extension, however slight, of the facilities for primary schooling, but for consolidation and much-needed improvement in the present system. So strongly do we feel on this point that we would even recommend some curtailment, perhaps temporary, of the present facilities in order to make sure that the quality of education can be improved. Whilst fully recognising the difficulties inherent in the step we propose, we believe it would be in the best interests of Mauritius and of its children if for a period of years the minimum age for admission to primary schools were raised by one year, that is from five to six. This would remove from the schools, in the first year of its application, some 15,000 children and would release 300 teachers, who would immediately be available for use elsewhere in the schools and whose services could lead to a reduction in the size of classes and to other improvements in the schools which are at present unattainable. It would be for the Government of Mauritius to consider whether it should keep the school life within the shorter period of six years or whether the year taken away at the bottom should be added to the top, in other words whether the age for leaving the primary school should be raised to 13 plus. This would clearly have many advantages, since the present gap between the primary school leaving age and the minimum legal age for employment causes much embarrassment and complication. On balance, however, we are inclined to think that greater benefit would result from keeping the primary school enrolment down at the reduced figure until satisfactory standards have been restored.

8:34. Mauritius is faced with an increase in the number of children of primary school age of about 5,000 per annum until 1967. It is already short of school accommodation, of teachers, equipment, and nearly everything else, including an adequate inspectorate. It has also just suffered heavily from two disastrous cyclones, the bills for which have still to be met. In other words, the general conditions for Mauritian education are grim indeed, and intense effort will be needed if even today's low standards are to be maintained. It they are to be improved (that they need to be everybody would agree), drastic measures will be necessary. One such is the raising of the age of admission to primary schools to six plus, a step which would bring Mauritius into line with France, Canada, Australia, and most other countries with fewer problems to solve than she has and would leave her still ahead of many countries with problems similar to, but often less acute than, her own.

8:35. Any raising of the minimum age for admission will open in a very acute form the question of the education of children below normal school age. Already many parents, in pathetic efforts to help their children, are sending them to private schools where the process of cramming begins far too early. Obviously, therefore, there is already in many minds a willingness to contribute towards the cost. of a child's education, and we believe that this willingness might be led into much more useful channels, if parents could be given the right kind of guidance. It is always dangerous to suggest the transplanting from one country to another either of institutions or of ideas, but Mauritius might well profit by the experience of Jamaica in this particular matter.

8:36. In a situation not dissimilar to that now prevailing in Mauritius, some answer had to be found to an ever-growing clamour for the provision by the Government of Jamaica of schooling for children below the age of normal admission to primary schools. To satisfy this demand was at the time completely beyond the capacity and material resources of Jamaica, but such was the success of a campaign to enlist the efforts of parents in the education of their young children and to spread throughout the country sound ideas about the proper educational treatment of young children that several hundred small village "schools" came into being, established as a result of local initiative and supported in the main by local contributions augmented only by a small government grant. Of these schools, some are excellent, some fair, and a few bad, but the overall effect on the ideas of Jamaican parents and the relief of the strain on government resources have amply repaid the efforts put forth. It is important that if any attempt is made in Mauritius to enlist the active interest of local communities in infant education, the whole question should be approached not simply with a view to saving government expense but to combining that saving with real educational advance.

Examination Results

8:37. As a conclusion to this section on the primary schools, we quote the relevant figures from the recent Junior Scholarship Examination. The number of candidates was:—

boys	4,151	
girls	2,871	
total	—	7,022

The number adjudged "meritorious" was:—

boys	195	
girls	165	
total	—	360

The number of scholarships awarded was:—

boys	72	
girls	50	
total	—	122

A great deal of the whole pathetic story is told by those figures, the low standard prevailing in the schools when only one in 20 of the best pupils can be adjudged as "meritorious", and the pitifully small chances children have of getting to the approved secondary schools when there are only 122 scholarships for 7,022 candidates. The tortures of the English 11-plus examination pale into insignificance beside these figures. Since Mauritius presumably feels she cannot afford to provide scholarships on a more generous scale, it is at least open to question whether she is wise to grant free tuition, books, *and a cash maintenance allowance* to all scholarship winners. It would seem more reasonable to pay the allowance only to those children whose parents could prove need, and to use any money so saved to increase the number of scholarships.

215

The Private Schools

8:38. The main problem which the Government of Mauritius has to face in secondary education is that of the private schools. These schools have grown with amazing rapidity, some to incredible size, as the direct result of the provision of primary schooling for the majority of Mauritian children without any possibility of the provision by the government of secondary schooling for more than a small fraction of the total number of children wanting it.

Table LXIV. Increase in Number of Secondary School Pupils, especially in Private Schools, 1955-1959

	1955–56	1956–57	1957–58	1958–59	1959–60
In all schools	10,228	10,960	12,606	15,437	18,489
In government and aided schools	3,146	3,241	3,408	3,686	3,795
In private schools ..	7,082	7,719	9,198	11,751	14,694

This situation poses problems which are very grave indeed. As can be seen from Table LXIV, over 80% of secondary school places are in private schools which as one would expect vary from a standard very similar to that prevailing in the aided schools to a shocking level of incompetence.

8:39. In so far as examination results are a measure of school efficiency, the table of results in the Cambridge School Certificate Examination for 1959 (overleaf) is very revealing. (It should be noted that the schools listed as Provisional "B" schools are regarded as the best of the private secondary schools.) It is worth noting that the percentage of passes achieved by Mauritian candidates is lower than the corresponding figure for any country whose schools take the Cambridge Overseas Examination.

8:40. It is true that the Department of Education has the right to inspect all private schools and to call for the closure of any which do not reach reasonable standards in regard to accommodation, staffing and so forth, and no doubt many of the private schools ought to be closed. To close them, however, is really no solution of the problem, because the schools have come into existence through the determination of Mauritian parents to get the best education they can for their children. The only satisfactory solution in the long run is, therefore, for the government to provide good secondary education for all children who are qualified to receive it, but this would be such a costly process that the government should not think of embarking upon it for several years.

Table LXV. 1959 *Cambridge School Certificate Results in Government and Better-Class Secondary Schools*

Schools	No. of candidates	No. of passes Division I	Division II	Division III	Total	Percentage of Passes
Government "A" Schools						
Royal College, Curepipe ..	62	11	25	16	52	82·5
Royal College, P. Louis ..	98	7	32	36	75	76·5
Queen Elizabeth College ..	28	5	8	8	21	75·0
Aided "A" Schools						
Loreto Convent, Curepipe ..	34	9	11	10	30	88·2
College du St. Esprit ..	61	2	12	13	27	44·2
St. Joseph's College ..	46	1	12	8	21	45·6
St. Andrew's School ..	92	1	10	13	24	26·1
Aided "B" Schools						
Loreto Convent, P. Louis ..	55	3	10	16	29	52·7
Loreto Convent, Q. Bornes ..	36	3	11	9	23	63·8
Loreto Convent, Vacoas ..	21	6	7	5	18	85·7
Loreto Convent, St. Pierre ..	6	—	1	1	2	33·3
Non-Aided "B" Schools						
Loreto Convent, R. Hill ..	34	2	8	15	25	73·5
St. Mary's College ..	26	1	4	9	14	53·8
New Eton College ..	78	2	23	10	35	44·8
Trinity College ..	170	—	5	23	28	16·4
Cul. du Bonet P. Secours ..	14	3	3	6	12	85·7
Provisional "B" Schools						
Bhujoharry College ..	508	2	23	56	81	15·9
Mauritius College ..	89	—	9	8	17	19·1
Neo College ..	392	—	2	22	24	6·1
University College ..	93	—	1	12	13	13·9
Hindu Girls' College ..	13	—	2	5	7	53·8
Tutorial College ..	148	—	5	11	16	10·8
Islamic Cultural College ..	56	—	6	17	23	41·1
Eastern College ..	55	—	—	3	3	5·5
Notre Dame School ..	23	—	1	6	7	30·4
Windsor College ..	23	—	—	3	3	13·0
Lycee Leoville L'Homme ..	58	—	—	2	2	4·1
Dhanjee College ..	69	—	2	8	10	14·4
Presidency College ..	64	—	3	9	12	18·7
Adventist College ..	37	—	2	11	13	35·1
Total	2,480	58	238	361	657	26·5

8:41. For the time being, therefore, we recommend that the government must be hard-hearted and resist the temptation to accept direct responsibility for any great expansion of secondary schooling. There is every justification for the payment of grant-in-aid to a few of the best private schools. (It should be a condition of the payment of a grant that schools are non-profit-making. One or two schools already exist which are administered by boards of trustees, and their quality is such that the immediate payment of grant would be

9

justified. The proprietors of some of the other schools might be encouraged to think of setting up boards of trustees to run their schools, becoming themselves salary-earning principals paid by the trustees.)

"Comprehensive" and "Multi-lateral" Schools

8:42. The other measures of expansion contemplated in the plan for Mauritius again are fully justified, and in particular we welcome the intention to establish one or more schools in rural areas. Whether the so-called "comprehensive" pattern is suitable for Mauritius is a much more open question. A "comprehensive" school is essentially a school which offers a wide variety of courses *and which every child of appropriate age in the area served by the school attends.* Certainly Mauritius has great need of secondary schools where more varied courses will be available than are available in the present government and grant-aided schools. Mauritius, on the other hand, simply cannot at this stage afford the luxury of universal secondary schooling, and it should not therefore provide secondary schooling in a few districts for all children irrespective of their mental abilities.

8:43. It seems likely that there has been some confusion between the terms "comprehensive" and "multilateral" or "bilateral". Though we could not at present support a proposal to provide free secondary education and therefore feel that genuinely comprehensive schools would not at present fit the Mauritian situation, we would support strongly the idea of introducing technical and perhaps even direct vocational courses into a secondary school on terms of complete parity with the traditional "grammar" studies. We should therefore like to see one bilateral grammar-cum-technical school established on an experimental basis, in the hope that it could succeed and lead later to the establishment of other bilateral schools and help to break down the present bias against practical courses. We suggest that in any school of this type now established, fees should be charged, just as they are charged universally in Mauritius in the normal secondary schools.

8:44. If a bilateral school is to succeed it will be essential to build up the prestige of the technical courses so that there is an even distribution of ability between the technical and the grammar streams. It would probably be advisable therefore to appoint as the first principal of such a school a man who was himself brought up in the technical education field rather than someone whose background is completely academic.

8:45. Unhappily, it is very far from certain that any new type of secondary school would be acceptable to parental opinion in Mauritius, largely because of the effect on pupils, teachers, and parents of the relentless competition which characterises secondary education and which has as its goal the glittering prize of an English Scholarship. It would be a very good thing for Mauritian education if there were no such thing as English Scholarships, and if there were neither glamour nor profit to lure children on throughout their school careers like blinkered donkeys seeing only the dangling carrot. We are not sufficiently naïve to suggest, however, that the English Scholarship should be abolished, because we know that its hold on public opinion is far too strong for such a suggestion ever to be accepted. We do, however, urge strongly that the conditions for the award of the English Scholarship should be so amended as to give the government considerable rights in selecting or at least approving the courses to be pursued by successful candidates and to remove some of the financial benefits. (The value of the scholarship should be such as to cover costs of tuition, maintenance, and reasonable out-of-pocket expenses, but should certainly not allow a scholarship-holder to send money home and to regard the scholarship as a prize won rather than as the means to a further course of study.)

8:46. Some of the evil effects of the English Scholarship system might be ended or reduced by an increase in the number of scholarships awarded by the Government of Mauritius to able and deserving students to meet the cost of their studies at universities abroad. As the Titmuss Report also concludes, some of the cost of these additional scholarships could be found in the savings which would result from the elimination of the income tax allowance at present granted for the education of children overseas (paragraph 7:12). The allowances masquerade as aid for the educationally deserving, but are in fact granted not to those who are intellectually most fitted to receive them but to those whose parents can afford to meet the remaining costs of university or college education.

8:47. There is on general grounds every justification for the award of more university scholarships, since it seems clear that for some years at least the needs of Mauritius for higher education will have to be met by sending its best students abroad. It may prove feasible at a later date (how much later we would not care to guess) to establish an institution of university status in the island, and we have no wish to pre-judge the results of the investigation into university education in Mauritius which we believe is shortly to be undertaken. Until or unless it has a university of its own, however, Mauritius is far from making the best use of the funds it professedly devotes to higher education.

8:48. One thing which could be done to help the private schools improve their quality and which need not be very expensive would be to offer the possibility of part-time training for existing secondary school teachers at the Teacher Training College. There is urgent need to provide facilities for improving the teaching as well as the general education of many of the young men and women who are at present struggling with little or no assistance to prepare pupils for examinations which they themselves have with difficulty managed to pass. Help for the teachers through the Training College and more regular and closer contact between the Education Department and the schools could do much to improve a situation which is already very grave and could easily get out of hand.

Teacher Training

8:49. It is a platitude to say that in teacher training lies the key to most educational problems, but nowhere is the truth of this more evident than it is today in Mauritius. The island possesses a Training College pleasantly sited and attractively housed, which could be expected, if the quality of teaching in the schools was already satisfactory, to turn out annually the trained teachers necessary to keep the service fully manned. Unfortunately, however, as we pointed out earlier, rapid expansion has led to considerable deterioration in the quality of teaching particularly in the primary schools, whilst there is at the secondary level, particularly in the private schools a huge number of teachers who have had no professional training whatsoever and whose results are understandably quite deplorable.

8:50. We recommend, therefore, that two things should happen simultaneously, the first, that the normal course of training for entrants to the teaching profession should be lengthened to its original two-year period, and the second that intensive courses should be instituted for the benefit of the many teachers who have not had the opportunity hitherto of full college training.

8:51. In particular the greatest possible attention should be concentrated on the teaching of English, simply because an inadequate command of English and an imperfect knowledge of how to teach the subject are the main handicaps from which large numbers of young Mauritian teachers are suffering. It is in our view highly desirable that the English teaching at the College should be strengthened by the addition to the staff of one or possibly two well-qualified expatriates, *with first-hand experience of the problems of teaching English as a foreign language.* This is not to belittle in any way the efforts of those members of the staff, expatriate and

Mauritian, who are at present teaching English, but merely to recognise the extent to which their efforts are at present only in part successful. We believe that the problems of English teaching in Mauritius are so serious that the island should have a claim as strong as, or stronger than, that of any territory within the Commonwealth to any assistance which may now be available, or may become available, from Colonial Development and Welfare or other sources within the United Kingdom. We hope that the possible inability of Mauritius to pay salaries and provide conditions attractive to the best teachers of English will not be a bar to their recruitment, and that any forms of subsidy which may be available will be fully used on Mauritius' behalf.

8:52. We hope it will not be taken as a reflection on the capacity of Mauritians if we suggest that the Training College would for the next few years be best headed by an expatriate principal. We make this suggestion only because the College, sound though its general programme may be, is at present somewhat pedestrian in outlook and lacking in liveliness and inspiration, and because there does not seem to be anybody readily available in Mauritius who has the experience to enable him to initiate the kind of intensive and vigorous programme of a twofold nature which we think is essential. Again we should hope that if need be the appointment of a principal for a term of years could be assisted by whatever subsidies are available for "key" posts (see paragraph 9:9).

8:53. If any programme of teacher training is to have enduring success, there must be some provision whereby trained teachers, particularly young teachers, are enabled to keep in touch with modern ideas and to continue to draw inspiration from the College in which they were trained. In the absence of such provision, it is difficult indeed for a young teacher to retain either the ideas or the liveliness of mind and the devotion with which he first takes up his professional task. The greater his professional isolation, the more likely he is to fall a victim to the reactionary pressures of those who, by reason of their greater age, think they must be better than any youngster, although in fact they are often very out-of-date. This problem is very evident in Mauritius, where there is an obvious lack of understanding between, on the one hand the Training College and the majority of its young products, and on the other hand the group of older professionals known as Area Superintendents, including former successful teachers in primary schools who as a result of seniority and their own good work have entered the Education Department as supervisors of the primary school system.

8:54. Mauritius cannot afford the luxury of a full primary school inspectorate. She should therefore afford the comparatively inexpensive innovation of a small increase in the staffing establishment of the Training College in order to maintain contact between the College and its former students. We propose an addition of two tutors to the College staff, to be responsible to the Principal for liaison with the primary schools in general, and in particular to supervise the work of teachers who have left the Training College within recent years. There should be no suggestion that these additional members of the Training College staff should undertake any of the "watch-dog" activities which in the past used to fall on the School Inspectors. Their duties would simply be to help, advise, and guide the young teachers and to keep their colleagues on the Training College staff fully aware of all developments in the schools.

8:55. If the Training College could also undertake to put on occasional short courses or conferences for the Area Superintendents, we believe that the experience of the additional members of staff whom we are recommending could help greatly in breaking down the suspicion with which the Training College is apparently regarded at times by the Area Superintendents and some of the older teachers. Certainly the work of the College as a whole should benefit greatly from the closer contact with the school system.

8:56. Another activity which we believe ought to be centred on the College is the production of school text-books and readers, written for Mauritian children and based as far as possible on local material. There are at present widespread complaints of the unsuitability of the books in use. This is not surprising, since in most cases the books were produced to meet the needs of children in other countries, and not even skilful adaptation of foreign material can always make it suitable for use in Mauritius. The Training College is the logical place in which to develop a small production unit which should aim at turning out both school books and teaching aids in general. There are countless teachers in Mauritius capable of writing the simple texts which would at first be required, and the Training College is or should be in a position to try out proposed books on school classes and so ensure that the real needs of teachers and pupils are met. Such a production unit need not be costly even if Mauritius had to foot the whole bill. This kind of enterprise however is one in which U.N.E.S.C.O. is not only keenly interested but has developed considerable expertise in recent years, and we believe that an application for U.N.E.S.C.O. assistance in the establishment of such a unit and in the expense of running it in its early stages might well meet with a favourable response.

8:57. As was said at the beginning of this chapter, the complete absence of technical education is a very severe obstacle to economic development in Mauritius. Not only does the island suffer from a lack of trained personnel, but public opinion as a whole is unaware of the importance of technical training and remains obsessed with the academic schooling which has been the pattern for so long and which can only lead for most young people to clerical occupation or to unemployment.

8:58. The desirability and feasibility of a programme of technical education have been discussed almost *ad nauseam* both before and since the visit to the island in 1955 of Dr. Harlow, then Assistant Adviser (Technical) to the Secretary of State. Dr. Harlow's report contained recommendations which were accepted in general and which led to specific proposals for the establishment of a technical institute and a trade training centre. The former was meant to provide full-time junior technical and commercial courses, as well as part-time and evening courses for young men and women already employed in industry, whilst the latter would offer training in the following six trades, carpenter and joiner, mason/bricklayer, electrician, motor mechanic, fitter/machinist, and painter and decorator. Sufficient agreement was reached for a site to be chosen, funds to be voted for the building operations, a principal and the nucleus of a staff to be appointed, and for the first batch of students to be enrolled. Delays occurred for one reason and another however, and it has seemed recently that the whole future of the accepted scheme was in doubt.

8:59. We welcome very warmly therefore the renewed declaration of the government's intention to develop technical and vocational training by the establishment of the Technical Institute and the Trade Training Centre which have so long been in the planning stage. We do not regard ourselves as competent to advise on the details of the buildings, equipment, and staff which will be required, or on the details of the courses to be followed. The government has available, however, the views of its Technical Education Advisory Board, and in particular the recommendations of the sub-committee of that board, and has been able to draw upon the highly expert knowledge of Dr. Harlow's successor, Mr. J. C. Jones, who visited Mauritius in July 1960.

8:60. There will undoubtedly be considerable difficulty in building up the prestige of this new form of education and in getting parents in particular to regard admission to a technical institute or trade training centre as no less worth while than admission to one of the existing secondary schools, and on that account we see considerable merit in the proposal to establish some form of secondary school which, while enjoying all the prestige attaching to secondary schools as at present defined, will also provide some technical courses. We should however make it clear that these courses could not in any sense be a substitute for the Technical Institute and the Trade Training Centre, though they could be a useful adjunct.

8:61. Another difficulty which would have to be faced is that of ensuring that remunerative employment at the appropriate level is available for students on completion of their technical training. Here there will undoubtedly be considerable prejudice to overcome, since in a community where practical skill has been handed down from father to son, or at any rate from adult to boy, through unregulated and very informal schemes of apprenticeship, there is likely for some time to be a feeling of hostility towards young men who enter industry or seek promotion in it on the strength of training of a new kind received in a new institution. We are, however, satisfied as a result of enquiries amongst employers and workers in most of the industries now carried on in Mauritius that the need for formal training is acute and is also fully appreciated by very many people in industry, and we have no doubt ourselves that the first products of the Technical Institute and Trade Training Centre will be readily absorbed.

8:62. It is not perhaps so clear whether there is a real likelihood of industrial development in Mauritius on such a scale as to guarantee employment for the regular succession of young men who could be expected to pass through the training institution year by year. It may therefore be thought that there is something of a gamble involved in providing technical and vocational instruction, costly as they both are, in the absence of the fullest assurances regarding future employment.

8:63. We believe, however, that it would be folly to adopt this attitude. If the other measures necessary for Mauritian economic development are in fact taken, then those who are technically trained will be readily absorbed into productive employment. If on the other hand the other measures necessary for economic development are not carried out, the prospects for Mauritians will in any case be grim, and the fact that some trained technicians will be unemployed will be only a minor element in the general gloom. In brief, technical education is a necessary condition for Mauritian economic development and those who are responsible for technical education in Mauritius must plan on the assumption that the other measures necessary for economic development will in fact be taken.

CHAPTER 9

The Machinery of Government

9:1. In the course of our consideration of the measures necessary to stimulate the economic growth of Mauritius, it has become clear that in numerous ways the government will have a central role to play. Indeed the carrying into effect of the recommendations made in this report (and in the Titmuss Report) will, if adopted, make heavy calls on the public services. We have not ourselves been able to examine the structure of the public service in great detail but we have been able to reach certain broad conclusions concerning the way in which we think it should be strengthened or helped to meet the demands that will be placed upon it.

9:2. As Mauritius has progressed towards a parliamentary and cabinet system on the lines of the United Kingdom, it has adopted a similar administrative organisation. In particular the introduction of a ministerial system has as usual been accompanied by the creation of ministries with administrative heads, known in Mauritius as Principal Assistant Secretaries, who are the ministers' immediate advisers. The superimposition upon established departments of government staffed by experienced technical officers, of newly created ministries whose officers in many cases began with little knowledge of the technical administrative and financial problems of the departments for which they have become responsible, has inevitably produced difficulties of a personal as well as an administrative kind. Such arrangements often mean that an experienced technical officer with considerable administrative ability has to transact his business with the minister through a new officer who has no more administrative ability and much less experience than himself. Moreover, in a small territory the scale of business is often such that it is pure waste to have both a fully competent technical officer and a fully competent administrative officer at the head of affairs.

9:3. Similar difficulties have been experienced by almost every territory in which the transition to a ministerial system has taken place, but for two main reasons they are more than usually acute in Mauritius—with the result that it is particularly important that they should be solved. In the first place there is a noticeable lack of administrative experience in Mauritius. All major policy decisions have to be translated into action by a handful of senior officials and it is largely true to say that the pace of development in the past has

225

been dictated by the enormous load which has fallen upon them. In the second place Mauritius contains within a small area many differences of race, religion, and language, and sectional interests that would tax a body of seasoned and experienced administrators. These sectional interests not only create problems of tact and understanding, they also create a tendency for people to look to government to perform functions which in other societies are undertaken by private individuals or established institutions which enjoy the confidence of the community. We gave one example of this in the request made from all four chambers of commerce that government should undertake the business of supplying commercial information (paragraph 7:30), but it has general application in as much as, given the general lack of institutional organisation in the island except on a communal basis, people inevitably look to government as the only organisation from which they have any hope of effective and dispassionate assistance or redress. It is also a problem of poverty, and lack of opportunity. Lacking either the skill or the opportunity for remunerative and satisfying work the only alternative for many people is to look to the government or to give up hope altogether. The result is that departments of government tend to assume functions which would not normally be regarded as governmental and to employ inflated staffs.

9:4. The problem of administration in Mauritius is, therefore, twofold. It is on the one hand how to bring together the administrative officers serving in ministries and the professional and technical heads of departments, so as to produce the most effective and efficient amalgam of their respective qualities and experience and ensure that the minister receives, by co-operation between all the members of his staff, the best administrative and technical advice that the ministry and department can together command. On the other hand, it is how to staff the administration so that it can efficiently fulfil the additional functions which will be put upon it without further encouraging the existing tendency to look to the government for everything and without aggravating the existing over-staffing of government departments.

9:5. It is impossible to lay down any generally applicable rule of thumb. The full integration of ministries and departments may well be possible where related subjects come within a single portfolio, as in the case of the Ministry of Education where integration has already been achieved. Where different subjects come within a single portfolio, however, as in the Ministry of Labour and Social Security, it is unlikely that integration either could or should be achieved. In fact each ministry of each department will have, by day-to-day experience, to evolve a method of co-operation best suited to its own needs. This would be entirely consistent with what happens in the United Kingdom where there is much variation of practice and where a considerable number of departments are not integrated with their respective ministries. In short the right policy for Mauritius is to treat integration as one among several administrative organisational problems directed towards improved efficiency.

9:6. There are, in fact, a number of measures falling short of complete integration whereby efficiency might be improved. There would seem, for example, to be little justification for maintaining separate "ministry" files and the issue of letters from departments to ministries often separated by little more than fifty yards. Submission by the head of a department to the ministry could be by a simple minute or memorandum on the file addressed to the Principal Assistant Secretary. Where integration is considered practicable the aim should be for the administrative division of the ministry to be responsible for advising the minister on policy and on the handling of financial and establishment matters, with the professional and technical officers giving technical advice and being responsible for execution. It is important in this connection, however, that the key posts of Principal Assistant Secretary should go to the ablest and most experienced officers irrespective of whether they are administrative officers or professional or technical officers. And once appointed officers should only exceptionally be transferred to other ministries.

9:7. We had little opportunity in the time available to us to examine in any detail the procedures for the staffing of both ministries and departments, except in the case of the Department of Agriculture, on which we have already made a number of specific suggestions (paragraph 5:136 ff). We did however form a firm opinion that there would be advantage in a thorough review of present methods and procedures and a reorganisation of staff training. To this end we recommend that the Establishment Secretary's office should be strengthened by the creation of an organisation and methods section which would be charged with eliminating much of the present waste from the administration and which would also assume responsibility for staff training.

9:8. In order to be effective, however, we are bound to say that this organisation and methods section would need the closest co-operation of both ministers and administrators. There is an unfortunate tendency at the moment for both continually to be troubled with individual cases and for decisions on them to be taken against a communal and political background which makes dispassionate judgment and decision on those cases very difficult. As we have already observed this is to some extent a reflection of the intimacy of Mauritian society, but if any lasting improvement in the quality of the public service and of its morale is to be gained there is little doubt that it must be overcome. Those in positions of authority should learn to disregard family, communal, and political ties in the exercise of their political and administrative duties.

9:9. Above all we would emphasise the need to ensure that there is a sufficient number of able and experienced men in the top ranks of the public and similar services in Mauritius to make possible the great revolution in economic policies which our proposals will involve. A casual glance at the Gorvin Report of 1948 or the Report of the Royal Commission of 1910 will show that we make few proposals that are wholly new, and whether or not our proposals are effectively translated into action will largely depend upon the presence of sufficient and sufficiently able senior officials to see that they are. In the course of our enquiries we came across many cases in which failure to achieve effective action in economic policy was due to the overloading with work and responsibility of the handful of men at the top who would effectively handle such matters. We have already said that we think the Government of Mauritius should be prepared to offer high salaries to obtain the best men for posts like Chairman of the Industrial Development Board (see paragraphs 2:68 and 6:98), and we are likewise convinced that it should accept —to the interests of Mauritians whose opportunities will be ultimately enlarged—the continuing assistance in the immediate future of United Kingdom officials. If Mauritius itself cannot afford the salaries required to attract such officials we believe the United Kingdom Government should be requested to pay the addition (see also paragraphs 8:51 and 52).

9:10. Finally, we believe that there is one particular arrangement that would make a valuable contribution to the solution of this problem. In our opinion great benefit could be gained over the next decade or so by a system of interchange of officers between the public services of Mauritius and of the United Kingdom. If, for example, three or four selected Mauritian officers in the Principal Assistant Secretary and Assistant Secretary grades were now sent to the United Kingdom for a period of, say, a year to eighteen months, and were temporarily replaced by officers from the United Kingdom, a double advantage might be gained. On the one hand the Mauritian officers would gain experience in administrative methods in the United Kingdom. This experience should cover administrative work in the comparable Ministry in the United Kingdom and where appropriate administrative work carried on in particular fields such as education by local authorities.[1] On the other hand, the resulting vacancies in the Mauritian administration would be filled by Officers seconded from the Administrative Class of the Home Civil Service in the United Kingdom. These officers would be valuable in the training of locally recruited junior administrative staff and would provide a useful stiffening of the local public service during the testing period of the next few years. It is our view that the provision of facilities of this kind for the interchange of administrative officers between the Mauritian and the United Kingdom administrative services, together with the payment by the United Kingdom of the additional charge of employing expatriate officials, represents one of the most valuable forms of technical assistance which the United Kingdom can render to Mauritius at the present time.

[1] Ministries in the United Kingdom exercise rather more limited functions than in the case of Mauritius. As an example, the Ministry of Education in the United Kingdom does not run any schools, the execution of policy being left to the local education authorities.

CHAPTER 10

Summary of Recommendations

10:1. In the course of the preceding chapters we have made a number of recommendations which, if accepted and put into effect, will, we believe, go far towards solving the problems set out in our terms of reference. We would like to stress once more that these recommendations should be treated as a single whole. Together they constitute that revolution in economic affairs in Mauritius which is essential to start a process of economic development on a scale which will absorb the growing population of Mauritius without a serious fall in the present standard of living. Others who have been concerned on earlier occasions with Mauritian problems have already made many of our proposals, only to find them ignored or their implementation indefinitely delayed. But with the present rapid growth of population in Mauritius, time is now very short; and disaster will ensue unless the Government of Mauritius can on this occasion promptly take the necessary, though in some cases unpopular, measures to bring into effect in all its aspects the necessary economic and social revolution.

10:2. In order to provide the framework within which the economic problem may become manageable, we recommend that the government should take immediate measures to tackle the population problem along the lines laid down in the Titmuss Report (paragraph 2:90). As we have made clear, the proposals of the Titmuss Report have serious implications for the budget; but if their acceptance is a necessary part of an effective check to the rise in population, without which we see no future for the Mauritian economy, we regard them as deserving the fullest support (7:29).

10:3. In order to achieve an expansion of the openings for the productive employment of labour on the required scale it is essential that for an initial period of several years at least labour costs should not rise higher than they now are (2:17-28). Together with population control this element of stable wage rates constitutes the essential background to our other recommendations. If moderate measures of social security and of cost-of-living stabilisation are necessary for the achievement of a policy of wage restraint, the budgetary cost involved should be accepted.

10:4. So far as the recruitment of labour and conditions of work are concerned, we recommend that a concerted attack should be made on the problem of casualisation in the sugar industry and, in particular, that:—

1. The sugar industry (*inter alia*) should be encouraged to experiment with financial incentives designed to stimulate decasualisation and to reduce the rate of absenteeism (4:17).

2. The Labour Ordinance should be amended to empower the Labour Commissioner to charge a fee for licences issued to job contractors and to rescind as well as to issue licences (4:18).

3. Labour should so far as possible be employed directly by the sugar estates (4:20).

4. The Labour Ordinance should be amended to prohibit the payment of labourers through job contractors (4:20).

We also recommend that:—

5. The system of priority by date of registration in employment exchanges should be abandoned (4:22).

6. In the coming two or three years the Department of Labour should launch an intensive recruitment drive directed at young people (4:24).

7. As recommended in the Luce Report, a specialised youth movement with an experienced youth movement service officer should be established (4:25).

8. The government should give all possible encouragement to existing youth movements (4:26).

9. The trade union movement should be given the opportunity, wherever possible, of serving on advisory committees and other bodies set up to help to plan economic development (4:28).

10. The government should examine the possibility of promoting emigration, including emigration into the United Kingdom (2:6-12 and 4:37).

10:5. So far as the sugar industry is concerned much of our comment has been in the nature of description rather than recommendation. With the exception of its attitude to labour recruitment, the industry is extremely efficiently run. Apart, therefore, from our recommendations about labour recruitment, we have only three other recommendations, one extremely important, the other two rather less so:—

11. In view of marketing limitations and the need to provide more employment, we are of the opinion that no further large-scale expansion of sugar production should take place. As a disincentive to expansion we recommend a 5% *ad valorem* tax on sugar should

be imposed and that the subsequent adjustment of the rate of this tax should be regarded as the main instrument for controlling the output of sugar (2:38-39 and 7:22-23).

12. A soil physicist should be added to the strength of the Sugar Industry Research Institute (5:19).

13. The Board of the Cyclone and Drought Insurance Fund should consider whether it is necessary for compulsory insurance to cover such a high proportion of losses incurred as a result of cyclone or drought, and whether the present definition of a "normal" year is entirely satisfactory (5:33).

10:6. In agriculture there are a number of steps which need to be taken, particularly in the spheres of marketing and research, if alternative activities to the growing of sugar are to be developed. We therefore recommend that:—

14. Legislation should be enacted against the misuse of land (5:6-9).

15. Owners of land used for the breeding of stags which is suitable for cultivation should be required by sale or lease to make such land available to those willing and able to undertake approved development (5:10).

16. A statutory Water Resources Authority should be established and legislation introduced for the control of surface and underground water resources (5:11 and 6:88).

17. A qualified officer should be appointed for tea research (5:40).

18. An expert to advise on protection works for tea should be sought from Kenya (5:41).

19. The government should exercise greater control over new tea projects, either by taking over new project planters' land (employing private contractors, where possible, for specific jobs) or through a non-profit-making Tea Development Authority (5:42 and 43).

20. The Tea Board should consider ways and means of satisfactorily insuring tea plantations and installations (5:44).

21. A study should be made of the form of development and the supporting legislation for smallholding tea in Ceylon and Kenya (5:45).

22. The government should encourage the expansion of the tobacco industry. It should adjust import and excise duties to give greater protection to local manufacturers, without any sacrifice of revenue from tobacco duties (5:47).

23. So long as the quota system persists the price guaranteed to producers of tobacco should be reduced (5:50).

24. Agronomic research on tobacco growing should be continued with a view to improving the quality and to lowering the cost of tobacco (5:51).

25. There should be no major expansion in the production of ginger (5:52).

26. The government should encourage the production of food-stuffs by establishing a central Agricultural Marketing Board (see recommendation no. 61), providing adequate storage and (if necessary) processing facilities, improving the agricultural extension and research services (see recommendation no. 53), reviewing the legislation on security of tenure for small planters, and by tightening the law against praedial larceny (5:59-61).

27. The Agricultural Marketing Board should for the time being concentrate on non-perishable crops (5:60-61).

28. The government should give moderate financial assistance towards an assessment of the value of more intensive methods of cultivation of aloe (5:68).

29. Mechanical methods of processing aloe fibre should be examined (5:69).

30. In the light of recommendations nos. 28 and 29, the government should not, at present, consider closing the sack factory and the present, or similar, arrangements for subsidisation should continue (5:70 and 6:20-21).

On forestry we recommend that:—

31. Action should be taken on the recommendations contained in the recent report of the Secretary of State for the Colonies' Adviser on Forestry (5:72).

32. The Forestry Department should be relieved of burdens unnecessarily placed upon it (5:73).

33. A modern sawmill, seasoning, and preservation plant should be established (5:74 and 6:50).

On livestock we recommend that:—

34. Efficient milk production methods should be demonstrated on a government farm (5:88).

35. Encouragement should be given to small-scale milk production (5:89).

36. The Palmar Settlement should be re-organised to make possible the examination of the problems of milk production and an improvement in the extension services (5:90).

37. The government should guarantee loans to individual milk producers to enable them to provide proper facilities for their cows (5:91).

38. The cost of the artificial insemination service should be reduced by operating it through a series of district centres (5:92).

39. The Livestock Division of the Department of Agriculture should endeavour to reduce the cost of feeding-stuffs. Abattoir material and condemned material from the fishing industry should be utilised for stock feed and, if necessary, the government should furnish a loan for the establishment of a processing plant (5:93 and 114).

40. The marketing of milk should be improved and the government should give positive encouragement to any well-considered scheme for the establishment of a milk-processing plant, and of producers co-operatives (5:95).

41. There should be a reduction in the number of calves slaughtered for meat (5:101).

42. There should be a concerted effort to eradicate T.B. among cows (5:102).

43. A decision should be taken on the future of the Pas Geometriques on the basis of the grazing leases drawn up by the Director of Agriculture (5:106).

44. The prices of meats should be re-arranged on the basis of quality (5:111).

45. Abattoir facilities should be improved, particularly by the installation of cold-storage facilities and weighbridges (5:110 and 113).

46. The Department of Agriculture should intensify its research work on pastures and fodder (5:93 and 108).

47. Encouragement should be given to the establishment of new breeds of goats (5:120-121).

48. The establishment of a small bacon factory should be considered (5:125).

49. The Department of Agriculture should consider the importation of suitable rabbits for sale as breeding stock (5:126).

50. The Reduit poultry unit should pay greater attention to the production and provision of poultry feed (5:129).

In order to encourage the expansion of the fishing industry we recommend that:—

51. The proposal that a joint Japanese-Mauritian Company should be formed for deep-sea fishing should be examined by United Kingdom fisheries experts and, if their report is favourable, the government should give the Company financial backing (5:134).

52. If private capital is not forthcoming the government should give financial backing to the definite proposal which has been made for the establishment of adequate cold-storage facilities for fish (5:135).

On the administrative and research sides of agriculture we recommend that:—

53. One post of Deputy in the Department of Agriculture should be abolished. One or more posts of assistant Director and one of Chief Research Officer should be created and every effort should be made to secure a high-class officer to take charge of the extension services (5:136).

54. The Department of Agriculture should divest itself of all activities that can as well be carried on by private enterprise (5:137 and 140).

55. Two streams should be instituted in the College of Agriculture, one for the sugar technologists and the other for general agriculture (5:138).

56. An expert agriculturist should be appointed as head of the Agricultural College (5:138).

57. The functions and composition of the Board of Agriculture should be reviewed (5:139).

58. The Department of Agriculture should review its policy of land settlements (5:140).

59. The limit on membership of co-operatives should be raised or co-operatives should in some way be grouped (5:142).

60. The Department of Co-operation should be strengthened with staff trained in co-operation (5:143).

61. A central Agricultural Marketing Board should be established to assist and improve the marketing and processing of agricultural and fishery produce. It should receive a recurrent government grant to enable it to offer guaranteed minimum prices for crops other than sugar (5:59-61 and 144-151).

10:7. As we have already made clear the successful encouragement of new and additional industrial activities in Mauritius will largely depend upon fiscal measures. There are, however, a number of ways in which we think direct encouragement should be given to industrial development in the form of financial aid to particular industries, reforms in the tariff structure, the establishment of an Industrial Development Board, and an increase in the borrowing powers of the Agricultural Bank. In this connection we make the following specific recommendations:—

62. The law should be amended to permit the distillation of good-quality rum (6:24).

63. If the project for the establishment of a distillery is supported by overseas customers it should also receive official support (6:25).

64. The tariff on the importation of machine tools, and on workshop and foundry equipment should be abolished and the duties on machinery should be standardised at a fairly low level (6:32 and 7:18).

65. The government should assist producers to obtain import licences into Reunion and Madagascar (6:32).

66. The government should cease to import metal goods, machinery, and equipment that can be made locally (6:32).

67. Tariff protection should be provided for the local production of household utensils (6:34).

68. The organisation and centralisation of the leather and shoe industries should be encouraged by the modification or rationalisation of the present duties (6:40).

69. Consideration should be given to the protection that would be required if a soap factory were to be established again (6:41).

70. Whatever decision is taken concerning the future of the Oil Islands, the oil extraction plant should be kept in good repair (6:44).

71. The excise duty on matches should be abolished (6:47).

72. Failing the construction of a factory by private enterprise, a co-operative factory for furniture production should be established with government help (6:51).

73. All possible encouragement should be given to the idea of establishing a brewery (6:55).

74. Financial assistance should be given to the person proposing the production of instrument jewels to enable him to make a thorough study of the possibilities (6:57).

75. Encouragement should be given to the idea of making Indian jewellery (6:58).

76. The tariff should be adjusted to encourage, rather than discourage, the production of fabrics made from artificial fibres (6:61).

77. The legislation regarding building works should be tightened (6:62).

78. The possibility of producing pozzolanic cements should be kept in mind (6:65).

79. Financial help should be given to the company engaged in the production of lime (6:69).

80. Advice should be sought from a United Nations Agency on the establishment of cottage industries (6:71).

81. The proposal to construct an hotel at Grande Baie should be deferred and in the immediate future efforts should be concentrated on improving the existing hotel and making a success of the hotel at La Chaland (6:76).

82. If sufficiently promising, the scheme for producing electricity from sea-wave energy should be referred to the United Nations for financial assistance (6:83).

83. An expert controller of traffic should be appointed (6:87).

84. An Industrial Development Board should be established to promote, and to advise the government on the details of, industrial development (6:98 and 99).

85. The Industrial Development Board should not itself act as a bank. Loans to industry should be channelled through the Agricultural Bank, acting on the advice of the Industrial Development Board (6:101).

86. A Government Advisory Committee should be established to receive applications by industrialists for concessions (e.g. tariff concessions, tax holidays, etc.) and to make recommendations to the relevant ministers as to whether such concessions should be given (6:101).

87. The government should act in concert with the Industrial Development Board to establish a trading estate. A town and country planning organisation should be established in sufficient time to ensure that this estate forms part of a larger area reserved for industrial development (2:60, 6:51 and 102).

88. The government should review the policy of local purchase (6:105).

89. Company tax should be reduced from 40% to 30% (7:8).

90. The investment allowance should be withdrawn (7:9).

91. The government should be empowered to offer tax holidays for five out of the first eight years of a company's operation. Such concessions should be given on the advice of the Industrial Development Board working through the Government Advisory Committee (7:10).

92. The tax allowance for children should be restricted to the first three children (7:13).

93. The overseas leave privilege for local civil servants should be

greatly curtailed, the tax allowance for overseas leave should be withdrawn, and for purposes of income tax assessment leave passages should be regarded as a part of income (2:83 and 7:14).

94. We welcome the fact that the tariff schedule is being revised and suggest that this revision should be carried out in accordance with certain definite principles (2:70-72, 6:96, and 7:15 and 21).

95. The advice of the Government Advisory Committee should be statutorily required before concessions are made under Section 4 of the Customs Tariff Ordinance of 1954 (7:17).

96. The government should consider giving tariff protection to suitable industries, subject to the advice of the Government Advisory Committee (6:94-6, 7:16-20).

97. The government should aim at an annual surplus of £20 million on current account to help finance capital development, to service the public debt, and to build reserves against disasters (7:39).

98. Recurrent government expenditure should be closely scrutinised with a view to eliminating unnecessary spending and the annual increase should not exceed 5% (7:36 and 42).

99. The government should continue to control the rice trade but hand over financing of it to private hands (7:31-35).

100. The new five-year Capital Expenditure Programme should give priority to projects leading directly to productive employment or providing urgently needed social services, and should be subject to annual revision (7:49, 51 and 59).

101. The construction of the road from Trianon to Cluny should be postponed (7:50).

102. The Colonial Development Corporation and United Nations Agencies should be approached for financial assistance (6:82 and 93 and 7:61).

103. The government should consider raising further loan funds (7:62).

104. The Agricultural Bank ordinance should be amended to make it clear that the Bank should not lend to borrowers who can raise the money from other sources. The Bank should lend more to branches of agriculture other than sugar and to manufacturing industry (7:85-86).

105. The borrowing powers of the Agricultural Bank should be increased (see recommendation No. 85) and attempts should be made to attract outside capital. The Bank might be renamed the Mauritius Agricultural and Development Bank (7:89 and 90).

10:8. In order that the education system of Mauritius should help rather than hinder the programme of economic development we make the following recommendations:—

106. A strong effort should be made through the medium of the education system to change the current attitude of young people that it is undignified to work with their hands (8:8).

107. A firm decision should be taken on the complex question of language teaching. English should be taught as early as possible in the primary schools and no other language except English should be formally taught at the primary level (8:28).

108. A series of Central Schools should be established in which an interest in agriculture and manual skills should be fostered (8:31).

109. The government should not at present press the idea of compulsory primary schooling (8:33).

110. The age of entry into primary school should be raised from five to six years (8:33).

111. The idea of parental contributions to the cost of education and to the establishment of village schools (as in Jamaica) should be examined (8:35).

112. The temptation to expand (rather than to improve) secondary education should be resisted (8:40).

113. Bilateral or technical-grammar schools should be established, as and when possible (8:43).

114. The present small number of English scholarships should be replaced with a larger number of less expensive scholarships (8:46).

115. Intensive refresher courses should be provided at the Teacher Training College (8:50).

116. Training Courses at the Teacher Training College should be lengthened from one to two years (8:50).

117. Greater attention to the teaching of English should be paid in the Teacher Training College (8:50).

118. Every effort should be made to secure sufficient good teachers of English. If Mauritius cannot afford to pay the salaries required to attract them, assistance should be sought from the United Kingdom (8:51).

119. The Teacher Training College should be headed by an expatriate principal (8:52).

120. The staff of the Teacher Training College should be increased by two teachers responsible for improving liaison between the College and the teachers (8:54).

121. Courses for Area Superintendents should be provided at the Teacher Training College (8:55).

122. An attempt should be made, with the possible help of U.N.E.S.C.O., to produce at the Teacher Training College text books specifically designed for Mauritius conditions (8:56).

123. Great concentration should be aimed at the establishment of the services for technical training and the Technical Institute should be established at once (8:58 and 59).

10:9. Finally in order to improve the efficiency of government we recommend that:—

124. A greater ruthlessness should be exercised in pruning government departments of unnecessary staff (7:28 and 9:7 and 8).

125. The government should so far as possible cease to carry out functions which can be better performed by private individuals or agencies (9:3 and 7 and recommendation no. 54).

126. Careful thought should be given to problems of either integrating or of ensuring close co-operation between ministries and departments (9:5 and 6).

127. An organisation and methods division should be set up within the Establishment Secretary's Office (9:7).

128. The government should be prepared to pay high salaries to attract the best men to key posts and to accept continuing help from United Kingdom officials. The United Kingdom Government should be requested, if necessary, to pay a proportion of the salaries of these officials (9:9).

129. Arrangements should be made for the interchange on a temporary basis of a small number of officials between the public services of Mauritius and of the United Kingdom (9:10).

Extract from the Report on Mauritius of the Secretary of State's Adviser on Forestry, October 1959

2. *Forest Policy and Land Planning*

In a small country with a large and rapidly rising population and almost complete economic dependence on the products of the land, it is axiomatic that every acre should be put to its optimum use. In Mauritius the need for proper land capability surveys is clamant, as a basis for the formation of a land and forest policy and for the allocation of rural land for optimum use.

Nothing has done more to discourage the Forest Department and undermine the morale of its staff than the excision of considerable areas of forest land, much of it already planted with timber trees. Forestry is such a long-term undertaking and the planning of timber production has to be undertaken so many years in advance that reasonable security of tenure of the forest estate is an absolute essential.

The three fundamentals before this security can be obtained are:—

(*a*) a formally approved statement of forest policy;

(*b*) a land-capability survey on which allocation of land for permanent forestry can be scientifically based; and

(*c*) adequate legislation.

The admirable "White Paper on Crown Forest Land and Forestry" by Allan and Edgerley was published by the Government in 1950. As far as I am aware it has not been formally adopted by the Government, though in general its recommendations have been followed. What is required now is a condensed statement of forest policy, brought up to date and incorporating a statement of the specific areas:—

(*a*) needed to meet the forest products requirements of the island;

(*b*) required for water conservation;

(*c*) required as nature reserves.

The Conservator's estimates of the afforestation programme

needed to meet the island's timber needs during the next 30 years are based on the following:—

Current local annual production	520,000 cu. ft.
Imports (annual)	1,280,000 cu. ft.
Total	1,800,000 cu. ft.

Present population 600,000.

Annual *per capita* consumption 3 cu. ft.

Allowing for a 50% increase in population within 30 years and *no increase* in *per capita* consumption, the gross consumption by 1990 is unlikely to be less than 2,700,000 cu. ft. It might well be very much more.

Assuming a mean annual increment of 200 cu. ft./acre, an area of 13,500 acres of fully stocked productive forest will be needed. The current level of timber importation of Rs. 4 million per annum will certainly rise in the future if this target is not achieved.

These estimates seem most conservative and it is vital that the land required at least for this should be permanently dedicated. Some of this can be found in areas required also for water conservation and there is nothing incompatible with water conservation and commercial forestry: there will remain however areas of steep mountain-land incapable of permanent agriculture or economic forestry which must be maintained under forest cover for protection purposes. The vital necessity also for maintaining substantial reserves for cyclone relief is underlined by the very heavy demands likely to be made on the forest as a result of cyclone "Alex" on January 19th, 1960.

There are certain areas of Crown forest land of mild topography which are being released for tea cultivation and, provided adequate soil and water conserving techniques are used, and provided the full acreage required for commercial timber growing is retained, one could not seriously challenge this. However, in some of the areas of new tea which I saw the cultural methods employed were *not* in my opinion adequate to prevent soil wash and loss of water control. Clean cultivation, no contour draining and open drainage channels up and down the slope are methods of cultivation (with rainfall of 120″) which surely can be improved upon.

Tephrosia hedges and the planting of Iris appeared to be inadequate and I do urge that normal soil-conserving techniques should be statutorily required on such land. The proper use of contour bunds and grassed water disposal outlets is excellently demonstrated in the Forest Department nurseries (e.g. at Askaran nursery).

In view of the strong pressure being exerted on the Government for release of forest land for agricultural purposes, one would assume that all privately held land was being fully developed: this is far from

242

being the case and there must be thousands of acres of private land which are contributing nothing to the island's economy. Any rationalisation of land use on government-controlled land must be accompanied by optimum development of private land through appropriate legislation, and based on the land capability surveys which I hope will be undertaken.

Further there are a number of enclaves of private land within the Crown forests: this makes for unnecessary administrative complications and they should be acquired by the Government.

3. *River Reserves*

It is with some diffidence that I comment on these areas, but it appears to me that they involve the staff (including the Surveyor) in the expenditure of time and money out of all proportion to their value. They obviously have an amenity value, if properly maintained, but on superficial observation I found it difficult to believe that bank erosion was a serious problem. However, I am in no position to comment on this with any degree of confidence and I merely suggest that the whole question of the purpose, status and administration of these River Reserves should be reviewed. It is possible that in some places these areas contain reliot fragments of the native vegetation.

4. *Pas Geometriques*

It is difficult to avoid the conclusion that the status of these lands is a picturesque anachronism: they form a traditional aspect of the Mauritian scene but I cannot see that present-day conditions justify their special status (unique perhaps in the Commonwealth). Here again this must be taken as a superficial observation but the unsatisfactory administrative position of these lands suggests that their status and utilisation should be reviewed.

5. *Nature Reserves*

I was extremely gratified to see something of the work being undertaken in protecting the relics of the indigenous Mauritian flora: these vegetation types are part of the national heritage and contain many plants and animals unknown in any other part of the world. It would be a tragedy if they were to go the way of the Dodo. In view of the highly aggressive character of a number of the naturalised exotic species, particularly Chinese Guava (*Psidium Cattleyanum*) and *Ardisia*, I am sure it is the right policy to set aside limited areas, where all exotic species are artificially eradicated.

Since these species coppice very freely they are being dug out by hand: I am sure that it is worth trying the new hormone arboricides (2,4,D and 2,4,5,T) as a basal spray or brush treatments, in order to eliminate subsequent coppicing. It should be cheaper.

243

This complete protection will only be possible over limited areas, and, provided adequate areas of the vegetation types are retained, it would be difficult to justify the retention of large areas of potentially productive land as Nature Reserves.

6. *Forest Legislation*

There is urgent need to consolidate and modernise the mass of legislation dealing with forestry matters: in particular, the legislation is fundamentally defective in that it makes no provision for the declaration of Forest Reserves or a dedicated forest estate. This is the cornerstone on which forest policy must rest. Further, it is essential that the Forest Department should be empowered to issue licences to cut timber etc. on Crown Lands and that fees and royalties should be prescribed. Apart from the many modern colonial forestry enactments, Gordon's "The Law of Forestry" indicates what should be aimed at.

7. *Forest Utilisation*

The utilisation of the products of the Crown Forests is undertaken on a most unusual system: all produce is felled and extracted departmentally (lorry haulage of logs to mill by contractor): it is then custom-sawn at a private mill (at fixed rates) and the output re-delivered to the Forest Department who arrange for its haulage to a Forest Department depot where it is retailed by the Department.

Throughout this whole process the movement of each piece of wood is laboriously recorded on standard "Government stores" procedure lines, an incredibly costly and cumbersome undertaking.

The only sawmill which I saw was pretty inefficient, the only equipment being four circular saw benches, with no crosscut: the standard of sawing was poor, though probably as good as could be obtained with the equipment available.

On arrival at depot much of the timber is sold before it is seasoned: proper air seasoning facilities should be available and no unseasoned sawn material sold. It is also essential that preservative treatment plant should be available. Unless the locally produced timber is properly sawn, seasoned, treated and graded it will continue to have difficulty in competing with imported lumber (itself not of outstanding quality, I believe).

As I understand that there is little immediate prospect of private enterprise providing these services, there should be no further delay in setting up the mill and processing plant for which, I understand, funds have already been provided in the 1957-62 Capital Budget. I am convinced that the present system combines the worst features of both public and private operative and involves the Department in much unnecessary waste of time and staff and money.

The plant should be operated on commercial accounting lines, paying royalty to the Department on standing timber.

8. *Working Plans*

In order to achieve continuity of forest management, the preparation of formal working plans is an essential part of forest administration. In Mauritius the absence of proper cadastral surveys and the uncertainty of tenure in certain areas have discouraged the Department from undertaking the preparation of Working Plans. I do not consider that the preparation of one Working Plan for the whole forest estate is desirable, and I cannot do better than repeat what my predecessor said in 1953.

"Working plans of the type required in Mauritius, one for the Timber Working Circle, one or more for the Local Supply Working Circles, and one for the Natural Forest Working Circle, should not take more than nine months to prepare. All that is really *essential* can be covered by concise and brief prescriptions for the total area of the Working Circle, for the rotation, for yield control, and for regeneration operations with brief notes on species and tending. At its simplest an annotated map will satisfactorily carry a great deal of this. Where a prescription cannot be made with absolute accuracy it must be made by intelligent forecast. The Plan which waits for perfection will never reach the stage of application."

Although preparation of a Working Plan for the central afforestation areas must await a decision on the extent of future tea areas, it should be possible to prepare Working Plans for the other areas.

A proper framework of cadastral surveys and the demarcation of all forest boundaries is an essential prerequisite to proper forest management and I hope this will not be further delayed.

9. *Plantations*

I have already recorded my views on the admirable exotic plantations of the Department and they represent a very solid achievement. Further notes on these areas are included in other parts of the report.

10. *Research*

With the wide range of tree species now being successfully grown in Mauritius there would appear to be no need at this stage to concentrate on species trials: in due course provenance and varietal

245

trials will no doubt be necessary and perhaps further introduction on an arboretum basis.

Perhaps the most important immediate line of investigation is plant espacement and thinning intensity trials: these must be considered in relation to:—

(*a*) objects of management;

(*b*) weed control;

(*c*) markets for thinnings;

(*d*) game damage;

(*e*) cyclone damage.

For example, is the standard 6′ × 6′ spacing for *E. robusta* really the answer? A properly laid out series of spacing and thinning trials with the main species would be well worth while. A further line of investigation which is necessary is in site classification and recognition in relation to species suitability. In view of the diversity of sites and species already established the delineation of provisional site quality classes should present little difficulty.

I hope it will be possible for Mr. Brouard, when he does his Oxford course, to undertake a special study of silvicultural research procedures, techniques and layout.

Another urgent matter is to compile a performance report on all economic exotic forest trees established in Mauritius: few tropical territories have such a diversity of experience in exotics, and documentation on this is badly needed, to ensure that the accumulated knowledge of the Department is fully recorded.

Printed and bound by CPI Group (UK) Ltd, Croydon, CR0 4YY

08/05/2025

01864354-0001